Palgrave Studies in Agricultural Economics and Food Policy

Palgrave Textbooks in Agricultural Economics and Food Policy

Series Editor

Christopher B. Barrett, Charles H. Dyson School of Applied Economics & Management, Cornell University, Ithaca, NY, USA

This book series provides instructors and students with cutting-edge textbooks in agricultural economics and food policy.

More information about this subseries at http://www.palgrave.com/gp/series/16444

Jessica Fanzo · Claire Davis

Global Food Systems, Diets, and Nutrition

Linking Science, Economics, and Policy

Jessica Fanzo
Nitze School of Advanced International
Studies
Johns Hopkins University
Washington, DC, USA

Berman Institute of Bioethics
Johns Hopkins University
Baltimore, MD, USA

Bloomberg School of Public Health
Johns Hopkins University
Baltimore, MD, USA

Claire Davis
Berman Institute of Bioethics
Johns Hopkins University
Baltimore, MD, USA

ISSN 2662-3889　　　　　　ISSN 2662-3897　(electronic)
Palgrave Studies in Agricultural Economics and Food Policy
ISSN 2662-5474　　　　　　ISSN 2662-5482　(electronic)
Palgrave Textbooks in Agricultural Economics and Food Policy
ISBN 978-3-030-72762-8　　ISBN 978-3-030-72763-5　(eBook)
https://doi.org/10.1007/978-3-030-72763-5

© The Editor(s) (if applicable) and The Author(s), under exclusive license to Springer Nature Switzerland AG 2021

This work is subject to copyright. All rights are solely and exclusively licensed by the Publisher, whether the whole or part of the material is concerned, specifically the rights of translation, reprinting, reuse of illustrations, recitation, broadcasting, reproduction on microfilms or in any other physical way, and transmission or information storage and retrieval, electronic adaptation, computer software, or by similar or dissimilar methodology now known or hereafter developed.

The use of general descriptive names, registered names, trademarks, service marks, etc. in this publication does not imply, even in the absence of a specific statement, that such names are exempt from the relevant protective laws and regulations and therefore free for general use.

The publisher, the authors and the editors are safe to assume that the advice and information in this book are believed to be true and accurate at the date of publication. Neither the publisher nor the authors or the editors give a warranty, expressed or implied, with respect to the material contained herein or for any errors or omissions that may have been made. The publisher remains neutral with regard to jurisdictional claims in published maps and institutional affiliations.

Cover credit: Bartosz Hadyniak/getty images

This Palgrave Macmillan imprint is published by the registered company Springer Nature Switzerland AG
The registered company address is: Gewerbestrasse 11, 6330 Cham, Switzerland

Acknowledgments

We would like to thank Chris Barrett for the opportunity to contribute to this outstanding food policy series. We are also grateful to our colleagues at Johns Hopkins University, especially those involved in the Global Food Ethics and Policy Program, the Berman Institute of Bioethics, and the Nitze School of Advanced International Studies for their contributions to our thinking and scholarship in the area of food systems. We are grateful to the many scientists and experts whose work has been highlighted throughout the book. A special thanks to Michaela Paugh for helping us with early drafts. Jess would like to thank the UN Committee on Food Security's High Level Panel of Experts for the opportunity to work on the Food Systems and Nutrition report, which contributed to the conceptualization of this book, particularly Patrick Caron, Eileen Kennedy, and Lawrence Haddad. And finally, Jess would like to acknowledge with much gratitude the unending support of her husband, Derek, who not only keeps her inspired, but provides her nourishment (literally) every day. Claire is grateful to her partner, Walker, for his generous support, encouragement, and thoughtful insights on the content of this book throughout its evolution.

Contents

1	**Introduction**	1
	References	5

Part I Introduction to Major Concepts and Frameworks

2	**Food Systems, Food Environments, and Consumer Behavior**	9
	Introduction	9
	Food and Its Role in Society	9
	What Are Food Systems?	10
	What Are Food Systems Meant to Do?	12
	Who Influences and Engages with Food Systems?	12
	Components of Food Systems	15
	Key Messages and Conclusions	21
	References	22
3	**Food Policy**	29
	Introduction	29
	What Is Food Policy?	29
	What Is Food Governance?	30
	Who Influences Food Policy and Governance?	32
	Historical Transitions Toward a Holistic Food Policy	34
	Key Messages and Conclusions	35
	References	37

Part II Changing Food Systems and Diets for Nutrition

4	**Nutritious Foods, Healthy Diets, and Contributions to Health**	41
	Introduction	41
	What Are Diets?	41
	Health Consequences of Suboptimal Diets	47
	Key Messages and Conclusions	48
	References	48

5	**The Multiple Burdens of Malnutrition**	51
	Introduction	51
	Nutrition	51
	Malnutrition	52
	Causes of Malnutrition	59
	Consequences of Malnutrition	61
	Intergenerational Cycle of Malnutrition	63
	Key Messages and Conclusions	64
	References	65
6	**Transformations Across Diets and Food Systems**	71
	Introduction	71
	Changing Diets	71
	Food System Transformation	75
	Key Messages and Conclusions	80
	References	80
7	**Drivers Shaping Food Systems**	85
	Introduction	85
	Biophysical and Environmental Drivers	85
	Sociocultural Drivers	88
	Political and Economic Drivers	89
	Demographic Drivers	94
	Innovation, Technology, and Infrastructure	97
	Key Messages and Conclusions	99
	References	99

Part III The Influence of Food Policy on Diets and Nutrition

8	**Policies Affecting Food Supply Chains**	109
	Introduction	109
	Ideal Food Supply Chains for Diets and Nutrition	109
	Policies that Shape Food Supply Chains and Their Impacts on Diets and Nutrition	112
	Key Messages and Conclusions	123
	References	123
9	**Policies Affecting Food Environments and Consumer Behavior**	131
	Introduction	131
	How Food Environments Affect the Food Supply and Consumer Demand	131
	Ideal Food Environments	132
	Why Physical Spaces and Places Matter	134
	Policies That Focus on Food Environments and Consumer Demand to Better Shape Diets and Nutrition	135

Key Messages and Conclusions 145
References 146

Part IV New Challenges to Achieving Healthy Diets for Nutrition

**10 Sustainable Diets: Aligning Food Systems
 and the Environment** 155
 Introduction 155
 The Agriculture–Environment Connection 156
 The History of Sustainable Diets 157
 The EAT-*Lancet* Report 158
 Health and Environmental Implications of Sustainable Diets 160
 The Sustainable Diet Conundrum 162
 Research Limitations and Policy Opportunities 163
 Key Messages and Conclusions 164
 References 165

11 The Future of Food: Shaping Diets and Nutrition 169
 Introduction 169
 Agriculture 4.0: Revolutionizing Food Supplies for Better Diets .. 169
 The Disappearing Grocery Store, Restaurant, and Kitchen 173
 Changing Palates, Changing Demands 176
 The Implementation of Technologies 178
 Key Messages and Conclusions 178
 References 180

12 Conclusion and Ways Forward 183
 Importance of Food Policy for Diets and Nutrition 183
 Challenges Remain 184
 With Challenges Come Opportunities 185
 References 186

Index 189

Abbreviations

ASF	Animal Source Foods
BMI	Body Mass Index
BOP	Back-of-Package
CAFO	Concentrated Animal Feeding Operations
DALY	Disability-Adjusted Life Years
DBM	Double Burden of Malnutrition
DR-NCD	Diet-Related Noncommunicable Disease
FAO	Food and Agriculture Organization of the United Nations
FBDG	Food-Based Dietary Guidelines
FDA	Food and Drug Administration
FOP	Front-of-Package
GDP	Gross Domestic Product
GHGe	Greenhouse Gas Emissions
GM	Genetic Modification
GMO	Genetically Modified Organisms
LBW	Low Birth Weight
LMIC	Low-and Middle-Income Countries
NCD	Noncommunicable Disease
SBCC	Social and Behavior Change Communication
SSB	Sugar-Sweetened Beverages
UNICEF	United Nations Children's Fund
USDA	United States Department of Agriculture
WHO	World Health Organization

List of Figures

Fig. 2.1	Role of food (*Source* Created by authors, not previously published)	10
Fig. 2.2	Conceptualization of a food system in its simplest form [7]	11
Fig. 2.3	Food supply chains [37]	15
Fig. 2.4	Consumer engagement with the built environment (*Source* Created by authors, not previously published)	19
Fig. 2.5	Food environment [89]	20
Fig. 3.1	Various types of food policies enacted around the world [3]	31
Fig. 3.2	Food system stakeholders (*Source* Created by authors, not previously published)	33
Fig. 3.3	Washington, DC 2020 Food Policy [23]	36
Fig. 3.4	Holistic proposed food policy for the European Union [24]	37
Fig. 4.1	**a** and **b** Suboptimal infant and young children's diets [12]	44
Fig. 4.2	Suboptimal adult diets, globally and regionally [17]	45
Fig. 5.1	Food insecurity and its impacts [12]	54
Fig. 5.2	Malnutrition burden switch in children under five [16]	57
Fig. 5.3	Double burden of malnutrition shift from high- to low-income quintiles over the last 30 years [30]	58
Fig. 5.4	UNICEF framework on undernutrition [42]	60
Fig. 5.5	Malnutrition impacts opportunities throughout the entire life cycle [7]	62
Fig. 6.1	Trends and patterns in per capita packaged food category sales by region, 2005–2017 [3]	73
Fig. 6.2	The nutrition transition and patterns [15]	74
Fig. 7.1	Effects of climate change on the food supply chain [20]	87
Fig. 7.2	Impacts of trade on food systems and diets [61]	91
Fig. 7.3	Global population growth, 1950–2050 [96]	95
Fig. 7.4	Percentage of the world's population residing in urban areas, 1950–2050 [96]	96
Fig. 8.1	Entry and exit points for nutrition along food supply chains [1]	111
Fig. 8.2	Food supply policy levers [28]	112

Fig. 8.3	What we produce to what we eat [33]	114
Fig. 8.4	Fortification legislation around the world [100]	120
Fig. 9.1	The social determinants of healthy eating [5]	133
Fig. 9.2	Areas where policies can shape food environments [24]	135
Fig. 9.3	Overall effects of fiscal instruments on consumer behavior and industry [49]	138
Fig. 9.4	Impact of different fiscal instruments on diets and disease outcomes [49]	140
Fig. 9.5	Policy actions to support enhanced consumer behavior for high-quality diets [71]	141
Fig. 10.1	Food systems contribute to climate change [3]	156
Fig. 10.2	Impact of food groups on five environmental pressures [64]	161
Fig. 11.1	Technologies and their readiness for markets [6]	170
Fig. 11.2	Technological innovations across the food system [57]	179

List of Tables

Table 2.1 Classification by degree of processing of food and beverage products [72, 73] 18
Table 3.1 History of nutrition policy and politics [21] 35

List of Boxes

Box 2.1	Golden Rice, a vision unrealized	14
Box 2.2	Quinoa, an indigenous crop of the Andes, goes mainstream	16
Box 3.1	Food system stakeholders and the elimination of trans fats	33
Box 4.1	Components of diet quality	42
Box 4.2	Disappearing traditional diets	46
Box 5.1	Different forms of malnutrition	53
Box 5.2	Ethiopia's astounding efforts to tackle stunting	55
Box 5.3	India's challenge in dealing with the double burden of malnutrition	59
Box 5.4	Born undernourished to die overnourished	64
Box 6.1	Effects of the COVID-19 pandemic on food systems	75
Box 6.2	The globalization of food environments	77
Box 7.1	What are ecosystem services?	86
Box 7.2	Trade policies to reduce unhealthy meat consumption in Fiji, Samoa, and Tonga	91
Box 7.3	The effects of war on nutrition and food security in South Sudan	93
Box 8.1	Impact of agricultural subsidies on nutrition in the United States and Malawi	114
Box 8.2	How reformulation improves the nutrient content of different food products	117
Box 8.3	Sodium reformulation in the United Kingdom	118
Box 9.1	Policy actions for food environments that enable healthy eating	136
Box 9.2	Taxation of unhealthy foods in Denmark and Mexico	139
Box 9.3	Regulation of marketing, labeling, and the school environment in Chile: A comprehensive policy to tackle obesity and improve the food system	141
Box 10.1	The burning of the Amazon: Threats to human diets and health	157
Box 11.1	Effects of the COVID-19 pandemic on online food shopping and delivery	174

Chapter 1
Introduction

Food is highly valued by society for many different reasons. Not only is food critical to human survival, but it is also important for nourishment and health, livelihoods dependent on food systems, economies growing through shared food supply chains and trade, peace and prosperity, and thriving cultures and traditions. Food comes from "food systems," which encompass everything from food production to its consumption. Food systems are shaped by actors and policies that determine their functionality and priorities.

Food systems vary dramatically—some move food to the far reaches of the world in what are termed "globalized food systems," while others utilize very localized farm to fork-type community systems. Regardless, everyone, every day engages with the food system and makes choices that shape them in different ways. The means by which food systems function are not only shaped by people. Food systems are shaped by governments and policies, global shocks and trends, and relationships between countries and regions. Looking broadly, one could say that food systems have become incredibly efficient at moving and delivering food—lots of it and many types—around the world to feed a massive population. However, closer inspection reveals cracks and fissures in food systems that give rise to insufficiencies and inequities [1].

Constraints on food systems cause some of these fractures. The global population is rapidly expanding, with the expectation that our planet will be home to 9.7 billion people by 2050 [2]. Along with this growing human population, urbanization, changing diets, environmental degradation, and, most worryingly, climate change place unprecedented stresses on food systems that threaten food security, diets, and nutrition [3]. At the time of this writing, the world is also grappling with the COVID-19 pandemic, a global health system shock that has affected the functionality of many world systems, including food systems, and further exacerbated geopolitical strife, world disorder, and economic decline [4, 5].

Given these risks and constraints, the creation, implementation, and investment in effective policies are critical to support healthy, equitable, and sustainable food systems for improved diets and nutrition. Policy action is vital and indispensable, because the world must contend with a universal, complex burden of malnutrition from which no country is immune. Every country's population struggles with one or more forms of malnutrition—hunger, undernutrition, micronutrient deficiencies, or obesity—with some countries facing two, three, or even four forms of malnutrition [6]. The multiple burdens of malnutrition are rapidly rising in low-and middle-income countries [7]. At the same time, malnutrition in all its forms contributes to a significant proportion of global ill-health, with malnutrition as the leading cause of morbidity and mortality in the world [8].

Globally, 1 in every 11 people suffer from hunger and about 25% of the world's population experience food insecurity [9]. Given the vast economic growth experienced in our modern era, it seems unfathomable that people still struggle to put enough food on the table to feed their families. Children under the age of five represent an important marker of the overall population's health. Of this age group, 20% are chronically undernourished (stunted), while 6% are overweight worldwide [6, 10]. In recent decades, the prevalence of stunting has been on the decline, but overweight prevalence is rising within this age group. Micronutrient deficiencies, particularly vitamin A, iodine, iron, and zinc, affect billions of people around the world [11]. Although the true extent of micronutrient deficiencies is poorly understood, the link between deficiencies and disease is well established. The prevalence of overweight and obesity in adults has grown significantly in recent decades, with a staggering 2 billion adults affected by overweight and 678 million with obesity [6].

Diets are one of the major causes of malnutrition and its subsequent health outcomes. Food systems shape the types of foods people consume, which make up their overall diets [12]. Unfortunately, diets are moving in the wrong direction across a suite of metrics and trending toward unhealthy, unsustainable, and inequitable patterns [13]. Healthy diets are also proving to be unattainable for large segments of the world's population because of geographic and economic barriers to access. Systemic and societal justice issues also marginalize populations and prevent them from engaging with food systems, which results in catastrophic inequities in food availability, accessibility, and utilization [9].

Unhealthy diets are now one of the top risk factors globally for deaths and disability-adjusted life years (DALYs) lost. The risks posed by unhealthy diets surpass those of air pollution, tobacco smoking, and high blood pressure [14]. Unhealthy diets do not typically contain sufficient health-promoting foods, such as fruits, vegetables, whole grains, nuts and seeds, milk, seafood, and aquatic foods high in omega-3 fatty acids. Instead, unhealthy diets consist of foods like red meat, processed meat (smoked, cured, salted or chemically preserved), sugary drinks [15], and highly-processed foods characteristically high in salt, trans fats, added sugars, and additives with health effects that are less well known [16]. These diets, sometimes referred to "Western diets," increase the risk of heart disease, diabetes, some forms of cancer, and stroke [7], and put 11 million people at risk for death on an annual basis [14]. These dietary changes have largely occurred over the last 30 years as a result of lifestyle changes, migration to urban areas, shifting livelihoods, and economic growth [17]. In some parts of the world, diets are still insufficient in calories and/or diversity of foods, which serve as a risk factor for food insecurity, and child and maternal undernutrition [8, 14]. The COVID-19 pandemic will exacerbate these dietary insufficiencies [18].

This book aims to provide readers with an understanding of the landscape of food systems in high-, middle-, and low-income countries, and explain how food policies and interconnected food systems affect the diets and nutrition of populations all over the world. Ensuring food security and nutrition for the global population is a grand challenge fraught with many contentious issues. For the global population to be food secure, there is a need for functional, healthy, and sustainable food systems and policies that support those systems. Food systems and policies are contingent on a complex network of individuals and institutions. Depending on the policies enacted, food systems can direct and determine the availability, affordability, and nutritional quality of the food supply, which influences the amount and variety of foods that people are willing and able to consume.

The creation and implementation of public policies are influenced by the agriculture-led economic growth of countries, health and nutrition of populations, and environmental sustainability of landscapes [19]. Conflicts about land, technology, natural resources, subsidies, inequity, and trade all play out in the food policy arena. By choosing to read this book, you, the reader, will become familiar with both domestic and international food policy processes and typologies, along with the key players in the international food security landscape. This book empowers its readers to critically analyze and debate how policy and science interact to influence regarding nutrition outcomes.

Part I of this book, "Introduction to Major Concepts and Frameworks," lays the groundwork for understanding the changing landscape of food systems, diets, and malnutrition. Chapter 2 outlines the necessary concepts and frameworks that frame this landscape. Food systems, food supply chains, food environments, and other food policy terminology are delineated. The food system gathers all the elements—environment, people, inputs, processes, infrastructures, institutions, etc.—and activities that relate to the production, processing, distribution, preparation, and consumption of food, as well as the outputs of these activities, including health and nutrition, socioeconomic, and environmental outcomes.

Chapter 3 provides an overview of food policy and food politics. Making investments that orient food systems and food environments toward nutrition and health outcomes is a challenging task due to their complexity and trade-offs. Policymakers need access to the latest and most rigorous evidence when formulating policies that will best address malnutrition burdens and unhealthy diets. Instead, they are often functioning "in the dark," with limited data on what works for a specific context. Policymakers may be able to identify the core set of interventions needed for certain outcomes, but the path to implementing these interventions and achieving desired outcomes is riddled with uncertainties.

Part II, "Changing Food Systems and Diets for Nutrition," delves into the complex relationship between diets, nutrition, and health. Chapter 4 introduces the concept of diets and explains how diets affect health. Diets are composed of foods that range in healthfulness and nutrition. Many different factors influence a person's diet. Healthy diets meet an individual's nutritional needs and support overall health. Dietary patterns vary by region, but global diets are less than optimal. These suboptimal diets directly affect nutrition and health outcomes. Poor diets are now considered a top risk factor for death and disability.

Chapter 5 presents "the big picture" of malnutrition, starting with the historical context of the current nutrition situation. This chapter delineates the global burden of malnutrition, the causes, and the consequences for health. Malnutrition takes different forms: undernutrition (underweight, stunting, and wasting); micronutrient deficiencies; and overweight and obesity. These forms of malnutrition affect all countries, whether developed or developing, and can also co-exist within countries, communities, households, and individuals.

Chapter 6 provides an overview of global dietary patterns, explaining how demand has shifted dietary choices and affected nutrition. The chapter describes the "nutrition transition" and explains how various factors have influenced its evolution. The impacts of globalization, trade, and urban migration are also considered. The choices that individual consumers make are influenced by individual preferences and habits, culture, marketing, food availability, and price. These choices are important for shaping food systems, which have secondary effects on economies and the environment. Changing diets and consumption patterns have been influenced by many factors, including changes in demography and urbanization, unfriendly built environments that allow for less physical activity, food environments that are often unhealthy and misleading, and barriers to nutritious food access, such as food deserts and high food prices.

Chapter 7 describes the many drivers of food system change that influence nutrition and diets. These include biophysical and environmental factors; innovation, technology and infrastructure; and political and economic; sociocultural; and demographic influences. These drivers can shape food systems in both positive and negative ways, some of which are predictable, while others come as disruptive shocks.

Part III of the book, "The Influence of Food Policy on Diets and Nutrition," focuses on the food policy landscape and its influence on diets and nutrition. Chapter 8 focuses specifically on food supply chain policies. Food supply policies shape the way that food is produced, moved, traded, and consumed. However, political agendas and power struggles can influence supply chain policies and interventions. This chapter highlights risks for food policies that often result in contentious debates about how to feed the world well while ensuring economic growth. Key policy issues are discussed, including rising food prices, food assistance, agricultural subsidies, and trade policies.

Chapter 9 focuses on policies that impact the food environment, which is where people engage with food systems through local outlets or public procurement establishments. The chapter discusses "food politics" and the influence of trans-and multinational food and beverage companies and other private sector entities on regulations and guidelines that affect nutrition outcomes. It also delves into policies that inform and guide consumers toward healthier eating. Some countries have dietary guidelines that make recommendations about what types of foods to consume within a person's dietary pattern. These rarely align with what the food system can supply and are often pitted against environmental and sustainability limits. These guidelines do not always have a meaningful impact on consumer behavior or nutrition literacy.

Part IV of the book, "New Challenges to Achieving Healthy Diets for Nutrition," focuses on emerging challenges for food systems. Chapter 10 examines diets through the lens of environment and climate change. The global food system uses 40% of the earth's land, 70% of its freshwater, and many other natural resources. It contributes 11–24% of greenhouse gas emissions, as well as other air and water pollutants. This chapter considers the environmental impacts of food systems, the bidirectional relationship between food system activities and climate change, and the potential for climate-smart food systems to address these issues.

Chapter 11 focuses on new technologies across food systems that are shaping access to healthy diets. Emerging technologies hold the potential to improve storage, packaging, and preservation of foods, particularly perishable foods (often those considered healthy foods, like animal source foods, fruits, and vegetables) in transport and storage. Technology can also help consumers access food in different ways through smartphone apps, "walk in/walk out" technology, and shared economies. The chapter discusses how these technologies can shape diets and, ultimately, nutrition.

At the end of this book, we hope that the reader will have a deeper understanding of how food systems influence the types of diets that people consume and how critical food policy is to achieving benefits for human health, equity, and the environment. This book aims to convey the significance of food and diets for human health and nutrition, as well as their fundamental importance for the 2030 Sustainable Development Goals, the roadmap of 17 goals to guide nations toward future prosperity for people and the planet.

References

1. Béné C, Oosterveer P, Lamotte L, Brouwer ID, de Haan S, Prager SD, et al. When food systems meet sustainability – Current narratives and implications for actions. World Dev. 2019 Jan 1;113:116–30.
2. United Nations, Department of Economic and Social Affairs, Population Division. World Population Prospects 2019: Highlights [Internet]. 2019. Available from: https://population.un.org/wpp/Publications/Files/WPP2019_Highlights.pdf
3. Global Panel on Agriculture and Food Systems for Nutrition. Future Food Systems: For people, our planet, and prosperity [Internet]. 2020. Available from: https://www.glopan.org/wp-content/uploads/2020/11/Foresight-2_WEB_2Nov.pdf
4. Fanzo J. No food security, no world order. In: Brands H And Gavin F, editor. COVID-19 and World Order: The Future of Conflict, Competition, and Cooperation. 2020.
5. World Economic Forum. The Global Risks Report 2019, 14th Edition. 2019.
6. Global Nutrition Report - Global Nutrition Report [Internet]. Global Nutrition Report. 2020 [cited 2020 Jul 27]. Available from: https://globalnutritionreport.org/reports/2020-global-nutrition-report/.
7. Popkin BM, Corvalan C, Grummer-Strawn LM. Dynamics of the double burden of malnutrition and the changing nutrition reality. Lancet. 2020 Jan 4;395(10217):65–74.

8. Murray CJL, Aravkin AY, Zheng P, Abbafati C, Abbas KM, Abbasi-Kangevari M, et al. Global burden of 87 risk factors in 204 countries and territories, 1990–2019: A systematic analysis for the Global Burden of Disease Study 2019. Lancet. 2020 Oct 17;396(10258):1223–49.
9. Fao Ifad Unicef Wfp. The State of Food Security and Nutrition in the World 2020. Transforming food systems for affordable healthy diets. FAO; 2020.
10. United Nations Children's Fund (UNICEF), World Health Organization, International Bank for Reconstruction and Development/The World Bank. Levels and trends in child malnutrition: Key Findings of the 2020 Edition of the Joint Child Malnutrition Estimates. 2020.
11. Ritchie H, Roser M. Micronutrient deficiency [Internet]. Our World in Data. 2017. Available from: https://ourworldindata.org/micronutrient-deficiency
12. HLPE. Nutrition and food systems. A report by the High Level Panel of Experts on Food Security and Nutrition of the Committee on World Food Security [Internet]. HLPE; 2017. Report No. 12. Available from: http://www.fao.org/fileadmin/user_upload/hlpe/hlpe_documents/HLPE_Reports/HLPE-Report-12_EN.pdf
13. Fanzo J, Davis C. Can Diets Be Healthy, Sustainable, and Equitable? Curr Obes Rep. 2019 Dec;8(4):495–503.
14. Afshin A, Sur PJ, Fay KA, Cornaby L, Ferrara G, Salama JS, et al. Health effects of dietary risks in 195 countries, 1990–2017: A systematic analysis for the Global Burden of Disease Study 2017. Lancet [Internet]. 2019 [cited 2019 May 20]; Available from: https://www.fabresearch.org/viewItem.php?id=12559
15. Willett W, Rockström J, Loken B, Springmann M, Lang T, Vermeulen S, et al. Food in the Anthropocene: the EAT-Lancet Commission on healthy diets from sustainable food systems. Lancet. 2019 Feb 2;393(10170):447–92.
16. Baker P, Machado P, Santos T, Sievert K, Backholer K, Hadjikakou M, et al. Ultra-processed foods and the nutrition transition: Global, regional and national trends, food systems transformations and political economy drivers. Obes Rev. 2020 Dec;21(12):e13126.
17. Popkin BM. Relationship between shifts in food system dynamics and acceleration of the global nutrition transition. Nutr Rev. 2017 Feb 1;75(2):73–82.
18. Osendarp S, Akuoku J, Black R, Headey D, Ruel M, Scott N, et al. The potential impacts of the COVID-19 crisis on maternal and child undernutrition in low and middle income countries [Internet]. 2020 [cited 2021 Jan 7]. Available from: https://www.researchsquare.com/article/rs-123716/v1
19. Barrett CB, Benton TG, Cooper KA, Fanzo J, Gandhi R, Herrero M, et al. Bundling innovations to transform agri-food systems. Nature Sustainability. 2020 Dec 1;3(12):974–76.

Part I
Introduction to Major Concepts and Frameworks

Part 1

Chapter 2
Food Systems, Food Environments, and Consumer Behavior

Introduction

Food is critical to good nutrition and health, but it is also an essential part of culture, society, tradition, religion, and individual values. Food systems consist of everybody and everything involved in bringing food from "farm to fork." This chapter provides an overview of food systems and the key concepts necessary to understand how food systems function. Food systems consist of all the components and activities related to the production, processing, distribution, preparation, and consumption of food. Farmers and other food producers, consumers, businesses, civil society groups, and governments play major roles in the food system. These actors influence, direct, and engage with food systems in different ways. Food system activities affect health and nutrition outcomes, as well as socioeconomic status and the environment. Food supply chains, food environments, and consumer behavior represent three major components of food systems.

Food and Its Role in Society

In choosing what food to eat every day, people make decisions that extend beyond their immediate survival needs to participate in something much grander. The daily necessity to eat binds people to their food and dietary choices. Food is also integral to people's values, traditions, cultures, religions, and the everyday structures that comprise societies. The choice of food helps define a person's identity, habits, and aspirations. People make food choices based on their beliefs and values, preferences and desires, and relationship to the origins of food.

Food plays many roles in every aspect of society and culture. Food nourishes us and fuels our economies. It represents traditions and sustains heritages through culinary knowledge and eating practices. Food serves human life by providing sustenance

Fig. 2.1 Role of food (*Source* Created by authors, not previously published)

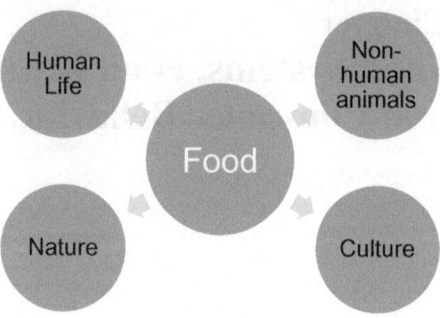

and facilitating relationships with others. It fosters relationships with food producers, sellers, sociocultural organizations, nature, and others. As Fig. 2.1 shows, food is vital to health, as well as connections to culture, non-human animals, and the environment.

Our dietary patterns consist of the foods and ingredients we regularly consume. These foods are made up of macronutrients, such as fats, proteins, and carbohydrates, and micronutrients, such as vitamins and minerals. These foods also contain chemicals that, when combined, can promote or impair health. Diets are shaped by a person's choices, habits, and lifestyle. The cost, convenience, desirability, and texture of certain foods also influence diets [1].

Healthy diets provide a sufficient quality and quantity of food, meaning that they are rich in both nutrients and energy. They also contain a diverse range of foods and are safe from foodborne pathogens. These diets should be affordable, accessible, and culturally acceptable [2, 3]. However, the ideal is not the norm. While the causes of malnutrition are multifaceted and complex, suboptimal dietary patterns contribute significantly to global malnutrition in all its forms [4].

What Are Food Systems?

Food systems consist of everybody and everything involved in bringing food from "farm to fork." This definition includes people who play a role in producing food, such as farmers and retailers, as well as people who are influenced by these activities, such as shoppers at a grocery store or market [5]. In addition to individuals, institutions and organizations are critical components of food systems. Food systems also include the environment; agricultural inputs, such as fertilizer and water; and infrastructure, such as roads, stores, and machinery on farms. Through the many activities and processes of the food system, food can be grown and produced, processed, distributed, prepared, and, ultimately, consumed [6].

Food systems are highly interconnected—any intervention or policy that addresses one part of the system will affect other parts. Health, politics, society, the economy, and the environment all intersect with food systems. As a result of this interconnectedness, any action can lead to unintended consequences. Figure 2.2 shows a

What Are Food Systems?

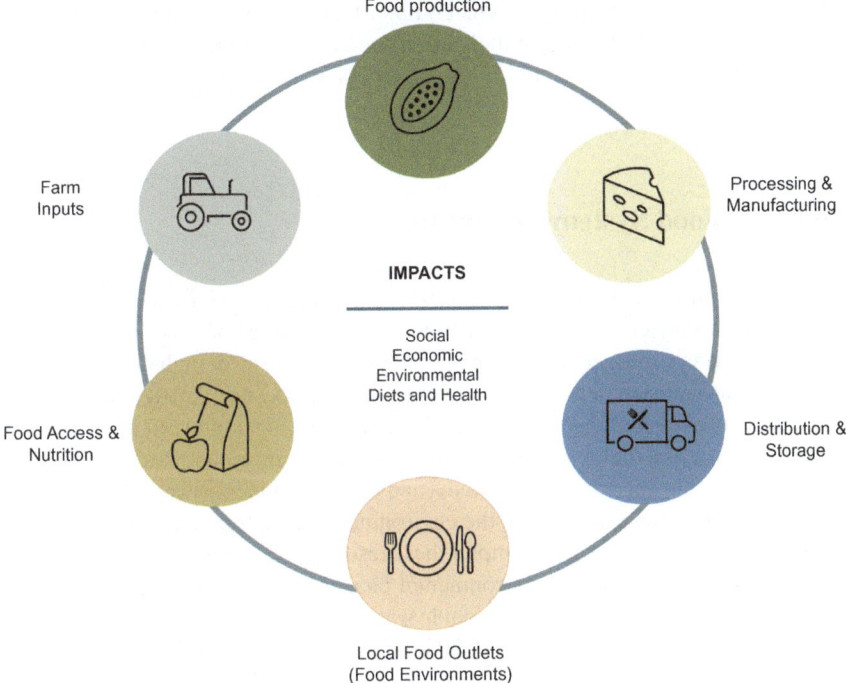

Fig. 2.2 Conceptualization of a food system in its simplest form [7]

conceptual diagram of a general food system.

There are three major definitions of the food system [8]:

- ***The* Food System:** "the interconnected system of everything and everybody that influences, and is influenced by, the activities involved in bringing food from farm to fork" [8].
- **A Food System:** the food system in a specific region or context.
- **Food *Systems*:** the entirety of all different forms and types of food systems in different regions and contexts. The concept of food systems describes the full diversity of food systems whose characteristics and operational scales vary.

A "food systems approach" is a departure from traditional approaches, which tend to be sectoral with a narrowly defined focus and scope. Instead, a food systems approach uses a holistic, comprehensive view of the entire system. This approach includes the actors within the food supply chain and governance mechanisms that shape their roles. A food systems approach requires "food systems thinking," which identifies and describes the influences, or "drivers," and relationships in the systems. Food systems thinking also considers how these influences intersect with each other in both positive and negative ways [8].

In order to implement this approach, it is important to understand the major components of food systems that shape their existence and direction. These components, which are a significant focus of this book, are food supply chains, food environments, and consumer behavior [3].

What Are Food Systems Meant to Do?

Food systems involve far more than producing enough food to feed the world. Through diets, they contribute to nutrition and health outcomes. Healthy diets are essential for preventing malnutrition in all its forms, which include undernutrition, micronutrient deficiencies, and overweight and obesity [9, 10]. Malnutrition contributes to poor health outcomes and diet-related noncommunicable diseases (DR-NCDs), such as diabetes, coronary heart disease, cancer, and stroke [11, 12].

The relationship between food systems and the environment is complex and bidirectional. Food systems depend on the environment and natural resources, but food system activities can degrade and impair these resources [13]. Food production alone is the largest cause of global environmental change [14]. The demand for certain foods and diets contributes to unsustainable water and land use, biodiversity loss, and increased greenhouse gas emissions (GHGe) [14, 15]. Current food system activities place unprecedented pressure on natural resources and lead to fundamental changes in ecosystems worldwide [14].

Food systems are also central to the lives of people around the world. Food systems improve social and gender equality and reduce rural poverty. They also help improve the resilience and livelihoods of vulnerable populations affected by conflict and natural disasters. Food systems provide income and employment for millions of people, particularly smallholders and poor people in rural areas. The agriculture sector employs an estimated one billion people worldwide, of whom 97% live in developing countries [16]. Food systems also impact social and cultural outcomes [17].

Who Influences and Engages with Food Systems?

Many different actors play a role in the food system: farmers and other food producers, governments, businesses, civil society, institutions, and consumers. Some actors are responsible for producing food, while others process, transport, sell, and prepare food products. Some actors may implement policies and take actions that directly affect the food system, while the influences and interests of other actors may be more subtle [8].

Collectively, these actors influence how food gets from farm to fork. They contribute to society's health and environmental sustainability issues, but they are also critical to solving these problems. Food system actors may be driven by different motivations: some act altruistically to help others and strengthen society, while others operate under political or financial incentives [18]. Some may be unaware that their actions have any influence on or consequence for the food system.

Within the food supply chain, the distribution of food system actors can be visualized as a misshapen hourglass. At one end of the hourglass, there are 1.5 billion producers. More than 70% of these producers operate on a small scale. The world's 7 billion consumers are at the other, wider end of the hourglass. The hourglass's narrow neck contains the system's food processing companies, traders, and retailers. The activity of transporting, processing, packaging, enhancing, and pricing food is concentrated among a few large private sector actors [19].

Farmers, livestock producers, and fishers: The global community of food producers is extremely diverse. Around the world, there are more than 570 million farms. Most of these farms are small and family-operated [20]. By some estimates, small and family farms manage 53% of the world's agricultural land and account for more than 50% of global agricultural production [20, 21]. Globally, 135 million people engage in fishing, aquaculture, and other related activities, such as processing and trading, as a source of employment. Most of the world's fishers and fish farmers are small-scale producers [22, 23]. Small-scale farms and fishers play an important role in food production and security.

Private sector: The private sector is highly influential within the food system: it affects food production, pricing and affordability, consumer attitudes and perceptions, and public policy. This sector includes the agriculture industry, food and beverage companies, food service, and retailers. Within this sector, small, mid-sized, and large enterprises operate at the local and global levels. Companies in the agrifood industry provide agricultural inputs, trade goods, process and package foods, and prepare and sell the final product to consumers. These businesses are involved in every stage of the food supply chain [8, 24, 25].

Consumers: Consumers influence food systems through their buying choices. Consumers are a diverse group that ranges in age, race, sex, geographic location, socioeconomic status, ethnicity, and culture, among other attributes. Food access, availability, price, and other contextual factors can affect consumer behavior and demand. As citizens, consumers can also express their beliefs and preferences about food system policies by voting, organizing, and engaging in other forms of civic activity [26].

Governments: Good governance is critical to building healthy, sustainable food systems. Governments develop and implement policies, enforce regulations, and offer incentives to different stakeholders to achieve desired outcomes. In some countries, governments directly manage and even participate in food production, while in other countries, the state regulates and facilitates the activities of food systems through policy. Food policies and programs include consumer and farm subsidies, food safety regulations, resource management, and trade policies, among others. These activities influence both the private sector and consumers. One government's food policies can also affect the activities of other countries, especially regarding trade [8, 18, 27].

Civil society: Around the world, many civil society groups act to promote food system goals. These non-governmental organizations may operate at the local or global level to support positive nutrition, health, and environmental outcomes. These groups can help initiate changes to food systems and shape public policy. The mission of these groups may differ—some focus on empowering women or small-scale farmers, while others advocate for health or the environment—but these varying goals are all connected to the food system. Civil society groups help to influence governmental policy and industry actions through advocacy, cooperation, and accountability [3, 18].

Collaboration between different food system actors can be critical to ensuring a well-functioning system. Effective partnerships require an understanding of the motivations and perspectives of different parties. Without this awareness, even well-intentioned pursuits can falter, as shown by the case of Golden Rice (Box 2.1). The failure of Golden Rice also illustrates the complex concerns that underpin people's decisions about what and how to eat.

Box 2.1 Golden Rice, a vision unrealized

In the 1990s, the Rockefeller Foundation funded the International Rice Research Institute and Syngenta to develop technologies that would address the scourge of vitamin A deficiency. At the time, vitamin A deficiency was causing death and blindness among women and children in many parts of the world [28]. The Rockefeller Foundation's vision was singular—use cutting-edge genetic plant breeding technology to insert beta carotene (a vitamin A precursor) into kernels of rice, a food highly consumed around the world.

Golden Rice was the result of this genetic modification (GM). Through various field trials, the new breed of fortified rice was found to be effective in reducing vitamin A deficiency [29]. While the technology worked miracles, the GM rice was met with significant resistance by countries and communities [30, 31].

Twenty years later, the controversies remain. There has been strong objection to GM technology in many parts of the world, and in places such as the Philippines, non-governmental agencies advocating for farmer and consumer rights groups destroyed Golden Rice crops. Both "top-down" government and policy dialogue and "bottom-up" community engagement are critical to ensure acceptance of such an intervention [30]. In the case of Golden Rice, policy engagement with various food system actors was not effectively done [32]. Instead, countries have tried to ban or postpone the technology, leaving Golden Rice mired in regulatory battles [33].

Components of Food Systems

Food Supply Chains

Food supply chains involve all the activities needed to bring food from farm to fork. These activities include producing, storing, distributing, processing, packaging, marketing, and selling food, as well as consuming it and disposing of food waste [34]. Actors in the public and private sectors play a role at every step in the food supply chain [35].

The structure and operation of food supply chains depends on local context. Some supply chains are long and engage many actors, while others are short and involve fewer actors [36]. In some places, food supply chains have become both longer and more efficient because of increasing urbanization, income growth, and globalization. Figure 2.3 shows the different steps of the food supply chain, along with the various actors engaged at each stage.

Like food systems, food supply chains are highly interconnected. The word "chain" implies that activities are closely connected. An individual actor's decisions at one stage in the chain can affect the actions of someone at a different stage in the chain. These decisions affect the way that food is produced and processed along the supply chain, all of which has consequences for food security, safety, and nutritional value [38].

Most of the world's food is produced on farms. Around the world, there are more than 570 million farms [39]. Nearly 40% of the world's labor force is engaged in agriculture [40]. Farming systems, or "agroecosystems," differ in their size, capacity, and methods. Some systems have a global reach, while others cater to

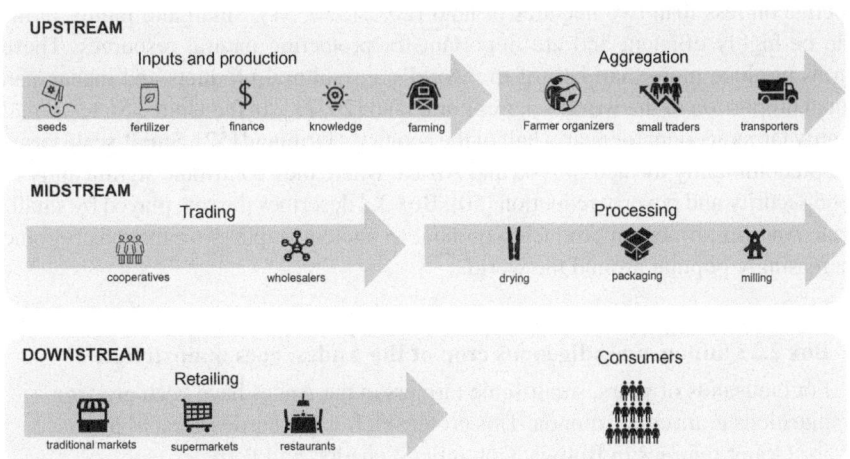

Fig. 2.3 Food supply chains [37]

local markets. Production methods are diverse and may include organic, conventional, and biodynamic approaches. Some producers grow only one type of crop, known as monocropping, while others grow a mixed set of crops.

Livestock production systems, aquatic ecosystems, fisheries, and aquaculture are also important for diets and nutrition. This sector represents an estimated one-third of global agricultural gross domestic product (GDP) and employs an estimated 1.3 billion people [40]. Animal products are an important source of protein and essential micronutrients for the world's population: meat, milk, and eggs provide at least 31% of dietary protein, and aquatic animal products like fish provide at least 16% of protein [41, 42]. Animal source foods (ASF) are produced in a wide range of farming systems that include grazing systems, concentrated animal feeding operations (CAFOs), fishing, and aquaculture. These production methods have serious implications for the environment: producing ASF requires more than three-quarters of the world's agricultural land and generates 14–20% of total GHGe [43].

The vast array of farming systems can be envisioned as a spectrum with industrial agricultural systems at one end and small-scale, subsistence farming at the other end. Industrial agricultural systems often involve the large-scale, intensive production of monoculture crops or livestock [44]. These systems tend to maximize yields and labor productivity through equipment and mechanization that operate at economies of scale. "Scale economies" mean that, given the production expenses, such methods are only economical when used in large operations. Industrial systems also extensively use external inputs like synthetic fertilizers, pesticides, and antibiotics [44]. While there are variations across industrialized systems, these systems typically have the capacity to quickly and efficiently produce a significant amount of food [45–49].

Small-scale farming is practiced by millions of smallholders and family farms throughout the world. Many different definitions exist for "smallholder agriculture," "family farms," and "subsistence agriculture," but most concur that small-scale farms operate on less than two hectares of land [20, 21, 50, 51]. Small and family farms can be highly efficient and are important for protecting natural resources. These farms produce more than half of the world's agricultural products and manage an equal proportion of the world's agricultural land [20, 21]. In the United States, small family farms account for nearly half of the country's farmland [52]. Small-scale farms are predominantly located in Asia and Africa, where they contribute significantly to food security and poverty reduction [50]. Box 2.2 describes the role played by small-scale Andean farmers in producing quinoa, an ancient staple grain that has become increasingly popular around the world.

> **Box 2.2 Quinoa, an indigenous crop of the Andes, goes mainstream**
>
> For thousands of years, small-scale farmers in the Andes have been growing a nutritious grain called quinoa. This protein-rich staple carries great importance for farmer families in Bolivia, Colombia, Ecuador, and Peru.
>
> Until a decade ago, quinoa was largely unknown to the rest of the world. Quinoa's popularity rose rapidly and demand for the "superfood" began to

grow in places like the United States and Europe. Imports of quinoa to the United States grew ten-fold and its price tripled [53].

As quinoa became increasingly sought-after around the world, some worried about the Andean farmers who grew the staple grain. Would Andean farmers see the financial benefits of quinoa going mainstream? Would they continue to consume the food themselves? Fortunately, the answer to both questions was "yes." Studies suggest that not only did quinoa farmers in the Andes continue to consume the food as part of their diet, but they also benefited from the growth of the commodity in international markets [53].

Despite its growing popularity, there are regulations and restrictions on how quinoa seeds and germplasm are traded across countries. As a result, Andean smallholder farmers remain responsible for conserving the biodiversity of quinoa species and their cultivation [54].

Mixed crop-landscape systems combine crop agriculture with livestock or aquaculture. Also known as "diversified farming," this integrated system can produce a diverse range of different foods [55]. Mixed or diversified systems produce approximately half of the world's food and more than half of the nutrients in the global food supply [56, 57]. Producers in these systems often grow many different crop species and varieties that include protein-rich crops, such as lentils; traditional foods, such as leafy greens; and underutilized crops, such as fonio and sorghum [3]. These systems can have a reduced impact on the environment and natural resource base, but may face many challenges, such as low productivity and limited connection to markets [58, 59].

Organic farming aims to promote agro-ecological balance and biodiversity. This production method uses few, if any, synthetic chemical inputs, such as pesticides, insecticides, and herbicides, in order to protect natural resources [60]. Some argue that organic foods have fewer pesticides and chemical residues than conventionally-grown products [61], a claim that is supported by several systematic review studies [62, 63]. Research on the nutritional value of organic foods has led to mixed results, and the long-term health benefits of diets high in organic foods remain unclear [63–66]. The demand for organic food has increased in recent decades, although these products are often much more expensive than conventionally-grown foods [67, 68].

After the initial production stage, most food products move to the processing and packaging stage of the supply chain. Food that is not immediately consumed by the producer must be stored for later consumption or distributed. First and foremost, food processing can help extend shelf life and avoid food loss. Processing can also contribute to nutrition outcomes by improving nutritional qualities, increasing the bioavailability of nutrients, and improving the sensory characteristics and functional properties of foods. It can also eliminate toxins that are harmful to health, such as foodborne microbes [69–71]. Common means of food processing include milling, cooling or freezing, smoking, heating, canning, fermenting and extrusion cooking

Table 2.1 Classification by degree of processing of food and beverage products [72, 73]

Category	Definition	Examples
Unprocessed or minimally processed	Single foods, no or very slight modifications	Fresh or frozen fruits and vegetables, milk, eggs, fresh fish, fresh meat
Basically processed	Single foods, processed as isolated food components or modified by preservation methods	Sugar, oil, unsweetened canned fruit, unsalted canned vegetables, white rice, flour, pasta
Moderately processed	Single foods with the addition of flavour additives	Sweetened canned fruit, salted canned vegetables, salted nuts, whole-grain bread, cereals with no added sugar
Highly processed	Multi-ingredient, industrially formulated mixtures	Sugar-sweetened beverages, salty snacks such as chips and crackers, cookies, cakes, candy, refined-grain bread, ready-to-eat cereals with added sugar, pre-prepared meals, margarine, ketchup, mayonnaise

Source Created by authors, not previously published

[71]. Table 2.1 illustrates the different categories of processed foods and examples of those foods.

Food value chains are a specialized type of supply chain. Although "food value chain" is often used synonymously with "food supply chain," there is a clear distinction between the two terms. Food value chains refer to the more specific process of adding value to a food product. In a food value chain, a product's value increases as it moves through each stage of the chain. This value can be achieved by improving the food product's functionality, safety, or nutritional value through processing. This change is then often reflected in the price of the product [74].

After the processing stage, food products are transported to markets and retail outlets. These spaces may be formal, such as stores, or informal, such as street vendors [75]. Informal markets are an important source of food for poor populations in low-and middle-income countries (LMICs), but supermarkets and fast-food chains have expanded significantly to reach the mass market in these countries [76, 77]. The retail landscape directly affects the food environment where consumers make their purchasing decisions [40].

Food Environments

Food environments are the places where people engage with food. These environments are where consumers make decisions about what to order, buy, or consume. These environments include the physical, economic, political, and sociocultural contexts that affect people's food choices. In addition, food environments include opportunities and conditions, all of which can influence dietary preferences, food choices, and nutritional status [78, 79].

For many communities, the food environment consists of the foods they produce and those they purchase from their local markets. For others, the food environment is more global, with increasingly interconnected local, regional, and international

Components of Food Systems

markets. Over time, food environments have become more complex as more actors shape food systems [80–82]. Fifty years ago, most food was grown for household consumption by small-scale producers in rural areas. Now, supermarkets that sell food grown in far-away locales are increasingly common [83, 84].

The food environment involves many different types of interactions. "Food entry points" are one type of interaction that represent opportunities—physical or otherwise—to support diets and nutrition along the food supply chain [38]. The built environment allows people to access these opportunities. It includes the human-made surroundings and infrastructure where people live, work, and play. Consumer engagement with the built environment depends on a range of factors, as shown in Fig. 2.4 [85]. Political, social, and cultural norms also play a role in food environments by influencing people's choices [86].

Interactions with the food environment can also be understood to occur in "external" or "personal" domains. As Fig. 2.5 shows, the external environment provides the available foods, their prices, properties, and marketing. The personal environment consists of a person's access to markets or the external food environment, their willingness or ability to pay for food, and the convenience and desirability of those foods [87, 88].

The availability and accessibility of food significantly influences the quality of diets. Food availability involves having a sufficient amount of high-quality food to satisfy a person's dietary needs. This food should be free of adverse substances and culturally acceptable [90]. Food access involves having the financial means to acquire food in a way that does not threaten or compromise other basic needs. Access means that adequate food is obtainable by all people, including vulnerable individuals and groups [90]. Food access includes both physical and economic access.

Physical access to food depends on the built environment. The lack of appropriate infrastructure in some LMICs can limit availability and access to foods, especially perishable foods. In addition, "food deserts" and "food swamps" can be found in all

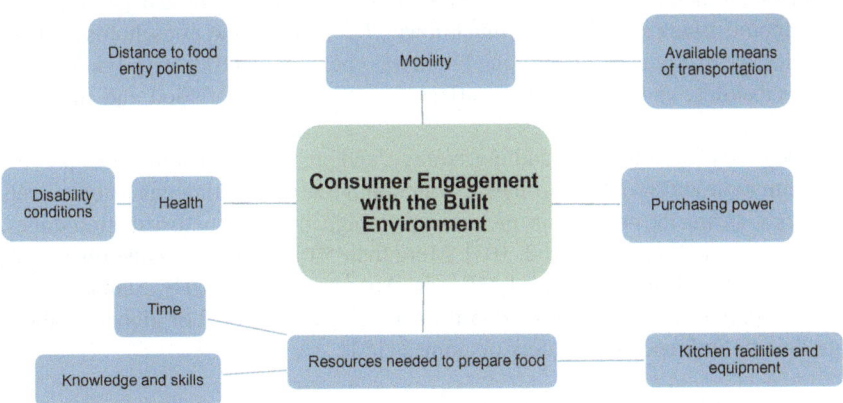

Fig. 2.4 Consumer engagement with the built environment (*Source* Created by authors, not previously published)

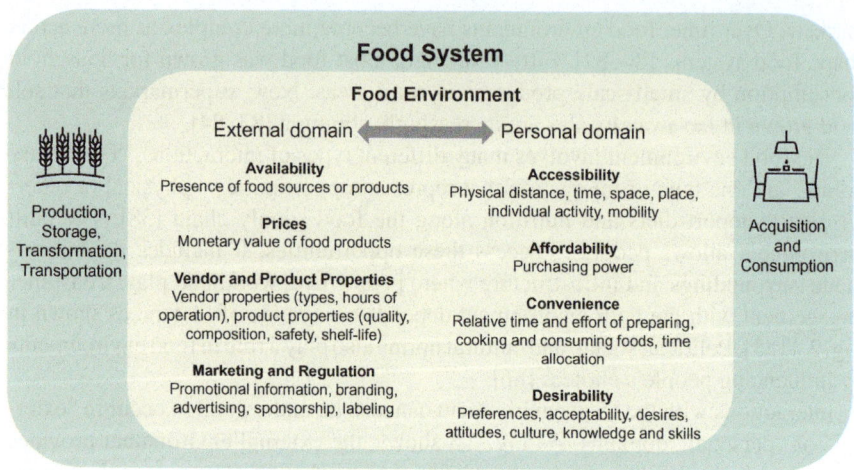

Fig. 2.5 Food environment [89]

countries. Food deserts are geographic areas where access to food is restricted or nonexistent due to the absence or low density of food entry points within a reasonable distance. Food swamps are areas where there is an overabundance of unhealthy foods but little access to healthy foods, especially fresh produce and minimally processed foods. Evidence from some high-income countries indicates that food deserts and food swamps are often found in low-income, underserved areas [91–93].

Economic access to food refers to food affordability and pricing. A household's income and purchasing power can be compared with the relative cost of food to understand their economic access to food [94–96]. Around the world, fresh and nutritious foods tend to be more expensive and less economically accessible than less nutritious, high-calorie foods [97]. In LMICs, people typically spend a significant proportion of their household budget on food [98, 99]. Relative food expenditures in high-income countries tend to be much lower, but low-income households in these countries spend a greater proportion of their income on food [100, 101]. Food prices, taxes, subsidies, and trade policies affect the affordability of food and influence consumption patterns [96].

Food safety refers to food handling, storage, and preparation practices that prevent contamination and foodborne illness. Contamination with pathogens or chemicals may occur during the production, processing, storage, transport or distribution stages, as well as in the household [102, 103]. More than 50% of all foodborne illness and 75% of related deaths occur in LMICs in Africa and Asia [104]. Standards and controls, policies, interventions, and investments at the national or global level can significantly influence food safety outcomes [104].

Consumer Demand

Consumer preference helps determine demand for certain foods and diets. This demand reflects people's choices about what foods to acquire, store, prepare, and eat, and how to share food within the household [105]. Income, education, taste preference, convenience, tradition, culture, and values determine consumer preferences and choices [106–108]. The external food environment also influences preference through various means of selecting, purchasing, preparing, and presenting food for consumption [78, 89].

Food purchasing and consumption decisions are influenced by information that people receive from advertising and marketing, labeling, and dietary guidelines. Food companies use branding, social media marketing, and advertisements to promote their food products. Product placement and signage in retail stores also influences dietary behavior. These promotional methods affect food acceptability, consumer preference, purchasing decisions, and consumption [109–112]. Labels, declarations, or warnings on food packaging, in food retail outlets, and on menus are other ways to inform consumers [113–115]. National food-based dietary guidelines provide recommendations on healthy diets that are adapted to the national context [116]. These guidelines can influence consumer preferences and inform both food supply chain actors and policymakers [117].

Convenience and preference are also critical to consumer decision-making. Sensory appeal and desirability are linked to the quality, safety, and familiarity of the food product, as well as the individual's own personal ideology, aspirations, and habits [118]. "Food quality" refers to the attributes of a food product that influence its value and enhance its acceptability to the consumer [103]. Social interactions, availability, and time constraints can affect a consumer's perceptions of convenience [118]. Other attributes that affect preference include the size, shape, and color of a food item or its presentation, the food's texture, flavor, odor, freshness and safety, ingredient and nutrient composition, production method (e.g., "organic" or "cage-free"), and level of processing [119].

Life events and personal experiences also influence food choice. Throughout life, people continuously consider and adjust their food values, preferences, and routines, though these deliberations are not necessarily conscious. These experiences affect consumer interactions with the food environment and guide eating behavior [120]. In turn, food choices influence nutritional status, health, and perceptions of identity, all of which can affect life experience [120].

Key Messages and Conclusions

Food systems are highly complex and interconnected. All the world's people interact with the food system: whether these interactions involve producing food on a farm, processing and selling it, monitoring safety and regulating, or buying and cooking food, everyone has a role to play. Food supply chains encompass all the disparate activities of the food system, while food environments represent places where people make decisions about what to buy and eat.

Food systems help to feed the world, but they also do so much more. These systems are interwoven with human society and the natural world. Food is critical to diets, nutritional status, and health, but it also carries importance for culture and tradition. Food systems provide employment and opportunity to millions of people around the world. Successful food production depends on the environment, but agriculture can also degrade and deplete natural resources, especially in the context of climate change.

Food systems must meet the increasing and evolving dietary needs of a growing global population in a sustainable way. Despite this daunting challenge, there is a tremendous opportunity to address food security and nutrition along with social justice and equality. To do this, a collective and integrated approach is imperative. Food systems need to become more inclusive, transparent, sustainable, and focused on providing healthier foods. Later chapters will discuss the importance of these goals and explore potential means of achieving them.

References

1. Mozaffarian D. Diets from around the world—Quality not quantity [Internet]. Vol. 378, The Lancet. 2011. p. 759. Available from: http://dx.doi.org/10.1016/s0140-6736(11)61362-7
2. Macdiarmid J. Healthy and sustainable diets [Internet]. Healthy and Sustainable Food Systems. 2019. pp. 125–34. Available from: http://dx.doi.org/10.4324/9781351189033-11
3. HLPE. Nutrition and food systems. A report by the High Level Panel of Experts on Food Security and Nutrition of the Committee on World Food Security [Internet]. HLPE; 2017. Report No.: 12. Available from: http://www.fao.org/fileadmin/user_upload/hlpe/hlpe_documents/HLPE_Reports/HLPE-Report-12_EN.pdf
4. Afshin A, Sur PJ, Fay KA, Cornaby L, Ferrara G. Health effects of dietary risks in 195 countries, 1990–2017: A systematic analysis for the Global Burden of Disease Study 2017. Lancet [Internet]. 2019; Available from: https://www.sciencedirect.com/science/article/pii/S0140673619300418
5. Parsons, K., Hawkes, C., Wells, R. What is the food system? A Food policy perspective [Internet]. Centre for Food Policy; 2019. Available from: https://www.city.ac.uk/__data/assets/pdf_file/0008/471599/7643_Brief-2_What-is-the-food-system-A-food-policy-perspective_WEB_SP.pdf
6. HLPE. Food losses and waste in the context of sustainable food systems. High Level Panel of Experts on Food Security and Nutrition of the Committee on World Food Security; 2014.
7. Food Systems | MNCFC [Internet]. Maine network of community food councils. 2020. Available from: https://www.mainefoodcouncils.net/food-systems
8. Hawkes C, Parsons K. Brief 1: Tackling food systems challenges: The role of food policy [Internet]. London: City University of London; 2019 [cited 2020 Aug 14]. Available from: https://openaccess.city.ac.uk/id/eprint/22793/
9. Hawkes C, Ruel MT, Salm L, Sinclair B, Branca F. Double-duty actions: Seizing programme and policy opportunities to address malnutrition in all its forms. Lancet. 2020 Jan 11;395(10218):142–55.
10. Webb P, Stordalen GA, Singh S, Wijesinha-Bettoni R, Shetty P, Lartey A. Hunger and malnutrition in the 21st century. BMJ. 2018 Jun 13;361:k2238.

11. Hawkesworth S, Dangour AD, Johnston D, Lock K, Poole N, Rushton J, et al. Feeding the world healthily: the challenge of measuring the effects of agriculture on health. Philos Trans R Soc Lond B Biol Sci. 2010 Sep 27;365(1554):3083–97.
12. Swinburn BA, Kraak VI, Allender S, Atkins VJ, Baker PI, Bogard JR, et al. The global syndemic of obesity, undernutrition, and climate change: The Lancet Commission report. Lancet. 2019 Feb 23;393(10173):791–846.
13. 13. Ericksen PJ. Conceptualizing food systems for global environmental change research. Glob Environ Change. 2008 Feb 1;18(1):234–45.
14. Willett W, Rockström J, Loken B, Springmann M, Lang T, Vermeulen S, et al. Food in the Anthropocene: The EAT-Lancet Commission on healthy diets from sustainable food systems. Lancet. 2019 Feb 2;393(10170):447–92.
15. Clark MA, Springmann M, Hill J, Tilman D. Multiple health and environmental impacts of foods. Proc Natl Acad Sci U S A. 2019 Nov 12;116(46):23357–62.
16. International Labour Organization. ILOSTAT database [Internet]. 2020. Available from: https://ilostat.ilo.org/data/
17. Allen T, Prosperi P. Modeling sustainable food systems. Environ Manage. 2016 May;57(5):956–75.
18. Pinstrup-Andersen P, Watson DD II. Food policy for developing countries: The role of government in global, national, and local food systems. Cornell University Press; 2011. 424 p.
19. IPES-Food. TOO BIG TO FEED Exploring the impacts of mega-mergers, consolidation and concentration of power in the agri-food sector. IPES Food; 2017.
20. Lowder SK, Skoet J, Raney T. The number, size, and distribution of farms, smallholder farms, and family farms worldwide. World Dev. 2016 Nov 1;87:16–29.
21. Graeub BE, Chappell MJ, Wittman H, Ledermann S, Kerr RB, Gemmill-Herren B. The state of family farms in the world. World Dev. 2016 Nov 1;87:1–15.
22. Food and Agriculture Organization of the United Nations. The State of World Fisheries and Aquaculture 2020. FAO; 2020.
23. Food and Agriculture Organization of the United Nations. The State of World Fisheries and Aquaculture. FAO; 2012.
24. Glopan. Improving diets in an era of food market transformation: Challenges and opportunities for engagement between the public and private sectors. Policy Brief No. 11. London, UK: Global Panel on Agriculture and Food Systems for Nutrition. 2018.
25. KPMG. The agricultural and food value chain: Entering a new era of cooperation. KPMG International; 2013.
26. Lusk JL, McCluskey J. Understanding the impacts of food consumer choice and food policy outcomes. Appl Econ Perspect Policy. 2018 Feb 16;40(1):5–21.
27. von Braun J, Birner R. Designing global governance for agricultural development and food and nutrition security. Rev Dev Econ. 2017 May 18;21(2):265–84.
28. Stokstad E. After 20 years, golden rice nears approval. Science. 2019 Nov 22;366(6468):934.
29. Stein AJ, Sachdev HPS, Qaim M. Can genetic engineering for the poor pay off?: An ex-ante evaluation of Golden Rice in India [Internet]. University of Hohenheim – Centre for Agriculture in the Tropics and Subtropics Institute of Agricultural Economics and Social Sciences in the Tropics and Subtropics; 2008 Mar [cited 2021 Jan 8]. Available from: http://opus.uni-hohenheim.de/volltexte/2008/261/
30. Glass S, Fanzo J. Genetic modification technology for nutrition and improving diets: An ethical perspective. Curr Opin Biotechnol [Internet]. 2017; Available from: https://www.sciencedirect.com/science/article/pii/S0958166916302488
31. Dubock A. Golden Rice: To combat vitamin a deficiency for public health. In: Zepka LQ, de Rosso VV, Jacob-Lopes E, editors. Vitamin A. Rijeka: IntechOpen; 2019.
32. Kettenburg AJ, Hanspach J, Abson DJ, Fischer J. From disagreements to dialogue: Unpacking the Golden Rice debate. Sustainability Sci. 2018 May 17;13(5):1469–82.
33. Wight AJ. The precautionary tale of golden rice. Science. 2019 Oct 11;366(6462):192–192.

34. Hawkes C, Ruel MT, Others. Value chains for nutrition. Reshaping agriculture for nutrition and health. 2012;73–82.
35. Porter ME, Millar VE, Others. How information gives you competitive advantage [Internet]. Harvard Business Review Reprint Service; 1985. Available from: https://www.gospi.fr/IMG/pdf/how_information_gives_you_competitive_advantage-porter-hbr-1985.pdf
36. 36. Renting H, Marsden TK, Banks J. Understanding alternative food networks: Exploring the role of short food supply chains in rural development. Environ Plan A. 2003 Mar 1;35(3):393–411.
37. Reardon T. Growing Food for Growing Cities. Chicago Council on Global Affairs; 2016.
38. Fanzo JC, Downs S, Marshall QE, de Pee S, Bloem MW. Value chain focus on food and nutrition security [Internet]. Nutrition and Health in a Developing World. 2017. p. 753–70. Available from: http://dx.doi.org/10.1007/978-3-319-43739-2_34
39. Lowder SK, Skoet J, Singh S. What do we really know about the number and distribution of farms and family farms in the world? Background paper for The State of Food and Agriculture 2014. 2014; Available from: https://ageconsearch.umn.edu/record/288983/
40. High Level Panel of Experts. Sustainable agricultural development for FSN: what roles for livestock? 2016.
41. Béné C, Barange M, Subasinghe R, Pinstrup-Andersen P, Merino G, Hemre G-I, et al. Feeding 9 billion by 2050–Putting fish back on the menu. Food Security. 2015;7(2):261–74.
42. Tacon AGJ, Metian M. Fish matters: Importance of aquatic foods in human nutrition and global food supply. Rev Fish Sci. 2013 Jan 1;21(1):22–38.
43. Ranganathan J, Vennard D, Waite R, Searchinger T, Dumas P, Lipinski B. Shifting diets: Toward a sustainable food future. In IFPRI; 2016. (2016 Global Food Policy Report, International Food Policy Research Institute (IFPRI)).
44. United States Department of Agriculture Economic Research Service. Farm Size and the Organization of U.S. Crop Farming. United States Department of Agriculture; 2013.
45. Foley JA, Ramankutty N, Brauman KA, Cassidy ES, Gerber JS, Johnston M, et al. Solutions for a cultivated planet. Nature. 2011 Oct 12;478(7369):337–42.
46. Garnett T, Appleby MC, Balmford A, Bateman IJ, Benton TG, Bloomer P, et al. Agriculture. Sustainable intensification in agriculture: Premises and policies. Science. 2013 Jul 5;341(6141):33–4.
47. Sachs JD, Remans R, Smukler SM, Winowiecki L, Andelman SJ, Cassman KG, et al. Effective monitoring of agriculture: A response. J Environ Monit. 2012 Mar;14(3):738–42.
48. 48. Pingali PL. Green revolution: Impacts, limits, and the path ahead. Proc Natl Acad Sci U S A. 2012 Jul 31;109(31):12302–8.
49. Cardinale BJ, Duffy JE, Gonzalez A, Hooper DU, Perrings C, Venail P, et al. Biodiversity loss and its impact on humanity. Nature. 2012 Jun 6;486(7401):59–67.
50. Hazell P. Five big questions about five hundred million small farms. In: Conference on New Directions for Smallholder Agriculture. researchgate.net; 2011. pp. 24–5.
51. High Level Panel of Experts. Investing in smallholder agriculture for food security. HLPE; 2013.
52. United States Department of Agriculture. America's Diverse Family farms [Internet]. 2019. Available from: https://www.ers.usda.gov/webdocs/publications/95547/eib-214.pdf?v=2023.2
53. Bellemare MF, Fajardo-Gonzalez J, Gitter SR. Foods and fads: The welfare impacts of rising quinoa prices in Peru. World Dev. 2018 Dec 1;112:163–79.
54. Bazile D, Jacobsen S-E, Verniau A. The global expansion of Quinoa: Trends and limits. Front Plant Sci. 2016 May 9;7:622.
55. Kremen C, Iles A, Bacon C. Diversified farming systems: An agroecological, systems-based alternative to modern industrial agriculture. Ecol Soc [Internet]. 2012;17(4). Available from: https://www.jstor.org/stable/26269193
56. Herrero M, Thornton PK, Notenbaert AM, Wood S, Msangi S, Freeman HA, et al. Smart investments in sustainable food production: Revisiting mixed crop-livestock systems. Science. 2010 Feb 12;327(5967):822–5.

57. Herrero M, Thornton PK, Power B, Bogard JR, Remans R, Fritz S, et al. Farming and the geography of nutrient production for human use: A transdisciplinary analysis. Lancet Planet Health. 2017 Apr;1(1):e33–42.
58. Chand R, Prasanna PAL, Singh A. Farm size and productivity: Understanding the strengths of smallholders and improving their livelihoods. Econ Polit Wkly. 2011;46(26/27):5–11.
59. van Tilburg A, Obi A. Factors unlocking markets to smallholders: Lessons, recommendations and stakeholders addressed [Internet]. Unlocking markets to smallholders. 2012. p. 243–54. Available from: http://dx.doi.org/10.3920/978-90-8686-168-2_11
60. Darnhofer I, Lindenthal T, Bartel-Kratochvil R, Zollitsch W. Conventionalisation of organic farming practices: from structural criteria towards an assessment based on organic principles. A review. Agron Sustain Dev. 2010;30(1):67–81.
61. Crinnion WJ. Organic foods contain higher levels of certain nutrients, lower levels of pesticides, and may provide health benefits for the consumer. Altern Med Rev. 2010 Apr;15(1):4–12.
62. United States Department of Agriculture. Pesticide Residue Monitoring Program Fiscal Year 2016 Pesticide Report. 2016; Available from: https://www.fda.gov/downloads/Food/Foodbo rneIllnessContaminants/Pesticides/UCM618373.pdf
63. Barański M, Srednicka-Tober D, Volakakis N, Seal C, Sanderson R, Stewart GB, et al. Higher antioxidant and lower cadmium concentrations and lower incidence of pesticide residues in organically grown crops: A systematic literature review and meta-analyses. Br J Nutr. 2014 Sep 14;112(5):794–811.
64. Dangour AD, Dodhia SK, Hayter A, Allen E, Lock K, Uauy R. Nutritional quality of organic foods: a systematic review. Am J Clin Nutr. 2009 Sep;90(3):680–5.
65. Smith-Spangler C, Brandeau ML, Hunter GE, Bavinger JC, Pearson M, Eschbach PJ, et al. Are organic foods safer or healthier than conventional alternatives?: A systematic review. Ann Intern Med. 2012 Sep 4;157(5):348–66.
66. Mitchell AE, Hong Y-J, Koh E, Barrett DM, Bryant DE, Denison RF, et al. Ten-year comparison of the influence of organic and conventional crop management practices on the content of flavonoids in tomatoes. J Agric Food Chem. 2007 Jul 25;55(15):6154–9.
67. Li J, Zepeda L, Gould BW. The demand for organic food in the US: An empirical assessment. Journal of Food Distribution Research. 2007;38(856-2016-57840):54–69.
68. Martin A, Severson K. Sticker Shock in the Organic Aisles. The New York Times [Internet]. 2008 Apr 18 [cited 2019 May 20]; Available from: https://www.nytimes.com/2008/04/18/bus iness/18organic.html
69. van Boekel M, Fogliano V, Pellegrini N, Stanton C, Scholz G, Lalljie S, et al. A review on the beneficial aspects of food processing. Mol Nutr Food Res. 2010 Sep 19;54(9):1215–47.
70. Weaver CM, Dwyer J, Fulgoni VL 3rd, King JC, Leveille GA, MacDonald RS, et al. Processed foods: Contributions to nutrition. Am J Clin Nutr. 2014 Jun;99(6):1525–42.
71. Augustin MA, Riley M, Stockmann R, Bennett L, Kahl A, Lockett T, et al. Role of food processing in food and nutrition security. Trends Food Sci Technol. 2016 Oct 1;56:115–25.
72. Poti JM, Mendez MA, Ng SW, Popkin BM. Is the degree of food processing and convenience linked with the nutritional quality of foods purchased by US households? Am J Clin Nutr. 2015 Jun;101(6):1251–62.
73. Moubarac J-C, Parra DC, Cannon G, Monteiro CA. Food classification systems based on food processing: Significance and implications for policies and actions: A systematic literature review and assessment. Curr Obes Rep. 2014 Jun;3(2):256–72.
74. Haq ZU. Food Value chain analysis: A review of selected studies for Pakistan and Guidelines for Further Research [Internet]. Working Paper; 2012. Available from: http://www.academia.edu/download/46134728/FVA.pdf
75. Food and Agriculture Organization. The informal food sector. FAO; 2003. Report No.: "Food in Cities" Collection, No. 4.
76. Resnick D. Governance: Informal food markets in Africa's cities. In: International Food Policy Research Institute, editor. 2017 Global Food Policy Report. 2017.

77. Reardon T, Gulati A. The rise of supermarkets and their development implications. International experience relevant for India [Internet]. 2008; Available from: https://citeseerx.ist.psu.edu/viewdoc/download?doi=10.1.1.141.1088&rep=rep1&type=pdf
78. Herforth A, Ahmed S. The food environment, its effects on dietary consumption, and potential for measurement within agriculture-nutrition interventions. Food Security. 2015 Jun 1;7(3):505–20.
79. Kraak VI, Swinburn B, Lawrence M, Harrison P. An accountability framework to promote healthy food environments. Public Health Nutr. 2014 Nov;17(11):2467–83.
80. Reardon T, Timmer CP. The economics of the food system revolution. Annu Rev Resour Econ. 2012 Aug 1;4(1):225–64.
81. Reardon T, Peter Timmer C. Transformation of the agrifood industry in developing countries [Internet]. Oxford Handbooks Online. 2014. Available from: http://dx.doi.org/10.1093/oxfordhb/9780195397772.013.026
82. Swinnen JFM. The dynamics of vertical coordination in agri-food supply chains in transition countries [Internet]. Global supply chains, standards and the poor: How the globalization of food systems and standards affects rural development and poverty. p. 42–58. Available from: http://dx.doi.org/10.1079/9781845931858.0042
83. Popkin BM, Reardon T. Obesity and the food system transformation in Latin America. Obes Rev. 2018 Aug;19(8):1028–64.
84. Minten B, Reardon T. Food prices, quality, and quality's pricing in supermarkets versus traditional markets in developing countries. Appl Econ Perspect Policy. 2008 Oct 1;30(3):480–90.
85. National Academies of Sciences, Engineering, and Medicine, Health and Medicine Division, Food and Nutrition Board, Roundtable on Obesity Solutions. Advancing obesity solutions through investments in the built environment: Proceedings of a workshop. National Academies Press; 2018. 100 p.
86. Swinburn B, Vandevijvere S, Kraak V, Sacks G, Snowdon W, Hawkes C, et al. Monitoring and benchmarking government policies and actions to improve the healthiness of food environments: A proposed Government Healthy Food Environment Policy Index. Obes Rev. 2013;14:24–37.
87. Caspi CE, Sorensen G, Subramanian SV, Kawachi I. The local food environment and diet: A systematic review. Health Place. 2012 Sep;18(5):1172–87.
88. Hawkes C, Smith TG, Jewell J, Wardle J, Hammond RA, Friel S, et al. Smart food policies for obesity prevention. Lancet. 2015 Jun 13;385(9985):2410–21.
89. Turner C, Aggarwal A, Walls H, Herforth A, Drewnowski A, Coates J, et al. Concepts and critical perspectives for food environment research: A global framework with implications for action in low- and middle-income countries. Global Food Security. 2018 Sep 1;18:93–101.
90. High Level Panel of Experts. Multi-stakeholder partnerships to finance and improve food security and nutrition in the framework of the 2030 Agenda [Internet]. HLPE; 2020. Available from: http://www.fao.org/3/CA0156EN/CA0156en.pdf
91. Walker RE, Keane CR, Burke JG. Disparities and access to healthy food in the United States: A review of food deserts literature [Internet]. Vol. 16, Health & Place. 2010. p. 876–84. Available from: http://dx.doi.org/10.1016/j.healthplace.2010.04.013
92. Beaulac J, Kristjansson E, Cummins S. A systematic review of food deserts, 1966-2007. Prev Chronic Dis. 2009 Jul;6(3):A105.
93. Rose D, Bodor JN, Swalm CM, Rice JC, Farley TA, Hutchinson PL. Deserts in New Orleans? Illustrations of urban food access and implications for policy. Ann Arbor, MI: University of Michigan National Poverty Center/USDA Economic Research Service Research [Internet]. 2009; Available from: http://citeseerx.ist.psu.edu/viewdoc/download?doi=10.1.1.189.2333&rep=rep1&type=pdf
94. Gibson J, Kim B. Do the urban poor face higher food prices? Evidence from Vietnam [Internet]. Vol. 41, Food Policy. 2013. p. 193–203. Available from: http://dx.doi.org/10.1016/j.foodpol.2013.05.003

95. Powell LM, Chaloupka FJ. Food prices and obesity: Evidence and policy implications for taxes and subsidies. Milbank Q. 2009 Mar;87(1):229–57.
96. Powell LM, Chriqui JF, Khan T, Wada R, Chaloupka FJ. Assessing the potential effectiveness of food and beverage taxes and subsidies for improving public health: A systematic review of prices, demand and body weight outcomes. Obes Rev. 2013;14(2):110–28.
97. FAO, IFAD, UNICEF, WFP. The state of food security and nutrition in the world 2020 [Internet]. 2020. Available from: http://www.fao.org/3/ca9692en/CA9692EN.pdf
98. Headey DD, Alderman HH. The relative caloric prices of healthy and unhealthy foods differ systematically across income levels and continents. J Nutr [Internet]. 2019 Jul 23 [cited 2019 Jul 23]; Available from: https://academic.oup.com/jn/advance-article-pdf/doi/10.1093/jn/nxz 158/28951648/nxz158.pdf
99. Clements KW, Si J. Engel's law, diet diversity, and the quality of food consumption. Am J Agric Econ. 2017;100(1):1–22.
100. Smith LP, Ng SW, Popkin BM. Trends in US home food preparation and consumption: analysis of national nutrition surveys and time use studies from 1965–1966 to 2007–2008. Nutr J. 2013 Apr 11;12(1):45.
101. Nord M. Food spending declined and food insecurity increased for middle-income and low-income households from 2000 to 2007. DIANE Publishing; 2009. 19 p.
102. Grace D. Food safety in low and middle income countries. Int J Environ Res Public Health. 2015 Aug 27;12(9):10490–507.
103. World Health Organization. Diet, nutrition, and the prevention of chronic diseases: Report of a joint WHO/FAO expert consultation. World Health Organization; 2003. 149 p.
104. Jaffee S, Henson S, Unnevehr L, Grace D, Cassou E. The safe food imperative: Accelerating progress in low-and middle-income countries. The World Bank; 2018.
105. Perry BD, Grace DC. How growing complexity of consumer choices and drivers of consumption behaviour affect demand for animal source foods. Ecohealth. 2015;12(4):703–12.
106. Glanz K, Basil M, Maibach E, Goldberg J, Snyder D. Why Americans eat what they do: Taste, nutrition, cost, convenience, and weight control concerns as influences on food consumption. J Am Diet Assoc. 1998 Oct;98(10):1118–26.
107. Furst T, Connors M, Bisogni CA, Sobal J, Falk LW. Food choice: A conceptual model of the process. Appetite. 1996 Jun;26(3):247–65.
108. Bisogni CA, Connors M, Devine CM, Sobal J. Who we are and how we eat: A qualitative study of identities in food choice. J Nutr Educ Behav. 2002 May;34(3):128–39.
109. Mazariegos S, Chacón V, Cole A, Barnoya J. Nutritional quality and marketing strategies of fast food children's combo meals in Guatemala. BMC Obes. 2016 Dec 8;3:52.
110. Popkin BM, Hawkes C. Sweetening of the global diet, particularly beverages: Patterns, trends, and policy responses. Lancet Diabetes Endocrinol. 2016 Feb;4(2):174–86.
111. Hawkes C, Harris JL. An analysis of the content of food industry pledges on marketing to children. Public Health Nutr. 2011 Aug;14(8):1403–14.
112. Cairns G, Angus K, Hastings G, Caraher M. Systematic reviews of the evidence on the nature, extent and effects of food marketing to children. A retrospective summary. Appetite. 2013 Mar;62:209–15.
113. Pomeranz JL, Wilde P, Mozaffarian D, Micha R. Mandating front-of-package food labels in the U.S. – What are the First Amendment obstacles? Food Policy. 2019 Jun 19;101722.
114. Singla M. Usage and understanding of food and nutritional labels among Indian consumers [Internet]. Vol. 112, British Food Journal. 2010. p. 83–92. Available from: http://dx.doi.org/10.1108/00070701011011227
115. Levy AS, Fein SB. Consumers' ability to perform tasks using nutrition labels. J Nutr Educ. 1998;30(4):210–7.
116. Herforth A, Arimond M, Álvarez-Sánchez C, Coates J, Christianson K, Muehlhoff E. A global review of food-based dietary guidelines. Adv Nutr [Internet]. 2019 Apr 30; Available from: http://dx.doi.org/10.1093/advances/nmy130
117. Dwyer JT. The importance of dietary guidelines [Internet]. Reference Module in Food Science. 2019. Available from: http://dx.doi.org/10.1016/b978-0-08-100596-5.22519-5

118. Pollard J, Kirk SFL, Cade JE. Factors affecting food choice in relation to fruit and vegetable intake: A review. Nutr Res Rev. 2002 Dec;15(2):373–87.
119. Grunert KG. Food quality and safety: Consumer perception and demand. Eur Rev Agric Econ. 2005 Sep 1;32(3):369–91.
120. Sobal J, Bisogni CA. Constructing food choice decisions [Internet]. Vol. 38, Annals of Behavioral Medicine. 2009. p. 37–46. Available from: http://dx.doi.org/10.1007/s12160-009-9124-5

Chapter 3
Food Policy

Introduction

This chapter introduces the concepts of food policy and governance. Food policy affects how food systems operate and how consumers, producers, and other stakeholders make decisions. Policy acts as a mechanism for governance by providing guidance for decision-making and measures for accountability. Food governance involves making and implementing policy decisions. Governments, consumers, producers, businesses, non-governmental organizations, civil society, and many others play a role in developing, implementing, and participating in food policy and governance. Food policy has changed significantly in recent decades to reflect emerging global trends. Consumer and civil society groups increasingly advocate for holistic food policies that integrate policy across different areas and sectors relevant to the food system.

What Is Food Policy?

Food policies are plans that affect the institutions, organizations, and actors working in food systems. These policies represent the collective efforts of governments to influence the operation of the food system and thus further social objectives. Food policies are meant to shape the decision-making environment of food producers, consumers, and retailers [1, 2].

Collectively, food policy affects who eats what, when, where, and at what cost. It affects nutrition and health, livelihoods and communities, urban and rural settings, and the environment and climate—now and into the future. Food policy is important for consumers as well as the people who grow, transport, process, and sell food: "Because everybody eats, food policy affects everyone" [3, p. 2].

Most often, food policies are closely connected to governmental actions. The policies of the private sector and civil society are also important for the food system [1, 4]. By setting regulations or changing stakeholder incentives, food policy is meant to shift the food system's structure and functionality toward a given country's intended goals.

Policy success is measured over time, though evaluating the direct impacts of policies is not always possible given the complexity of contributing factors. The success of a given policy can be assessed by its implementation within a specific context, achievement of intended effects, effective maintenance, and scalability over the long-term to improve diets and health of larger populations [5]. Despite policymakers' best intentions, sometimes actions can lead to unintended consequences or cause harm instead of improving the food system [4, 6].

Like any field of policy, food policy can be delivered at multiple levels from the local to the global. It can be highly specific or a general overarching approach. Food policies often involve a complex web of institutions, infrastructure, people, and processes [3]. Figure 3.1 shows the many types of food policies that exist. Some policies focus primarily on agriculture, while others concern urban food systems. Food policies can focus on very specific actions, such as food labeling or advertising, or provide broader guidance on diets for their populations.

Policies can be translated into action by using objectives that align with a country's needs, budgets, and specific, measurable targets. Thus, it is important for policies to be implemented as programs, such as national school meals or social protection programs, like food safety nets, or as helpful guidelines for the public, such as food-based dietary guidelines [7].

Laws and regulations also influence food policies. In the United States, for example, the Food, Drug, and Cosmetic Act of 1938 allowed the government to enforce food and drug regulations. The Meat Inspection Act, Poultry Products Inspection Act, and Egg Products Inspection Act are three major federal laws that govern adulterated foods. The Food and Drug Administration (FDA) and the U.S. Department of Agriculture (USDA) are the two major regulatory bodies that are responsible for enforcing these laws and regulations. The FDA oversees the regulation of 80% of the U.S. food supply. This agency has jurisdiction over domestic and imported foods, and it regulates all foods and food ingredients introduced into or offered for sale in interstate commerce. The USDA shares in the regulation of meat, poultry, and certain processed egg products.

What Is Food Governance?

Governance encompasses the process of making and implementing decisions. It also includes the structures through which these processes occur [8]. More specifically, food governance involves the effective delivery of food security and nutrition to all members of society, especially the most vulnerable. In countries with strong food

What Is Food Governance? 31

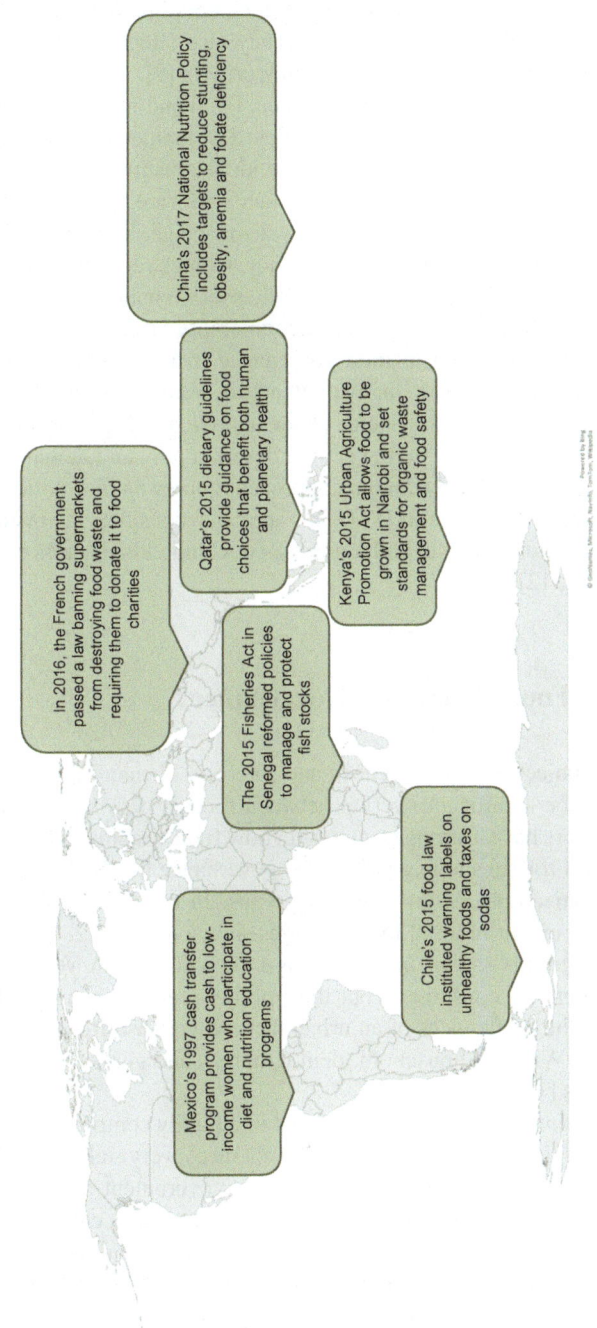

Fig. 3.1 Various types of food policies enacted around the world [3]

governance, governments commit to national food plans as part of the national development strategy. These countries convene intersectoral coordinating committees and maintain regular surveys and data collections. They also allocate funding in their budgets for food strategies and plans, among other criteria [9].

Policies are a critical component of governance. Food and nutrition policies are multisectoral, which means that successful policy development and implementation requires collaboration between different individuals, institutions, and systems. Effective policies require an understanding of which actors are "pulling the levers," or influencing outcomes in order to drive food system change. Interactions between actors can also influence the effectiveness of policy. Context also affects how well actors work together to develop and implement policies. In "enabling environments," actors share political will, coordination, and accountability [10].

A political economy approach to food governance focuses on actors and their power relationships. Over the years, many explanatory frameworks have been used to address challenges in the food system. Other approaches focus on the natural sciences, especially agronomy, or on the economics of supply and demand. Unlike these other approaches, a political economy approach focuses on how policies cause certain outcomes across food systems [11]. This approach considers the institutional framework in which actors operate, and it assesses how individual actors contribute to policy impacts [11, 12].

Who Influences Food Policy and Governance?

Food policies are subject to the influences and interests of many different stakeholders. There may be significant overlap between food system stakeholders and actors, but stakeholders have a stronger interest in how food systems function. These parties compete for a role in shaping policy and governance [3]. Stakeholders may be individuals, organizations, or unorganized groups. In most cases, food system stakeholders fall into one or more of the categories shown in Fig. 3.2.

The stakeholder groups shown in Fig. 3.2 are very diverse. A vegetarian and an omnivore may both be consumers, but their policy preferences might be very different. Likewise, the preferences of an urban factory worker differ from those of a rural farm laborer. Within a household, demographics and gender roles can also affect policy interests [13].

Food policy is meant to address the challenges of a highly complex food system. Given the enormity of this task, food policies may not meet every stakeholder's needs and interests. Food policies are negotiated between government agencies, which include ministries of finance, agriculture, health, commerce, trade, environment, and foreign affairs. Various bureaucracies and lobbying groups often attempt to shape policy negotiations. Because of these different influences, government action is likely to include conflicting goals and policy measures that may contradict each other. Policies may be influenced by certain parties that hold considerable power within food systems [13]. Box 3.1 describes how policies and interventions to eliminate trans fats from the food supply require the participation of many different stakeholders.

Fig. 3.2 Food system stakeholders (*Source* Created by authors, not previously published)

Box 3.1 Food system stakeholders and the elimination of trans fats

Trans fats are an artificial product contained in partially hydrogenated oils. In the early 1990s, trans fats entered the food supply as a key ingredient in processed foods due to their low cost and long shelf life. Consumption of trans fats, even at low levels of intake, is a major risk factor for cardiovascular disease, which is the leading cause of death globally and accounts for one in every three deaths [14]. Trans fats also increase the risk of other diseases, such as diabetes, cancer, and Alzheimer's disease [14, 15]. Removing trans fats from the food supply is an effective way to prevent cardiovascular disease.

Over time, many countries and jurisdictions have implemented policies to eliminate trans fats. Of these interventions, the most successful have been multicomponent approaches that involve different stakeholders. Since 1993, Denmark has attempted to reduce trans fat consumption through increasingly progressive strategies, which include food labeling and voluntary collaboration with industry. In 2003, the country implemented a ban on the use of industrially produced trans fats in food. As a result of these efforts, deaths from cardiovascular disease declined 3.2% more than in similar countries without trans fat restrictions. In the United States, Canada, and Costa Rica, multi-stakeholder interventions that involved food labeling and voluntary reformulation have also reduced the availability of trans fats and improved health outcomes, although to a lesser extent than strategies that involved legislation [15–19].

> In 2018, the World Health Organization (WHO) launched the REPLACE initiative to eliminate trans fats from the global food supply by 2023. Achieving this goal requires the participation of many different food system stakeholders. Policymakers need to implement and enforce regulation on trans fats, and governments must collaborate to monitor trans fat content in food products. Food companies need to work together with governments to reformulate their products and replace trans fats with healthier oils and fats [14]. By 2021, the WHO reports that 58 countries will have introduced legislation to reduce or eliminate trans fats from the food supply [20]. Despite this progress, two-thirds of the world's people remain unprotected from trans fats. The most comprehensive reforms have occurred in high-income countries, although low- and middle-income countries (LMICs) experience far more deaths associated with trans fat intake [14]. Without further action, trans fat intake will likely remain high among poor populations that consume more processed, packaged foods [15].

Historical Transitions Toward a Holistic Food Policy

Food policy has evolved significantly in recent decades to reflect changes in our world. Thirty years ago, food policies focused on reducing hunger, addressing rural needs, and increasing food productivity. Now, food policies focus more on urbanism, obesity, and global trade issues [13]. For example, nutrition policy has evolved from the 1970s, when nutrition policy focused on singular approaches that lacked intersectoral collaboration. In more recent years, nutrition policy became much more holistic, as Table 3.1 shows. The international development community has increasingly recognized the importance of nutrition, which has facilitated more cross-sectoral attention and an increasingly holistic view of nutrition [21].

Most food policies are intended to address specific aspects of the food system, instead of more comprehensively addressing challenges through a holistic food system policy. Existing policies are relatively narrow and focused in their scope: examples include dietary guidelines, subsidies, trade, taxes, and labeling schemes. However, many communities have advocated for a "systems approach" that would integrate relevant food policies. A "systems approach" to food systems explores how the entire system is connected in order to understand the influence of different activities across the system and the need for improved feedback mechanisms. A systems approach to food policy involves making these connections across discrete policy areas and different levels of government, as well as between the public and private sectors [22].

Holistic, integrated food policies have been implemented in some cities and regions around the world. In Washington, DC, for example, policy is integrated across the various food outcomes and actors that are needed to shape food systems

Table 3.1 History of nutrition policy and politics [21]

Evolution of nutrition policy and politics

From the protein era to multi-sectoral planning	From multi-sectorality to nutrition isolationalism	Micronutrient era	From obscurity to global priority	Increasing momentum
1970	**1980**	**1990**	**2000**	**2010**
International Conference on Nutrition, National Development and Planning (1971)	Sen on entitlements (1981)	UNICEF conceptual framework (1990)	MDG 1 (underweight target)	SUN Movement (2010 onwards)
Berg: *"The Nutrition Factor"* (1973)	Iringa Programme (Tanzania, 1985)	World Summit for Children (1990)	World Bank-UNICEF collaborations (Gillespie et al 2003)	Mainstreaming Nutrition Initiative (2011)
McLaren: *"The Great Protein Fiasco"* (1974)	Field (1987)	International Conference on Nutrition (1992)	Capacity focus (Heaver 2005)	Nutrition4Growth Summit (2013)
World Food Conference (1975)	Focus on micronutrient supplementation and breastfeeding	Micronutrient Initiative formed (1993)	Lancet Nutrition Series (2008)	Lancet Nutrition Series (2013)
1976 World Bank study			Food price spikes (2007-8)	
Nutrition planning cells (mandate without power)			Copenhagen Consensus (2008)	
			Increased focus on the "double burden"	

for urban residents (Fig. 3.3). The policy focuses not only on better diets, but also on more equitable access, livelihoods, and sustainability.

The International Panel of Experts on Sustainable Food Systems established a Common Food Policy that the European Union region could use to develop a more holistic food policy and align relevant policies that impact food. The proposed policy would implement a new "governance architecture" for policies related to food production, processing, distribution, and consumption, as shown in Fig. 3.4. The Common Food Policy aims to support the development of a more sustainable food system for the region.

The Common Food Policy recommends policy integration to resolve the inefficiencies of the current policy space. The policy's authors argue that the ad hoc development of Europe's current food policies have resulted in confusion. They advocate for integration across policy areas and governance levels, as well as across government levels. The authors suggest that policies should consider long-term solutions and ways in which holistic food systems can incorporate sustainability. This proposed policy would also involve democratic decision-making to reclaim public policies for the good of public health and manage the influence of powerful interest groups [24].

Key Messages and Conclusions

Food policy and governance play a critical role in determining how food systems operate. Policymakers use policy to address the challenges of a highly complex food

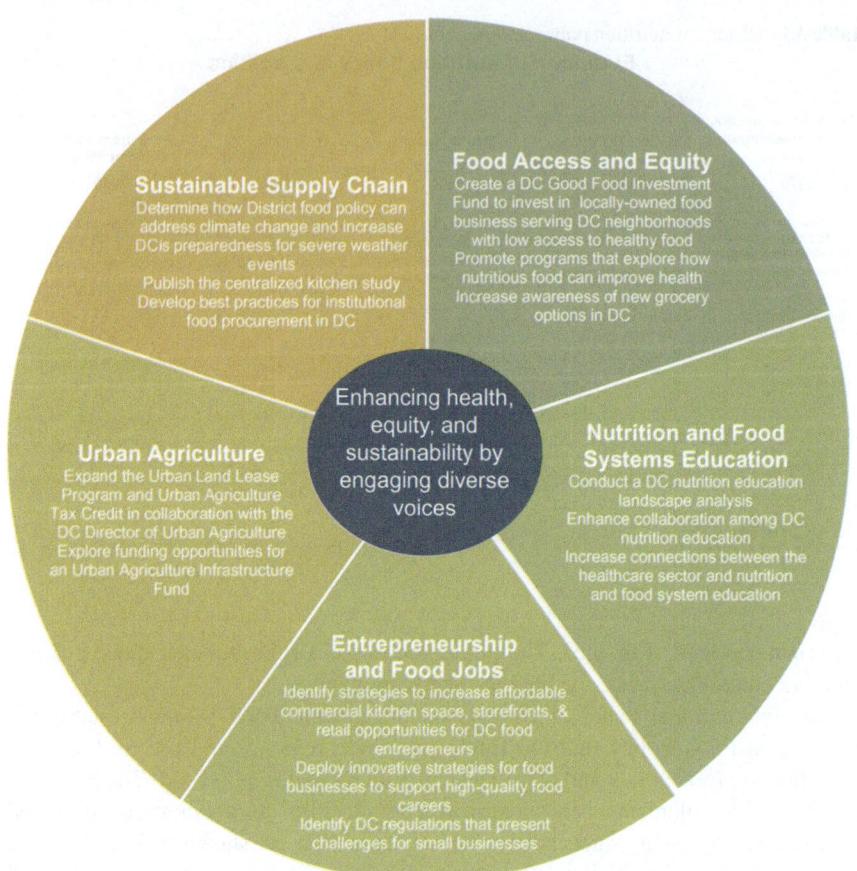

Fig. 3.3 Washington, DC 2020 Food Policy [23]

system. Governments, consumers, non-governmental organizations, businesses, and many others influence the development and implementation of food policy. These policies matter for everybody, because everybody eats.

Over the years, food policy has evolved to focus on obesity, urbanization, and global trade. A holistic policy approach is increasingly needed to address the complex challenges within the food system. Investments are needed to orient food systems toward better diets, nutrition, and health outcomes. Yet making these investments is a challenging task, because of the inherent complexity of implementation and potential trade-offs [25]. Policymakers need access to the latest and most rigorous evidence to best address food system challenges, but they are often forced to deliberate with limited data about what works in a specific context [26]. They may be aware of the core set of interventions needed to achieve a certain set of outcomes, but the path to implementing these interventions is full of uncertainties due to factors outside of their control [27].

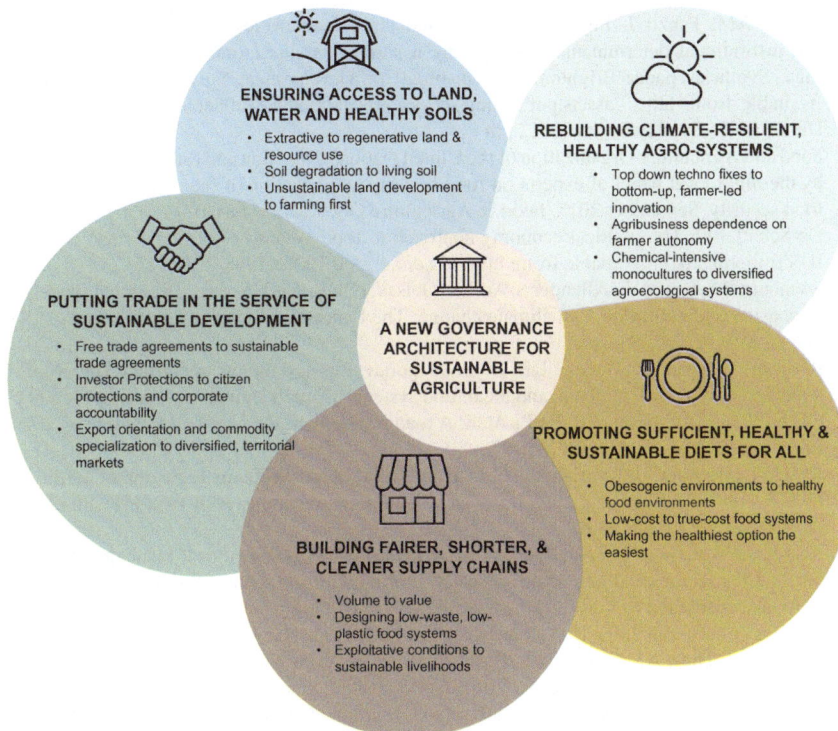

Fig. 3.4 Holistic proposed food policy for the European Union [24]

References

1. Buse K, Walt G. Globalisation and multilateral public-private health partnerships: Issues for health policy. Health Policy in a Globalising World. 2002;41–62.
2. Haddad L, Hawkes C, Waage J, Webb P, Godfray C, Toulmin C. Food systems and diets: Facing the challenges of the 21st century. London, UK: Global Panel on Agriculture and Food Systems for Nutrition; 2016.
3. Hawkes C, Parsons K. Brief 1: Tackling food systems challenges: The role of food policy [Internet]. London: City University of London; 2019 [cited 2020 Aug 14]. Available from: https://openaccess.city.ac.uk/id/eprint/22793/
4. Swinburn B, Kraak V, Rutter H, Vandevijvere S, Lobstein T, Sacks G, et al. Strengthening of accountability systems to create healthy food environments and reduce global obesity. Lancet. 2015 Jun 20;385(9986):2534–45.
5. Peeters A. Obesity and the future of food policies that promote healthy diets. Nat Rev Endocrinol. 2018 Jul;14(7):430–37.
6. Haddad L. Reward food companies for improving nutrition. Nature. 2018 Apr 5;556(7699):19–22.
7. Mozaffarian D. Dietary and policy priorities for cardiovascular disease, diabetes, and obesity: A comprehensive review. Circulation. 2016 Jan 12;133(2):187–225.
8. Srivastava M. Good Governance - Concept, meaning and features: A detailed study [Internet]. 2009 [cited 2020 Feb 2]. Available from: https://papers.ssrn.com/abstract=1528449

9. Acosta AM, Fanzo J. Fighting maternal and child malnutrition: Analysing the political and institutional determinants of delivering a national multisectoral response in six countries. Synthesis paper Brighton, UK: Institute for Development Studies [Internet]. 2012; Available from: https://assets.publishing.service.gov.uk/media/57a08a6840f0b649740005a2/DFID_ANG_Synthesis_April2012.pdf
10. Food and Agriculture Organization of the United Nations. Nutrition and food systems: A report by the night level panel of experts on food security and nutrition of the committee on world food security. September 2017. Food & Agriculture Org.; 2018. 152 p.
11. De Schutter O. The political economy approach to food systems reform [Internet]. Vol. 50, IDS Bulletin. 2019. Available from: http://dx.doi.org/10.19088/1968-2019.115
12. Swinburn BA, Kraak VI, Allender S, Atkins VJ, Baker PI, Bogard JR, et al. The global syndemic of obesity, undernutrition, and climate change: The Lancet Commission report. Lancet. 2019 Feb 23;393(10173):791–846.
13. Pinstrup-Andersen P, Watson DD II. Food policy for developing countries: The role of government in global, national, and local food systems. Cornell University Press; 2011. 424 p.
14. Ghebreyesus TA, Frieden TR. REPLACE: A roadmap to make the world trans fat free by 2023. Lancet. 2018 May 19;391(10134):1978–80.
15. Hyseni L, Bromley H, Kypridemos C, O'Flaherty M, Lloyd-Williams F, Guzman-Castillo M, et al. Systematic review of dietary trans-fat reduction interventions. Bull World Health Organ. 2017 Dec 1;95(12):821–30G.
16. Ratnayake WN, Swist E, Zoka R, Gagnon C, Lillycrop W, Pantazapoulos P. Mandatory trans fat labeling regulations and nationwide product reformulations to reduce trans fatty acid content in foods contributed to lowered concentrations of trans fat in Canadian women's breast milk samples collected in 2009-2011. Am J Clin Nutr. 2014 Oct;100(4):1036–40.
17. Downs SM, Thow AM, Leeder SR. The effectiveness of policies for reducing dietary trans fat: A systematic review of the evidence. Bull World Health Organ. 2013 Apr 1;91(4):262–9H.
18. Ratnayake WMN, L'Abbe MR, Mozaffarian D. Nationwide product reformulations to reduce trans fatty acids in Canada: when trans fat goes out, what goes in? Eur J Clin Nutr. 2009 Jun;63(6):808–11.
19. Mozaffarian D, Stampfer MJ. Removing industrial trans fat from foods. BMJ. 2010 Apr 15;340:c1826.
20. World Health Organization. More than 3 billion people protected from harmful trans fat in their food [Internet]. 2020. Available from: https://www.who.int/news/item/09-09-2020-more-than-3-billion-people-protected-from-harmful-trans-fat-in-their-food
21. Nisbett N, Gillespie S, Haddad L, Harris J. Why worry about the politics of childhood undernutrition? World Dev. 2014 Dec 1;64:420–33.
22. Parsons K HC. Brief 4: Embedding food in all policies. Centre for Food Policy City University of London; 2019.
23. DC Food Policy Council. 2020 DC food policy priorities [Internet]. DC Food Policy Council. 2020. Available from: https://dcfoodpolicy.org/2020-dc-food-policy-priorities-2/
24. De Schutter O. The political economy approach to food systems reform. IDS Bull [Internet]. 2019;50(2). Available from: http://dx.doi.org/10.19088/1968-2019.115
25. Pinstrup-Andersen P. Guiding food system policies for better nutrition. Background paper for the State of Food and Agriculture. 2013;
26. Mozaffarian D, Angell SY, Lang T, Rivera JA. Role of government policy in nutrition—Barriers to and opportunities for healthier eating. BMJ [Internet]. 2018 Jun 13 [cited 2020 Feb 2];361. Available from: https://www.bmj.com/content/361/bmj.k2426.abstract
27. Balarajan Y, Reich MR. Political economy challenges in nutrition. Global Health. 2016 Nov 5;12(1):70.

Part II
Changing Food Systems and Diets for Nutrition

Part II

Chapter 4
Nutritious Foods, Healthy Diets, and Contributions to Health

Introduction

This chapter introduces the concept of diets and explains how diets affect health. Diets are composed of foods that range in healthfulness and nutrition. Many different factors influence a person's diet. Healthy diets meet an individual's nutritional needs and support overall health. Dietary patterns vary by region, but global diets are less than optimal. These suboptimal diets directly affect nutrition and health outcomes. Poor diets are now considered a top risk factor for death and disability.

What Are Diets?

Diets are made up of foods, which can be categorized as "nutritious" or "less nutritious," and these, in turn, make up either a "healthy" or "unhealthy" diet. Nutritious foods include whole grains, fruits, vegetables, nuts and seeds, beans and legumes, fish and seafood, and dairy. Foods rich in total polyunsaturated fatty acids, omega-three fatty acids, and dietary fiber are in this group.

Less nutritious foods may be known as "highly-processed and packaged," "ultra-processed," or "junk" foods. This group of foods includes excessive amounts of unprocessed red meats, processed meats (e.g., sausage, bacon, ham, hot dogs), highly-processed starches (e.g., chips, crackers, breakfast cereals, baked goods like cookies or pastries, instant noodles), added sugars (e.g., candy and sweets), and sugar-sweetened beverages (SSBs). Foods that contain high levels of saturated fat, trans fat, dietary cholesterol, and sodium are in this group [1].

As discussed in Chapter 2, an individual's food choices and diet are affected by many factors throughout life. In addition to physiological needs, social, psychological, and economic factors also play a role in determining what foods people eat. These factors also change over time. For example, a parent or caregiver makes most food decisions for young children. During adolescence, body image concerns and others' opinions can influence what teenagers eat. Adults are more likely to consider price, healthfulness, convenience, and preference when they choose what foods to purchase and eat [2].

Healthy Diets

A healthy diet consists of a diverse set of nutritious foods and ingredients that meet an individual's nutritional needs. Healthy diets support a healthy body weight and overall health. Diets can also help prevent or reduce the risk of chronic and noncommunicable diseases (NCDs) throughout life [3–5].

The World Health Organization (WHO) recommends that an optimal diet contain a variety of foods that are sufficient in quantity, high in quality, diverse, and free from harmful pathogens [10]. Dietary diversity is an important component of a healthy diet, but it does not always indicate that the overall diet is healthy. A diverse set of foods can be a combination of less healthy foods [6, 7].

There are many ways to assess diet quality, as Box 4.1 shows. In addition to the recommendations from the WHO, moderation and balance are other indicators of a high-quality diet. Diet quality can be difficult to define, partly because diets vary depending on cultural customs, individual needs, and local availability of food items [8].

> **Box 4.1 Components of diet quality**
> - *Sufficient quantity*, or "adequacy," means that food should meet energy needs in the form of calories. These needs are based on an individual's age, weight and size, sex, activity level, and overall life stage;
> - *Quality* refers to the types and varieties of foods that an individual eats;
> - *Diversity*, or "variety," means an assortment of foods both within food groups and across the range of food groups;
> - *Safety* involves minimizing the risk that food might be contaminated with pathogens or diseases during any stage of the food supply chain. These stages include production, processing, storage, transport, and distribution, as well as storage, preparation, and cooking within households;
> - *Moderation* means that people should limit their consumption of foods and nutrients that are associated with chronic disease. Foods that are high in fat, saturated fat, sodium, cholesterol, and sugar should be eaten in moderation;
> - *Overall balance* refers to the proportionality of each element in the diet [9, 10].

In 2019, the *Lancet* journals created the Eat-*Lancet* Commission on Food, Planet, and Health to determine targets for healthy diets and sustainable agriculture. The

Commission, a team of diverse, multidisciplinary scientists, explored the potential for a diet that could maintain and improve human health while remaining within the boundaries of planetary sustainability. This new reference diet complements but is distinct from the WHO's recommended healthy diet. In the *2019 Eat-Lancet Report on Healthy Diets for Sustainable Food Systems*, the Commission described a universal healthy reference diet, or "Planetary Health Diet," that includes more healthy foods, such as fish, vegetables, fruit, legumes, whole grains, and nuts, and fewer unhealthy foods, such as red meat, sugar, and refined grains. Optional foods to be consumed in moderation include eggs, poultry, and dairy foods. The Commission's findings on diets and sustainability are discussed in greater detail in Chapter 10.

Current Diets

Diets contribute to nutrition and health outcomes for people throughout all stages of life. Nutritional needs are highest during periods of rapid growth, such as early life and adolescence. Despite their importance, diets remain suboptimal for populations around the world. For most people, their diets do not fully support their nutritional needs.

Healthy diets are critical in the very beginning of life because infants and young children have high nutritional and energy needs. Breast milk is a vital source of nutrients and contains biologically active components that aid in the development of the infant's immune system and intestinal microbiota [11]. Exclusive breastfeeding involves feeding only breastmilk, not any other liquids or solids, for the first six months of a child's life. Despite the nutritional value of breastmilk, only 42% of children around the world are exclusively breastfed [12].

After six months of age, other foods can be incorporated into a child's diet. However, these foods are often insufficient in energy or quality: Globally, 59% of young children do not eat animal source foods (ASF) on a daily basis and 44% do not eat any fruits and vegetables [12, 13]. More young children in upper-middle-income countries consume at least seven food groups than do children in low-and lower-middle-income countries (Fig. 4.1a) [12]. In upper-middle-income countries, twice as many children are fed eggs, meat, poultry, and fish than in low-and lower-middle-income countries (Fig. 4.1b) [12].

Dietary constraints continue as children grow older. A school-based survey conducted in 83 countries found that 33% of children aged 10 to 17 do not eat fruit daily and 86% do not consume vegetables daily. However, 44% of children report consuming soda every day [14]. Some studies have also shown that adolescent girls, particularly those living in South Asia, have inadequate intakes of iron, iodine, vitamin A, zinc, and calcium due to their diets [15, 16].

Suboptimal diets remain prevalent in adulthood. The consumption of nuts and seeds, milk, and whole grains falls below optimal levels, whereas the global consumption of less nutritious foods and unhealthy nutrients exceeds the optimal level, as shown in Fig. 4.2. In every region of the world, consumption of sodium and SSBs

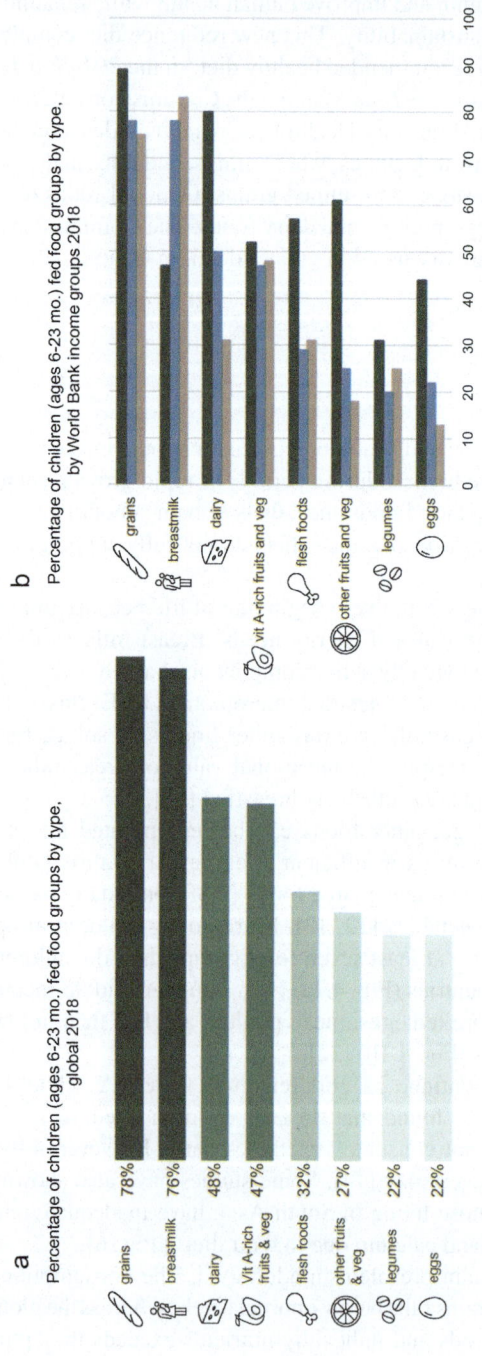

Fig. 4.1 a and b Suboptimal infant and young children's diets [12]

What Are Diets?

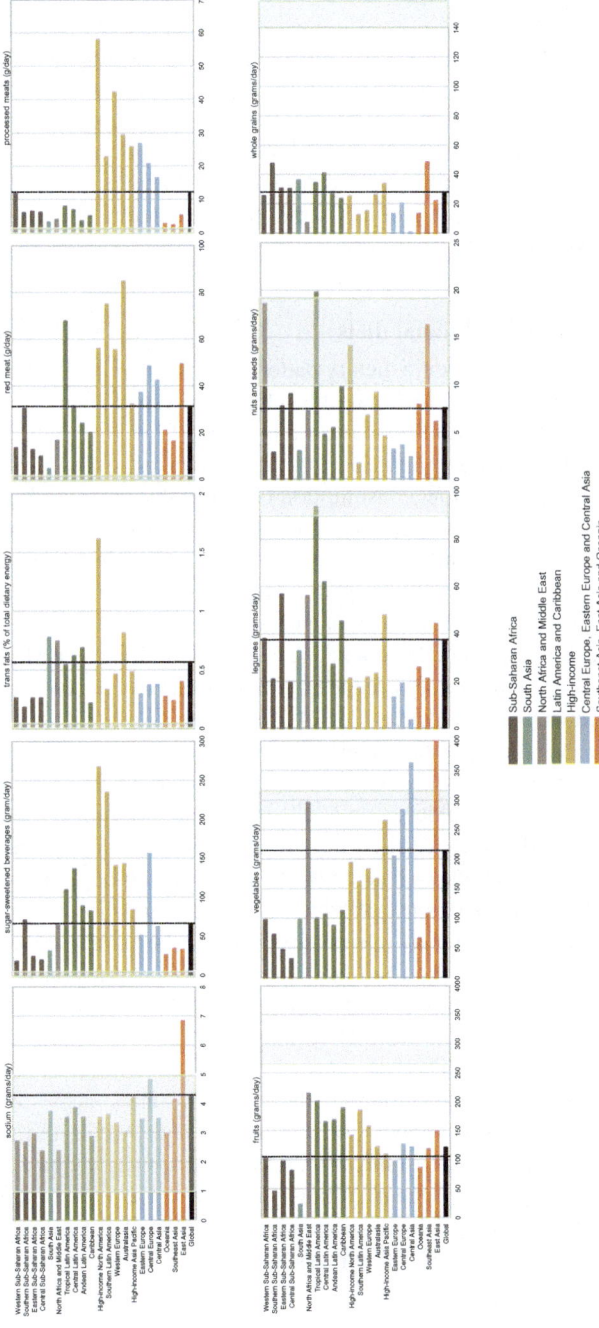

Fig. 4.2 Suboptimal adult diets, globally and regionally [17]

surpasses the recommended intake. The consumption of processed meat is 90% higher than the recommended intake, while red meat consumption is 18% higher than recommended [17].

Dietary patterns differ by region. The consumption of vegetables is highest in Central Asia, while legume consumption is high in the Caribbean, tropical Latin America, South Asia, and sub-Saharan Africa. Red meat consumption is high in Australia and parts of Latin America. Processed meat consumption is high in North America, Western Europe, and high-income countries in Asia Pacific. The highest intake of trans fats occurs in high-income North America, central Latin America, and Andean Latin America [17].

> **Box 4.2 Disappearing traditional diets**
>
> Certain traditional, region-specific dietary patterns can positively affect health and well-being. These diets, which may be called "blue zone" diets, include the Mediterranean, Nordic, and Okinawan diets [18, 19]. These traditional, regional diets tend to be more plant-based with high intakes of fruits, vegetables, legumes, and nuts and low consumption of unhealthy, processed, packaged foods. Other shared characteristics of these diets include "slow eating," local procurement of foods, and dietary moderation, as well as lifestyle factors like physical activity and quality time spent relaxing [20]. These patterns have been shown to beneficially influence human health, longevity, social cohesion, and in some cases, environmental resilience [21, 22]. For example, the Mediterranean diet has been found to help reduce the risk of cardiovascular disease, some forms of cancer, and dementia [23, 24], while the Nordic diet has been shown to reduce the risk of cardiovascular disease [25].
>
> Although these region-specific diets are critically important, they are disappearing. In Okinawa, many older people still follow the traditional diet that focuses on plants and energy restriction, but younger Okinawans consume more Westernized diets. Okinawa has the world's highest number of fast-food establishments per capita and, since World War II, the population has transitioned from having the lowest body mass index (BMI) to the highest among the Japanese population [19, 26]. The Nordic diet is also disappearing, as it is too expensive for many to consume on a daily basis [27]. Dietary shifts in Mediterranean regions, such as southern Italy, Greece, and Spain, have contributed to rising rates of obesity and NCDs [28].
>
> Other traditional diets around the world are also disappearing quickly. Indigenous populations living in the Arctic territories of Canada are increasingly consuming diets high in processed, packaged foods and experiencing more sedentary lifestyles. These changes are due to limits on whale hunting and mechanization of hunting, as well as food policies that shift food environments and allow mass media advertising of unhealthy

> foods [29, 30]. Among the Maasai of East Africa, pastoralists are becoming less nomadic and dependent on animals for food. As a result, their diets are shifting from milk and meat to starchy, staple grains provided by food assistance programs [31].

Health Consequences of Suboptimal Diets

Suboptimal diets are considered a major risk factor for negative health outcomes. Poor diets have long been considered the greatest avoidable cause of death and disability [32]. Suboptimal diets are now a top risk factor for deaths and disability-adjusted life years (DALYs) lost. Around the world, various dietary risk factors contribute to 11 million deaths and 255 million DALYs [17, 33, 34]. Of these deaths, cardiovascular disease caused 10 million. More than 45% of diet-related deaths occurred among people aged younger than 70 years [17].

Poor diets can directly lead to malnutrition. As Chapter 5 discusses, malnutrition can carry lifelong ramifications for disease burden, income earnings, and productivity [35–37]. Malnutrition in all its forms contributes to more lost DALYs than tobacco smoking, high blood pressure, and high fasting plasma glucose (high blood sugar). Globally, nutrition and dietary risks combined contribute significantly to disability, regardless of a country's wealth status. NCDs are the primary cause of disabilities associated with nutrition and dietary risk [17, 34].

Globally, diets low in health-promoting properties present the greatest risk to health. The top dietary risk factors are diets low in whole grains, fruits, vegetables, and nuts and seeds, and diets high in sodium. This research on dietary risk factors suggests that not eating healthy foods is more detrimental to health than eating unhealthy foods [6, 17, 38].

Dietary risks vary across different regions of the world. For much of Asia, the main dietary risk factor is cured, high sodium meats. For sub-Saharan Africa, low consumption of vegetables presents the greatest risk for disease and disability. In Latin America, low consumption of nuts and seeds represents the most significant dietary risk factor for deaths and DALYs [17].

Dietary shifts are also associated with an increasing prevalence of overweight and obesity and NCDs worldwide [39]. Dietary trends and resulting health outcomes are an issue for all countries, regardless of wealth status. Low-and middle-income countries (LMICs) face additional burdens as they transition from undernutrition to overweight and obesity, and experience the risk of NCDs [40–44]. Changes to lifestyles and activity levels also have important implications for the onset of overweight, obesity, and NCDs, such as cardiovascular disease and diabetes.

Key Messages and Conclusions

Diets are intertwined with food systems and healthy, optimal diets support nutrition and overall health throughout life. Expert recommendations for optimal diets include a diverse range of healthy foods that are of sufficient quantity, quality, and safety, and limit the consumption of less nutritious foods.

Despite their importance, diets remain suboptimal around the world. Many people do not consume enough healthy foods, like whole grains, fruits, vegetables, and nuts. The consumption of less healthy foods high in sugar, salt, and fat, often presented in packaged, highly-processed foods, far exceeds recommended intakes. As a result, current suboptimal diets are responsible for more deaths globally than any other risk factor [17]. To help counteract these risks, diets need to incorporate more healthy, nutritious foods that come from sustainable, well-functioning food systems.

References

1. Imamura F, Micha R, Khatibzadeh S, Fahimi S, Shi P, Powles J, et al. Dietary quality among men and women in 187 countries in 1990 and 2010: A systematic assessment. The Lancet Global health. 2015 Mar;3(3):e142.
2. Mozaffarian D. Diets from around the world—Quality not quantity [Internet]. Vol. 378, The Lancet. 2011. p. 759. Available from: http://dx.doi.org/10.1016/s0140-6736(11)61362-7
3. Hu FB, Willett WC. Optimal diets for prevention of coronary heart disease. JAMA. 2002 Nov 27;288(20):2569–78.
4. Mozaffarian D. Dietary and policy priorities for cardiovascular disease, diabetes, and obesity: A comprehensive review. Circulation. 2016;133(2):187–225.
5. Lim SS, Vos T, Flaxman AD, Danaei G, Shibuya K, Adair-Rohani H, et al. A comparative risk assessment of burden of disease and injury attributable to 67 risk factors and risk factor clusters in 21 regions, 1990-2010: A systematic analysis for the Global Burden of Disease Study 2010. Lancet. 2012;380(9859):2224–60.
6. Forouzanfar MH, Afshin A, Alexander LT, Anderson HR, Bhutta ZA, Biryukov S, et al. Global, regional, and national comparative risk assessment of 79 behavioural, environmental and occupational, and metabolic risks or clusters of risks, 1990–2015: A systematic analysis for the Global Burden of Disease Study 2015. Lancet. 2016;388(10053):1659–724.
7. Mozaffarian D, Fahimi S, Singh GM, Micha R, Khatibzadeh S, Engell RE, et al. Global sodium consumption and death from cardiovascular causes. N Engl J Med. 2014;371(7):624–34.
8. International Dietary Data Expansion Project. Quality: What is a quality diet and is it the same everywhere? Data4Diets.
9. Kim S, Haines PS, Siega-Riz AM, Popkin BM. The Diet Quality Index-International (DQI-I) provides an effective tool for cross-national comparison of diet quality as illustrated by China and the United States. J Nutr. 2003 Nov;133(11):3476–84.
10. World Health Organization. Healthy Diet [Internet]. World Health Organization. 2020. Available from: https://www.who.int/en/news-room/fact-sheets/detail/healthy-diet
11. Andreas NJ, Kampmann B, Mehring Le-Doare K. Human breast milk: A review on its composition and bioactivity. Early Hum Dev. 2015 Nov;91(11):629–35.
12. UNICEF. The state of the world's children 2019: Children, food and nutrition: Growing well in a changing world. UNICEF; 2019.
13. Infant and young child feeding - UNICEF DATA [Internet]. UNICEF DATA. [cited 2019 Apr 14]. Available from: https://data.unicef.org/topic/nutrition/infant-and-young-child-feeding/

References

14. Development Initiatives. 2018 Global nutrition report: Shining a light to spur action on nutrition. Development Initiatives; 2018.
15. Keats EC, Rappaport AI, Shah S, Oh C, Jain R, Bhutta ZA. The dietary intake and practices of adolescent girls in low- and middle-income countries: A systematic review. Nutrients [Internet]. 2018 Dec 14;10(12). Available from: http://dx.doi.org/10.3390/nu10121978
16. Nadia Akseer, Sara Al-Gashm, Seema Mehta, Ali Mokdad, Zulfiqar A. Bhutta. Global and regional trends in the nutritional status of young people: A critical and neglected age group. Annals of the New York Academy of Sciences. 2017;1393(1):3–20.
17. Afshin A, Sur PJ, Fay KA, Cornaby L, Ferrara G, Salama JS, et al. Health effects of dietary risks in 195 countries, 1990–2017: A systematic analysis for the Global Burden of Disease Study 2017. Lancet [Internet]. 2019 [cited 2019 May 20]; Available from: https://www.fabresearch.org/viewItem.php?id=12559
18. Bere E, Brug J. Towards health-promoting and environmentally friendly regional diets–a Nordic example. Public Health Nutr. 2009;12(1):91–6.
19. Willcox DC, Scapagnini G, Willcox BJ. Healthy aging diets other than the Mediterranean: A focus on the Okinawan diet. Mech Ageing Dev. 2014 Mar 1;136–137:148–62.
20. Trichopoulou A, Benetou V. Impact of mediterranean diet on longevity. In: Caruso C, editor. Centenarians: An example of positive biology. Cham: Springer International Publishing; 2019. p. 161–8.
21. Appel LJ. Dietary patterns and longevity: Expanding the blue zones. Circulation. 2008 Jul 15;118(3):214–5.
22. Buettner D, Skemp S. Blue zones: Lessons From the world's longest lived. Am J Lifestyle Med. 2016 Sep;10(5):318–21.
23. Dinu M, Pagliai G, Casini A, Sofi F. Mediterranean diet and multiple health outcomes: an umbrella review of meta-analyses of observational studies and randomized trials. Nutr Metab Cardiovasc Dis. 2017;27(1):e21.
24. Park J, Kim J. Meta analysis of relation between mediterranean diet and overall mortality. Atherosclerosis. 2015 Jul 1;241(1):e195.
25. Massara P, Viguiliouk E, Glenn A, Khan T, Chiavaroli L, Mejia SB, et al. Nordic dietary pattern and cardiometabolic outcomes: A systematic review and meta-analysis of prospective cohort studies and randomized controlled trials. Curr Dev Nutr. 2020 May 29;4(Supplement_2):546–546.
26. Willcox BJ, Willcox DC. Caloric restriction, CR mimetics, and healthy aging in Okinawa: Controversies and clinical implications. Curr Opin Clin Nutr Metab Care. 2014;17(1):51.
27. Jensen JD, Saxe H, Denver S. Cost-Effectiveness of a new nordic diet as a strategy for health promotion. Int J Environ Res Public Health. 2015 Jun 30;12(7):7370–91.
28. Vilarnau C, Stracker DM, Funtikov A, da Silva R, Estruch R, Bach-Faig A. Worldwide adherence to Mediterranean Diet between 1960 and 2011. Eur J Clin Nutr. 2019 Jul;72(Suppl 1):83–91.
29. Browne J, Lock M, Walker T, Egan M, Backholer K. Effects of food policy actions on Indigenous Peoples' nutrition-related outcomes: a systematic review. BMJ Glob Health [Internet]. 2020 Aug;5(8). Available from: http://dx.doi.org/10.1136/bmjgh-2020-002442
30. Kuhnlein HV, Receveur O, Soueida R, Egeland GM. Arctic indigenous peoples experience the nutrition transition with changing dietary patterns and obesity. J Nutr. 2004 Jun;134(6):1447–53.
31. Galvin KA, Beeton TA, Boone RB, BurnSilver SB. Nutritional status of maasai pastoralists under change. Hum Ecol Interdiscip J. 2015;43(3):411–24.
32. Black RE, Victora CG, Walker SP, Bhutta ZA, Christian P, de Onis M, et al. Maternal and child undernutrition and overweight in low-income and middle-income countries. Lancet. 2013 Aug 3;382(9890):427–51.
33. GBD 2016 Risk Factors Collaborators. Global, regional, and national comparative risk assessment of 84 behavioural, environmental and occupational, and metabolic risks or clusters of risks, 1990-2016: a systematic analysis for the Global Burden of Disease Study 2016. Lancet. 2017 Sep 16;390(10100):1345–422.

34. Swinburn BA, Kraak VI, Allender S, Atkins VJ, Baker PI, Bogard JR, et al. The global syndemic of obesity, undernutrition, and climate change: The Lancet Commission report. Lancet. 2019 Feb 23;393(10173):791–846.
35. Shekar M, Dayton Eberwein J, Kakietek J. The costs of stunting in South Asia and the benefits of public investments in nutrition. Matern Child Nutr. 2016 May;12 Suppl 1:186–95.
36. Dewey KG, Huffman SL. Maternal, Infant, and young child nutrition: Combining efforts to maximize impacts on child growth and micronutrient status. Food Nutr Bull. 2009;30(2_suppl2):S187–9.
37. Prado EL, Dewey KG. Nutrition and brain development in early life. Nutr Rev. 2014 Apr;72(4):267–84.
38. Willett W, Rockström J, Loken B, Springmann M. Food in the Anthropocene: the EAT–Lancet Commission on healthy diets from sustainable food systems. Lancet [Internet]. 2019; Available from: https://www.thelancet.com/journals/lancet/article/PIIS0140-6736(18)31788-4/fulltext?fbclid=IwAR2ftk_lpUKlVbQ-B93qUXmWnm6bA4dfFA5paVFCG0vExt5c516oikYOCsk
39. Goryakin Y, Lobstein T, James WPT, Suhrcke M. The impact of economic, political and social globalization on overweight and obesity in the 56 low and middle income countries. Soc Sci Med. 2015 May;133:67–76.
40. Aurino E, Fernandes M, Penny ME. The nutrition transition and adolescents' diets in low- and middle-income countries: A cross-cohort comparison. Public Health Nutrition. 2017;20(01):72–81.
41. Du SF, Wang HJ, Zhang B, Zhai FY, Popkin BM. China in the period of transition from scarcity and extensive undernutrition to emerging nutrition-related non-communicable diseases, 1949-1992. Obes Rev. 2014;15:8–15.
42. Wang Z, Gordon-Larsen P, Siega-Riz AM, Cai J, Wang H, Adair LS, et al. Sociodemographic disparity in the diet quality transition among Chinese adults from 1991 to 2011. Eur J Clin Nutr. 2017 Apr;71(4):486–93.
43. Popkin BM, Corvalan C, Grummer-Strawn LM. Dynamics of the double burden of malnutrition and the changing nutrition reality. Lancet. 2020 Jan 4;395(10217):65–74.
44. Popkin BM, Reardon T. Obesity and the food system transformation in Latin America. Obes Rev. 2018 Aug;19(8):1028–64.

Chapter 5
The Multiple Burdens of Malnutrition

Introduction

This chapter explains the importance of nutrition in the life cycle and the impact of malnutrition across generations. Malnutrition takes different forms: undernutrition (underweight, stunting, and wasting); micronutrient deficiencies; and overweight and obesity. These forms of malnutrition exist in all countries, whether developed or developing, and can also coexist within countries, communities, households, and individuals. The chapter discusses the global burden of malnutrition, its causes, and the consequences for health.

Nutrition

Nutrition is a critical component of health and development. Nutrients from food include macronutrients, such as carbohydrates, fats, fiber, and proteins, as well as minerals, vitamins, and water, some of which are considered micronutrients. Micronutrients are needed by the human body in smaller quantities.

To achieve optimal nutrition throughout life, an individual must consume and process nutrients and other substances contained in food. The digestion process involves the absorption and metabolism of nutrients, and the excretion of waste products. Nutrients in food are critical for energy, growth, cell repair, reproduction, and overall health.

Over the course of life, an individual's nutrients and energy needs change: during periods when the body is growing, the individual needs more nutrients. These growth periods occur during infancy, adolescence, and pregnancy. After these periods of intensive growth, the need for increased energy and certain nutrients declines [1, 2].

Nutritional Science

Nutritional research is a multidisciplinary field that has evolved to examine whole dietary patterns. Unlike some other scientific disciplines that conduct experiments with randomized control trials, nutritional science must often rely on observational studies and surveys. These research methods may lack precision and make it difficult, if not impossible, to prove causality. Globally, updated dietary intake and nutrition survey data remain limited. Conflicts of interest and bias also present issues for the discipline. Despite these challenges, independently funded research can provide strong evidence on the associations between diets, nutrition, and health [3].

Malnutrition

Malnutrition refers to an inadequate, unbalanced, or excess intake of nutrients in an individual's diet. Undernutrition, micronutrient malnutrition, and overweight and obesity are the three major forms of malnutrition. Undernutrition includes wasting (low weight for height), stunting (low height for age) and underweight (low weight for age). Wasting encompasses recent, severe weight loss, usually due to lack of food and/or infectious disease. Stunting is the result of chronic or recurrent undernutrition. Micronutrient-related malnutrition includes deficient or excess intake of important vitamins and minerals. Overweight and obesity result from an excess intake of energy [4].

Malnutrition is a serious condition that can adversely affect an individual's health. Poor nutrition negatively affects a person's physical and cognitive development, and it impairs the body's immune and cellular systems. Malnutrition can also increase the risk of developing communicable diseases and noncommunicable diseases (NCDs). Globally, unhealthy diets are major risk factors for diet-related noncommunicable diseases (DR-NCDs), such as cardiovascular disease, certain cancers, and diabetes. As a whole, malnutrition limits an individual's ability to achieve her full developmental potential and restricts productivity [5]. Different forms of malnutrition contribute to various health impacts and long-term development challenges [6]. Box 5.1 defines these different forms of malnutrition.

Malnutrition is a global challenge. Worldwide, every country is affected by one or more forms of malnutrition. Overweight and obesity is on the rise: globally, an estimated 1.9 billion adults and 38.3 million children are overweight or obese. Undernutrition remains a pressing concern, especially for low-and middle-income countries (LMICs). Approximately 462 million adults are underweight, while 144 million children experience stunting and 47.5 million experience wasting [4].

> **Box 5.1 Different forms of malnutrition**
> *Undernutrition*: chronic or acute condition when a person's energy and nutrient requirements are not met. Undernutrition results from under-consumption or impaired nutrient absorption and use. It includes deficits in energy intake, as well as micro-and macronutrient deficiencies.
> *Stunting*: low height for age. The WHO considers stunting to be a public health problem when 20% or more of the population is affected.
> *Wasting*: low weight for height. This situation often indicates recent, severe weight loss due to not having enough to eat or experiencing an infectious disease. Wasting becomes a public health problem when 5% or more of the population is affected.
> *Overweight and obesity*: abnormal or excessive accumulation of fat. This situation is caused by an energy imbalance between calories consumed and expended. Overweight and obesity is often combined with a sedentary lifestyle [4, 7, 8].

Hunger and Food Insecurity

Hunger refers to a state of not having enough food to meet physiological needs. The experience of hunger encompasses everything from short-term physical discomfort to a life-threatening lack of food [9]. Hunger can manifest through undernourishment, micronutrient deficiencies, stunting, and wasting.

After decades of progress, the global prevalence of hunger has risen in recent years. According to the Food and Agriculture Organization of the United Nations (FAO), hunger and undernourishment affects an estimated 690 million people, or 8.9% of the global population. Worldwide, Africa experiences the highest prevalence of hunger, affecting 20% of the continent's population. Asia also has a significant population of undernourished people, though the region has made significant progress in reducing hunger and the prevalence of undernourishment is less than half that of Africa. Since 2014, Latin America and the Caribbean have experienced a significant increase in hunger prevalence [10].

Food security encompasses the ability of all people to have physical, social, and economic access to sufficient safe, and nutritious food that meets their dietary needs and food preferences [10, 11]. The four dimensions of food security are food availability, access, utilization, and stability. Food access refers to the physical presence of food; access indicates whether a household can obtain the food; utilization encompasses optimal consumption of nutrients and energy; and stability measures whether a household is food secure over time [10]. Food insecurity is a highly complex outcome that can result from hunger, as well as poverty, conflict, and climate change, among other causal factors [12]. Food insecurity can contribute to multiple forms of malnutrition, as shown in Fig. 5.1.

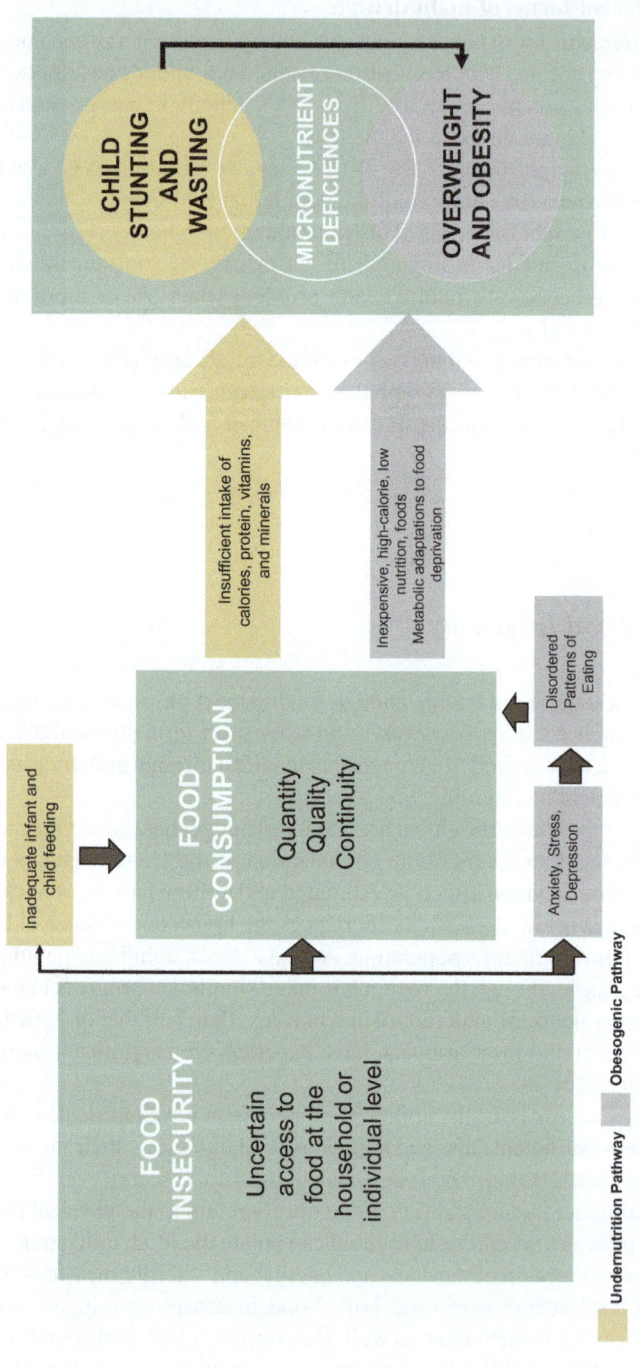

Fig. 5.1 Food insecurity and its impacts [12]

Globally, far more people experience food insecurity than hunger. More than 2 billion people, or 25.9% of the global population, suffer from moderate to severe levels of food insecurity [13]. As with hunger, the prevalence of food insecurity has risen worldwide since 2014 as a result of increased conflicts, often exacerbated by the effects of climate change, and economic slowdowns. Africa experiences the highest levels of food insecurity, though Latin America and the Caribbean are experiencing the fastest growth in food insecurity. Worldwide, women are more likely to experience food insecurity than men [10].

Undernutrition

Undernutrition is a widespread global concern with special implications for young children and women. Worldwide, 144 million children under the age of five are affected by stunting and 47.5 million are affected by wasting [14]. An estimated 9.4% of women and 5.7% of adolescent girls are underweight [15, 16]. Undernutrition is a critical issue for these populations because the first 1,000 days of a child's life are critical to growth and development. Poor nutrition during this period can lead to adverse health outcomes that can reverberate throughout life and even affect subsequent generations [17, 18].

The prevalence of childhood undernutrition is highest in Africa and Asia. The majority of children under the age of five who are stunted reside in Southern Asia (55.9 million), Eastern Africa (23.1 million), and Western Africa (17.8 million). Burundi, Eritrea, Timor-Leste, Niger, and Guatemala experience the world's highest prevalence of stunting. The most recent data indicates that in Burundi, Eritrea, and Timor-Leste, more than 50% of children under the age of five are stunted. The prevalence of wasting is highest in Southern Asia, where 25.2 million children are affected by wasting. More than half of the world's wasted children live in Southern Asia. The most recent data indicates that wasting prevalence in children under five years of age is highest in South Sudan, Djibouti, India, Yemen, and Sudan [14]. Box 5.2 illustrates how Ethiopia has addressed extremely high levels of stunting in children under the age of five.

> **Box 5.2 Ethiopia's astounding efforts to tackle stunting**
>
> Ethiopia is a country that has been grappling with undernutrition for centuries and knows how devastating deep, prolonged hunger can be. From 1983 to 1985, Ethiopia suffered from one of the last great famines the world has seen. An estimated 400–500,000 people died of starvation due to significant droughts and conflict [19]. Since that devastating event, Ethiopia has vowed to never face famine again. While the prevalence of children under the age of five who suffer from stunting remains incredibly high in the East Africa region, Ethiopia has reduced stunting from almost 70 to 40% since 1992 [20].

> How did a low-income country with minimal resources make such progress in tackling stunting? Nutritional status has improved due to increases in agricultural productivity, increased competency and coverage of community health workers (especially in rural areas), parental education, and reductions in open defecation, among other causes [20, 21]. Despite these gains, the improvements have been unequal. Many of the poor, uneducated, and rural still suffer disproportionately from stunting. A sub-regional analysis of Ethiopia shows that stunting prevalence among these vulnerable populations has not improved [22, 23].

Low birth weight (LBW) is another important indicator of poor nutritional status. LBW is defined as live births in a given population and over a given time period with a birth weight of less than 2.5 kg. Infants born with LBW experience an increased risk of morbidity and mortality. Although many newborns are not weighed at birth, estimates indicate that LBW affects more than 20 million infants [15].

Micronutrient Deficiencies

Micronutrient deficiencies affect billions of people around the world. These deficiencies in essential vitamins and minerals are also known as "hidden hunger." Micronutrient deficiencies are a major public health concern, especially for populations in LMICs. Deficiencies in vitamin A, iodine, iron, and zinc are the most common. More than 340 million children under the age of five experience deficiencies in essential vitamins and nutrients, though the full extent of micronutrient deficiencies across populations and age groups is poorly understood [16, 24].

Overweight and Obesity

Overweight and obesity is a fast-growing problem for populations around the world. A staggering 2.01 billion adults are affected by overweight and obesity, with a higher number of women being overweight and obese than men [15]. Additionally, 38.3 million children under the age of five are estimated to be overweight [14].

The prevalence of overweight and obesity has increased dramatically in recent decades. Between 1980 and 2013, the proportion of overweight adults increased from 28.8 to 36.9% in men and from 29.8 to 38.0% in women [25]. Between 1980 and 2008, obesity prevalence in adults increased from 4.8 to 9.8% in men and from 7.9 to 13.8% in women [26].

Overweight and obesity is a global concern. To date, not a single country has experienced a decline in obesity [27]. The prevalence of obesity is highest in American Samoa, Nauru, Cook Islands, Marshall Islands, and Palau, where the estimated prevalence of obesity exceeds 60% in men and/or women [28]. Urbanization has long been considered a major driver of overweight and obesity, but prevalence in rural areas is on the rise. Globally, rural areas experienced more than half of the increase in mean body mass index (BMI). Some LMICs experienced up to an 80% increase in mean BMI [29].

Multiple Burdens of Malnutrition

In recent decades, the epidemiology of malnutrition has shifted, and the overall global causes of morbidity and mortality have changed. While stunting remains high in some parts of the world, overall stunting among children under five years of age has slowly declined. At the same time, the prevalence of overweight among children has risen (Fig. 5.2), as well as among adolescents and adults. In LMICs, stunting and thinness in women are declining, while overweight is increasing in most age groups [16].

Around the world, populations are increasingly experiencing the multiple burdens of malnutrition. The "multiple burden of malnutrition" is understood as the coexistence of undernutrition and overweight, obesity, and DR-NCDs. Some experts characterize these burdens as "double" or "triple" burdens. The global increase in overweight and obesity prevalence has been the main driver of multiple burden growth [30]. Different forms of malnutrition can overlap in countries, households, and individuals, with some experiencing multiple burdens of different forms of malnutrition [30–32].

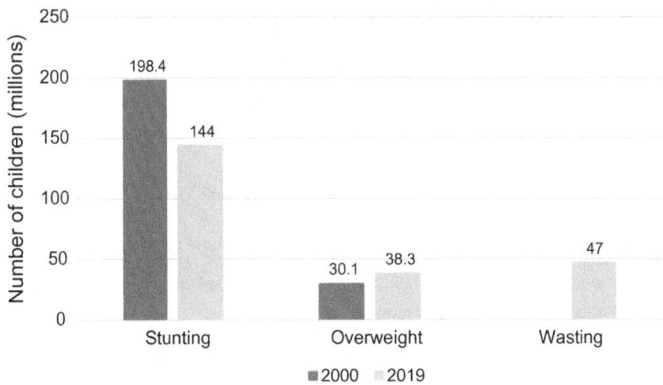

Fig. 5.2 Malnutrition burden switch in children under five [16]

The double burden of malnutrition (DBM) is largely concentrated in the world's poorest countries, as shown in Fig. 5.3. The figure shows the number of countries that changed DBM status from the 1990s to 2010s, by gross income quartile. Sub-Saharan Africa, South and East Asia, and the Pacific are especially affected by the DBM. In some areas, such as sub-Saharan Africa and South Asia, the prevalence of overweight and obesity is concentrated among wealthier populations and in urban areas. In many other areas, the risk of the DBM affects lower-income populations and those in rural areas [30].

The DBM also exists at the household and individual levels. Some households contain both overweight parents and undernourished children, though the prevalence of these "double burden" households varies considerably [30, 31, 33]. In Asia, for example, the prevalence of double burden households ranges from 5% in Vietnam to 30.6% in Indonesia [34]. Worldwide, it is estimated that 3.6% of children under the age of five (15.9 million) experience both stunting and wasting at the same time [16]. Approximately 1.8% (8.2 million) of children in this age group experience conditions associated with both stunting and overweight [16]. Box 5.3 describes the challenges faced by India in combating the DBM at both the population and household level.

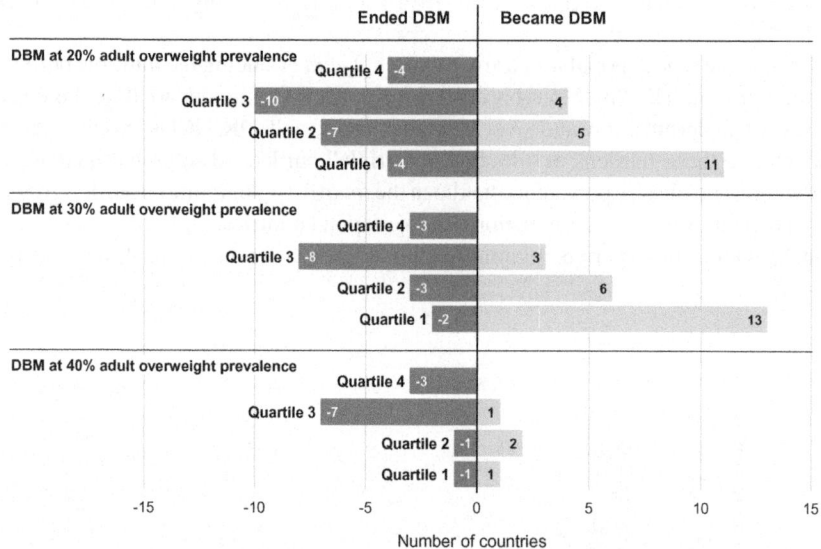

* Double burden of malnutrition (DBM) = at least 1 child, adolescent, or adult in household with severe levels of wasting/stunting/thinness and 1 with overweight/obesity (shown at 20%, 30%, or 40% adult overweight prevalence); countries only included here if they had DBM data available for both time periods (1990s and 2010s)
** Quartile (Qtl) 1 is lowest-wealth, Qtl4 is highest-wealth

Fig. 5.3 Double burden of malnutrition shift from high- to low-income quintiles over the last 30 years [30]

Box 5.3 India's challenge in dealing with the double burden of malnutrition

India struggles with a double burden of malnutrition. This burden is especially significant because India has the highest burdens of undernutrition in the world. With the rise in overweight and obesity, Indian populations are at significant risk for developing NCDs, and diabetes is already escalating at an alarming rate [35].

The DBM primarily affects adults, although it can also manifest across different generations within households. The latest national survey data indicates that 19.6% of adult men and 22.4% of adult women are underweight, while 17.1% of adult men and 18.6% of adult women are overweight and obese [36]. Over the last 20 years, both rural and urban residents have experienced increases in obesity [37]. An individual can demonstrate multiple burdens: a woman who is obese can be anemic, and a child who is stunted can also be overweight. Household-level evidence suggests that women are at risk of being overweight, whereas children living with their mothers tend to be underweight [36, 38].

India's DBM is largely the result of economic, epidemiological, and nutrition transitions. India's income growth is one of the major macro-trends of the country's transition. As India's economy and GDP has grown, the prevalence of overweight has increased and underweight has declined. Rising levels of education and wealth are positively associated with increases in overweight and obesity. Diets are also changing: increased consumption of processed, packaged foods are highly correlated with the rise in obesity and anemia, whereas intake of legumes, fruits, and vegetables are correlated with declines in undernutrition on the sub-continent [36, 39, 40].

Causes of Malnutrition

Malnutrition is caused by a range of complex, multifaceted determinants. In addition to a lack of nutritious food, malnutrition can be caused by illness, lack of access to healthcare, and poor care practices, as shown in Fig. 5.4. UNICEF's conceptual framework of child undernutrition identifies three major causes of malnutrition: basic, underlying, and immediate. Basic causes of undernutrition include broad societal, economic, and political contexts that have a long-term impact on food security and nutrition. These factors can perpetuate poverty and limit access to the resources needed to achieve optimal nutrition and health [41, 42]. Underlying causes of undernutrition affect an individual's dietary intake and exposure to disease. These causes include household food insecurity, inadequate childcare and feeding practices,

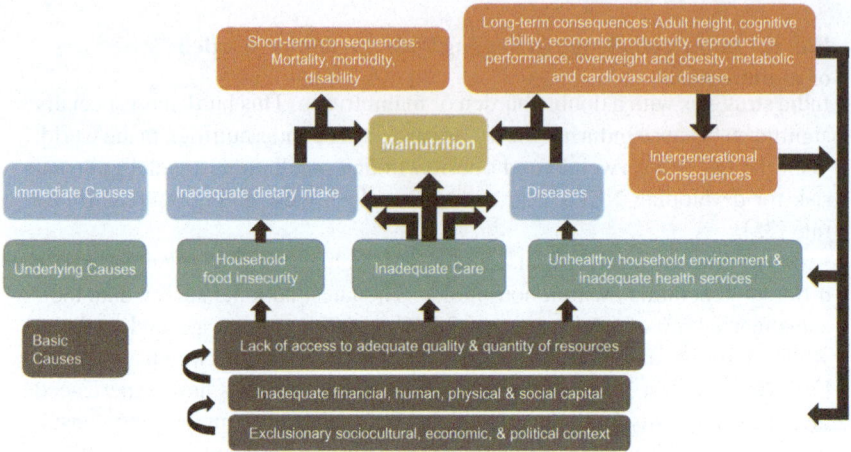

Fig. 5.4 UNICEF framework on undernutrition [42]

unhealthy living environments, and inadequate healthcare [42]. Lastly, immediate causes of undernutrition include inadequate dietary intake and disease [43].

The causes underlying the different forms of malnutrition are related and intertwined. Both undernutrition and overweight and obesity share many of the same underlying causes, such as poverty, inability to access healthy diets, poor infant and young child feeding practices, and unhealthy food environments. The increased consumption of ultra-processed food has been linked to increases in obesity and NCDs, although the impact of these foods on stunting prevalence is less clear. Consumption of these foods is increasing among young children, which could present a risk if these foods are replacing nutrient-rich foods [30, 44].

The gut microbiome, which is made up of microorganisms living in the digestive tract, is also important for preventing malnutrition. The relationship between diet, health, and the microbiome is reciprocal. Diets, nutrition, health, and the environment influence the health and diversity of the microbiome. In turn, the microbiome affects micronutrient uptake and metabolic pathways. Research suggests that the microbiome may help protect against infections that increase the likelihood of developing nutritional deficiencies.

Poor nutrition and health can harm the microbiome and perpetuate the cycle of malnutrition. Malnutrition can impair the microbiome's maturation or affect its functioning in a way that increases the risk of disease [45]. The microbiome can be harmed by diseases that lead to complications like intestinal inflammation, enteric infection, and nutrient malabsorption [46]. Disruption to the microbiome during childhood can also lead to metabolic syndromes, including obesity [45].

Consequences of Malnutrition

Malnutrition adversely affects health and well-being throughout the entire life cycle, as shown in Fig. 5.5. As discussed in Chapter 4, unhealthy diets are contributors to poor nutrition outcomes, as well as morbidity and mortality of many populations around the world. The consequences of malnutrition carry broad implications for societies and populations, as well as individuals and households. Some groups are particularly vulnerable to malnutrition, including those with specific nutrient requirements at critical stages of their life cycle, such as young children, adolescent girls, pregnant and lactating women, the elderly, and people who are ill or immunocompromised. Marginalized groups that have less control over their diets due to societal circumstances are also vulnerable to malnutrition. These groups include the urban and rural poor, those that are geographically isolated, and some Indigenous peoples. [47].

The emergence of undernutrition early in life is especially harmful to health. In the short term, undernutrition increases the risk of mortality and morbidity [48]. Undernutrition in women and children is the underlying cause of 3.5 million deaths and represents 35% of the disease burden in children under five years of age [5]. In the longer term, it is associated with shorter adult height, increased risk of overweight and related NCDs, lower life expectancy, and, for women, poor pregnancy outcomes [1, 18, 49–51]. Undernutrition affects brain development and motor skills, which may prevent undernourished children from reaching their full developmental potential [1, 18, 52, 53]. In adolescent and adult women, undernutrition can lead to diminished productivity, complications in pregnancy, and an increased risk of mortality [54].

Overweight and obesity is a major risk factor for a wide range of NCDs. These include heart disease, diabetes, musculoskeletal disorders, and some cancers, including breast, ovarian, prostate, liver, kidney, and colon cancer [8]. High BMI accounts for 4 million deaths globally: more than two-thirds of these deaths are linked to cardiovascular disease [55].

Micronutrient deficiencies can negatively affect growth and development, impair health, and lead to disease. These deficiencies can cause birth defects, growth impairment, reduced cognitive function, and greater vulnerability to infectious diseases [56, 57]. Micronutrient deficiencies are associated with specific health conditions: for example, iodine deficiency can lead to goiter, compromise mental health, and limit intellectual capacity [58, 59], while vitamin A deficiency can contribute to visual impairment, diarrheal disease, and measles [60]. Vitamin A deficiency contributes to 600,000 deaths worldwide, while deficiencies in zinc are responsible for 400,000 deaths [5].

Women and children are especially vulnerable to the effects of micronutrient deficiencies. Due to the physiology of menstruation and increased nutritional needs during pregnancy, adolescent girls and women experience a heightened risk of developing iron-deficiency anemia. The problem of anemia appears intractable among this population: prevalence in girls and women ages 15–49 is 32.8 and 40.1% among pregnant women [15]. Anemia is associated with maternal and child mortality, poor physical performance, and chronic kidney and heart disease [61]. Among children and adolescents, anemia is also the leading cause of years lived with disability [62].

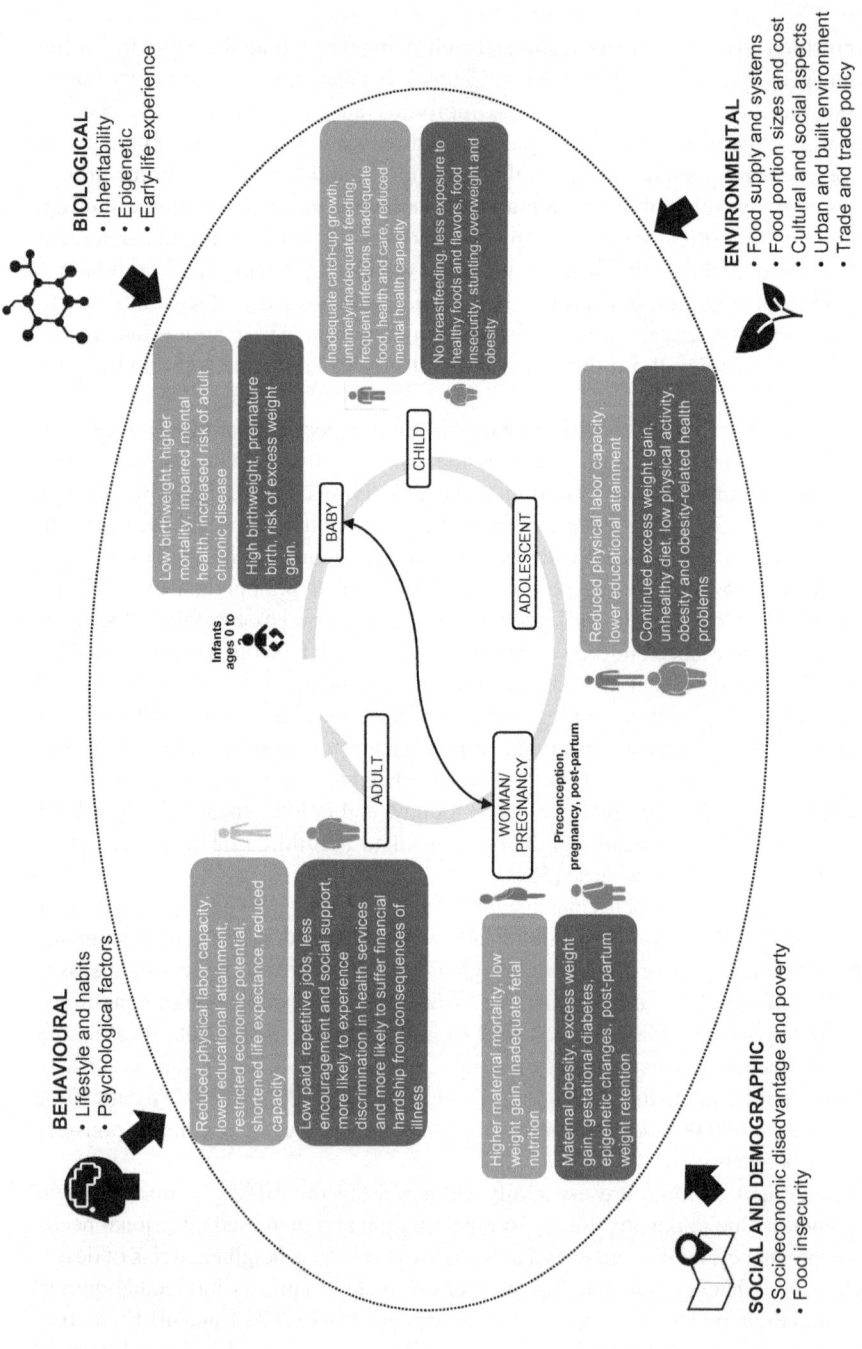

Fig. 5.5 Malnutrition impacts opportunities throughout the entire life cycle [7]

Malnutrition also carries economic and societal implications. Undernutrition increases the risk of impaired cognition, which can result in poor academic performance, less schooling, and reduced economic productivity [63]. Both undernutrition and micronutrient deficiencies can impair workforce productivity, which can lead to serious economic consequences that affect national development, particularly in LMICs [1]. Overweight and obesity can lead to higher health costs and lowered productivity. From 2011 to 2025, the global economic burden of NCDs is estimated to be USD 7 trillion, with cardiovascular disease accounting for most of that expense [64].

Intergenerational Cycle of Malnutrition

The effects of malnutrition can span generations, as maternal malnutrition affects the health of children. For the child, poor nutrition can begin in utero and extend into adolescence and adulthood. For girls, the cycle of malnutrition may continue with their children into the next generation. The intergenerational cycle of malnutrition is perpetuated by biological mechanisms, such as shared genetic traits, and sociocultural factors, such as intergenerational poverty, among others. The effects of this cycle can persist throughout several generations: birthweight is correlated across generations and many generations are required to fully "wash out" the consequences of poor nutrition [17].

The intergenerational cycle of malnutrition begins with maternal health and pregnancy. Although health and nutrition prior to conception influence pregnancy outcomes, many women around the world are not nutritionally prepared for the demands of pregnancy [2]. Maternal undernutrition can impair an unborn child's growth, lead to LBW, cause pregnancy complications, and increase the risk of infant death [2, 6, 17, 48]. It also increases the risk of childhood underweight, stunting, wasting, and micronutrient deficiencies [2, 6, 17]. Maternal overweight and obesity is associated with pregnancy complications, increased fetal adiposity, micronutrient deficiencies, congenital anomalies, and infant death [2, 6].

Malnutrition that occurs early in life can carry long-lasting consequences. The "Fetal Origins of Adult Disease" hypothesis, which is also known as the "Developmental Origins of Health and Disease" hypothesis, posits that early life factors, such as poor nutrition, can increase the risk for chronic conditions later in life [65–70]. Infants that experience intrauterine growth retardation and are born with LBW face a heightened risk of mortality and developmental deficits. LBW infants are more likely to experience underweight or stunting in early childhood [71]. Excessive nutrition in early life can also lead to adverse health outcomes. Higher birth weight and fast postnatal weight gain are associated with an increased risk of obesity, abdominal fat, and insulin resistance in adulthood [6]. Box 5.4 describes the Dutch famine birth cohort, a seminal case that illustrated the importance of maternal diets for a child's health throughout life.

> **Box 5.4 Born undernourished to die overnourished**
>
> The Dutch famine birth cohort was one of the most important epidemiological studies to show the relationship between undernourishment in early life and increased risk of obesity and NCDs in adult life. During World War II, food was rationed in Amsterdam due to wartime embargoes on food trade. The rations were insufficient to meet the population's caloric needs, leading to severe hunger and famine in the winter of 1944–1945 [72, 73]. The famine significantly affected the health of the general population, but vulnerable groups, including pregnant women, faced the worst impacts [74].
>
> After the war ended, rigorous obstetric records were collected to track the health of women and their offspring. This record-keeping resulted in the Dutch famine birth cohort, which consisted of approximately 2,400 children conceived during the famine and born between 1943–1947. These babies experienced lower birth weights than those who were not exposed to famine in utero. This cohort was studied into adulthood to better understand the long-term consequences of prenatal exposure to famine. One of the major findings was that those born in times of famine experienced increased risk of coronary heart disease, diabetes, and obesity as adults [75, 76]. The Dutch famine cohort is just one of many examples that show how maternal nutrition and diets affect a child's growth, both in utero and throughout life [77].

In addition to pregnancy and early life, adolescence is an important stage in the intergenerational cycle. Adolescence represents the transition from childhood to adulthood: this period can establish future dietary patterns and behaviors, all of which can affect the risk of NCDs in adulthood and the health of future generations [62, 78]. Sustained nutrition during this period can help compensate for malnutrition in early childhood, but undernourished children who rapidly gain weight in later childhood and adolescence are at heightened risk of chronic disease [50]. Catch-up growth during this period may not fully mitigate the effects of undernutrition on cognitive development and behavior [78, 79]. Without interventions that address maternal and child nutrition, a stunted girl is likely to become a stunted adolescent whose own children are born with LBW and thus continue the cycle of malnutrition (Fig. 5.5).

Key Messages and Conclusions

Malnutrition remains a serious issue in many parts of the world. Currently, 1 in 3 people suffers from some form of malnutrition. While stunting is declining, the number of people who are hungry is rising, as is the prevalence of overweight and obesity in children, adolescents, and adults. Many individuals, households, and countries are grappling with double or triple burdens of malnutrition, with an increase in malnutrition among poor and rural populations.

The causes of malnutrition are multifaceted. While poverty plays a significant role, poor access to diets and poor infant and young child feeding practices are also significant influences. Poor sanitation and hygiene, lack of access to healthcare, and increasingly, climate change and conflict all contribute to the malnutrition burden.

The challenge of combating global hunger and food insecurity has grown ever more difficult. Since 2014, the prevalence of hunger and food insecurity has risen worldwide as a result of conflict, climate change, and economic downturns [10]. The COVID-19 pandemic is worsening the global prevalence of hunger and food insecurity. Worldwide, between 83 and 132 million people likely joined the rolls of the undernourished in 2020. A subsequent economic recovery would reduce the number of undernourished, but the overall prevalence of hunger and undernourishment will still be higher due to the pandemic [10].

The consequences are dire. Because malnutrition can carry repercussions throughout the entire life cycle and even affect future generations, the impacts on growth, development, and productivity are debilitating. A significant malnutrition burden affects the economic growth of nations and income earnings of individuals. It also affects an individual's ability to learn, perform, and grow to his or her full potential, creating a lifelong malady that reverberates through future generations.

References

1. Alderman H, Gentilini U, Yemtsov R. The 1.5 billion people question: food, vouchers, or cash transfers? The World Bank; 2017.
2. Stephenson J, Heslehurst N, Hall J, Schoenaker DAJM, Hutchinson J, Cade JE, et al. Before the beginning: nutrition and lifestyle in the preconception period and its importance for future health. Lancet. 2018 May 5;391(10132):1830–41.
3. Tufford AR, Calder PC, Van't Veer P, Feskens EF, Ockhuizen T, Kraneveld AD, et al. Is nutrition science ready for the twenty-first century? Moving towards transdisciplinary impacts in a changing world. Eur J Nutr. 2020 May;59(Suppl 1):1–10.
4. World Health Organization. Malnutrition [Internet]. World Health Organization. 2020. Available from: https://www.who.int/news-room/fact-sheets/detail/malnutrition
5. Black RE, Allen LH, Bhutta ZA, Caulfield LE, de Onis M, Ezzati M, et al. Maternal and child undernutrition: global and regional exposures and health consequences. Lancet. 2008 Jan 19;371(9608):243–60.
6. Wells JC, Sawaya AL, Wibaek R, Mwangome M, Poullas MS, Yajnik CS, et al. The double burden of malnutrition: aetiological pathways and consequences for health. Lancet. 2020 Jan 4;395(10217):75–88.
7. Branca F, Piwoz E, Schultink W, Sullivan LM. Nutrition and health in women, children, and adolescent girls. BMJ. 2015 Sep 14;351:h4173.
8. World Health Organization. Obesity and overweight [Internet]. World Health Organization. 2020. Available from: https://www.who.int/news-room/fact-sheets/detail/obesity-and-overweight
9. Ballard TJ, Kepple AW, Cafiero, C. The Food Insecurity Experience Scale Development of a Global Standard for Monitoring Hunger Worldwide [Internet]. FAO; 2013. Available from: http://www.fao.org/3/a-as583e.pdf
10. FAO, IFAD, UNICEF, WFP. The State of Food Security and Nutrition in the World 2020 [Internet]. 2020. Available from: http://www.fao.org/3/ca9692en/CA9692EN.pdf

11. FAO. Declaration on world food security [Internet]. Rome Declaration on World Food Security. 1996 [cited 2020 Aug 21]. Available from: http://www.fao.org/3/w3613e/w3613e00.htm
12. FAO, WFP, UNICEF. The State of Food Insecurity in the World 2018. Building climate resilience for food security and nutrition. Rome, FAO (also available at http://www.fao.org/docrep/018/i3434e/i3434e.pdf); 2018.
13. Food and Agriculture Organization of the United Nations. The State of Food Security and Nutrition in the World 2019: Safeguarding against economic slowdowns and downturns. Food & Agriculture Org.; 2019. 239 p.
14. UNICEF-WHO-The World Bank. Joint child malnutrition estimates—levels and trends—2020 edition [Internet]. 2020. Available from: https://data.unicef.org/resources/jme-report-2020/
15. Global Nutrition Report. 2020 Global Nutrition Report: Action on equity to end malnutrition. 2020.
16. Development Initiatives. 2018 Global Nutrition report: shining a light to spur action on nutrition. Development Initiatives; 2018.
17. Martorell R, Zongrone A. Intergenerational influences on child growth and undernutrition. Paediatr Perinat Epidemiol. 2012 Jul;26 Suppl 1:302–14.
18. Nandi A, Bhalotra S, Deolalikar AB, Laxminarayan R. The Human Capital and Productivity Benefits of Early Childhood Nutritional Interventions. In: Bundy DAP, Silva N de, Horton S, Jamison DT, Patton GC, editors. Child and Adolescent Health and Development. Washington (DC): The International Bank for Reconstruction and Development/The World Bank; 2018.
19. Cohen R. Evil days: thirty years of war and famine in Ethiopia. Human Rights Quarterly. 1992 Nov;14:660–63.
20. Tasic H, Akseer N, Gebreyesus SH, Ataullahjan A, Brar S, Confreda E, et al. Drivers of stunting reduction in Ethiopia: a country case study. Am J Clin Nutr. 2020 Sep 14;112(Suppl 2):875S–893S.
21. Baye K. Prioritizing the scale-up of evidence-based nutrition and health interventions to accelerate stunting reduction in Ethiopia. Nutrients [Internet]. 2019 Dec 16;11(12). Available from: http://dx.doi.org/10.3390/nu11123065
22. Wirth JP, Matji J, Woodruff BA, Chamois S, Getahun Z, White JM, et al. Scale up of nutrition and health programs in Ethiopia and their overlap with reductions in child stunting. Matern Child Nutr [Internet]. 2017 Apr;13(2). Available from: http://dx.doi.org/10.1111/mcn.12318
23. Zegeye B, Shibre G, Idriss-Wheeler D, Yaya S. Trends in inequalities in childhood stunting in Ethiopia from 2000 to 2016: a cross sectional study. J Public Health [Internet]. 2020 May 19. Available from: http://dx.doi.org/10.1093/pubmed/fdaa051
24. UNICEF. The State of the World's Children 2019: Children, Food and Nutrition: Growing Well in a Changing World. UNICEF; 2019.
25. Ng M, Fleming T, Robinson M, Thomson B, Graetz N, Margono C, et al. Global, regional, and national prevalence of overweight and obesity in children and adults during 1980-2013: a systematic analysis for the Global Burden of Disease Study 2013. Lancet. 2014 Aug 30;384(9945):766–81.
26. Finucane MM, Stevens GA, Cowan MJ, Danaei G, Lin JK, Paciorek CJ, Singh GM, Gutierrez HR, Lu Y, Bahalim AN, Farzadfar F. National, regional, and global trends in body-mass index since 1980: systematic analysis of health examination surveys and epidemiological studies with 960 country-years and 9·1 million participants. The Lancet. 2011;377(9765):557–67.
27. Mozaffarian D. Dietary and policy priorities to reduce the global crises of obesity and diabetes. Nature Food. 2020 Jan 1;1(1):38–50.
28. Abarca-Gómez L, Abdeen ZA, Hamid ZA, Abu-Rmeileh NM, Acosta-Cazares B, Acuin C, Adams RJ, Aekplakorn W, Afsana K, Aguilar-Salinas CA, Agyemang C. Worldwide trends in body-mass index, underweight, overweight, and obesity from 1975 to 2016: a pooled analysis of 2416 population-based measurement studies in 128·9 million children, adolescents, and adults. The Lancet. 2017;390(10113):2627–42.
29. Bixby H, Bentham J, Zhou B, Di Cesare M, Paciorek CJ, Collaboration NRF, et al. Rising rural body-mass index is the main driver of the global obesity epidemic. Nature. 2019;(569):260–64.

References

30. Popkin BM, Corvalan C, Grummer-Strawn LM. Dynamics of the double burden of malnutrition and the changing nutrition reality. Lancet. 2020 Jan 4;395(10217):65–74.
31. Tzioumis E, Adair LS. Childhood dual burden of under- and overnutrition in low- and middle-income countries: a critical review. Food Nutr Bull. 2014 Jun;35(2):230–43.
32. Popkin BM, Slining MM. New dynamics in global obesity facing low-and middle-income countries. Obes Rev [Internet]. 2013. Available from: https://onlinelibrary.wiley.com/doi/abs/10.1111/obr.12102
33. Wojcicki JM. The double burden household in sub-Saharan Africa: maternal overweight and obesity and childhood undernutrition from the year 2000: results from World Health Organization Data (WHO) and Demographic Health Surveys (DHS). BMC Public Health. 2014;14(1):1124.
34. Rachmi CN, Li M, Baur LA. The double burden of malnutrition in Association of South East Asian Nations (ASEAN) countries: a comprehensive review of the literature. Asia Pac J Clin Nutr. 2018;27(4):736–55.
35. Atre S, Deshmukh S, Kulkarni M. Prevalence of type 2 diabetes mellitus (T2DM) in India: a systematic review (1994–2018). Diabetes & Metabolic Syndrome: Clinical Research & Reviews. 2020 Sep 1;14(5):897–906.
36. Dutta M, Selvamani Y, Singh P, Prashad L. The double burden of malnutrition among adults in India: evidence from the National Family Health Survey-4 (2015-16). Epidemiol Health. 2019 Dec 18;41:e2019050.
37. Biswas T, Townsend N, Magalhaes RJS, Hasan M, Mamun A. Patterns and determinants of the double burden of malnutrition at the household level in South and Southeast Asia. Eur J Clin Nutr [Internet]. 2020 Sep 2. Available from: http://dx.doi.org/10.1038/s41430-020-00726-z
38. Kulkarni VS, Kulkarni V, Gaiha R. Double Burden of Malnutrition: Why are Indian Women Likely to Be Underweight and Obese? [Internet]. Brooks World Poverty Institute. 2014 [cited 2021 Jan 8]. Available from: https://papers.ssrn.com/abstract=2374028
39. Swaminathan S, Hemalatha R, Pandey A, Kassebaum NJ, Laxmaiah A, Longvah T, et al. The burden of child and maternal malnutrition and trends in its indicators in the states of India: the Global Burden of Disease Study 1990–2017. The Lancet Child & Adolescent Health. 2019 Dec 1;3(12):855–70.
40. DeFries R, Chhatre A, Davis KF, Dutta A, Fanzo J, Ghosh-Jerath S, et al. Impact of historical changes in coarse cereals consumption in India on micronutrient intake and anemia prevalence. Food Nutr Bull. 2018 Sep;39(3):377–92.
41. Shekar M, Heaver R, Lee Y-K, World Bank. Repositioning Nutrition as Central to Development: A Strategy for Large Scale Action. World Bank; 2006. 246 p.
42. United Nations Children's Fund. UNICEF's approach to scaling up nutrition for mothers and their children. UNICEF; 2015.
43. Scrimshaw NS, Taylor CE, Gordon J. Interactions of nutrition and infection. Berita Jururawat. 1969 Nov;9(2):41–4 passim.
44. Popkin BM, Adair LS, Ng SW. Global nutrition transition and the pandemic of obesity in developing countries. Nutr Rev. 2012 Jan;70(1):3–21.
45. Cox LM, Blaser MJ. Pathways in microbe-induced obesity. Cell Metab. 2013 Jun 4;17(6):883–94.
46. Kau AL, Ahern PP, Griffin NW, Goodman AL, Gordon JI. Human nutrition, the gut microbiome and the immune system. Nature. 2011 Jun 15;474(7351):327–36.
47. Devine A, Lawlis T. Nutrition and vulnerable groups. Nutrients [Internet]. 2019 May 14;11(5). Available from: http://dx.doi.org/10.3390/nu11051066
48. Black RE, Victora CG, Walker SP, Bhutta ZA, Christian P, de Onis M, et al. Maternal and child undernutrition and overweight in low-income and middle-income countries. Lancet. 2013 Aug 3;382(9890):427–51.
49. Barker DJ. Maternal nutrition, fetal nutrition, and disease in later life. Nutrition. 1997 Sep;13(9):807–13.
50. Victora CG, Adair L, Fall C, Hallal PC, Martorell R, Richter L, et al. Maternal and child undernutrition: consequences for adult health and human capital. Lancet. 2008 Jan 26;371(9609):340–57.

51. Norris SA, Osmond C, Gigante D, Kuzawa CW, Ramakrishnan L, Lee NR, et al. Size at Birth, Weight Gain in Infancy and Childhood, and Adult Diabetes Risk in Five Low- or Middle-Income Country Birth Cohorts [Internet]. Vol. 35, Diabetes Care. 2012. pp. 72–79. Available from: http://dx.doi.org/10.2337/dc11-0456
52. Permatasari DF, Sumarmi S. Differences of Born Body Length, History of Infectious Diseases, and Development between Stunting and Non-Stunting Toddlers [Internet]. Vol. 6, Jurnal Berkala Epidemiologi. 2018. p. 182. Available from: http://dx.doi.org/10.20473/jbe.v6i22018.182-191
53. Crookston BT, Dearden KA, Alder SC, Porucznik CA, Stanford JB, Merrill RM, et al. Impact of early and concurrent stunting on cognition. Matern Child Nutr. 2011 Oct;7(4):397–409.
54. Ezzati M. Comparative Quantification of Health Risks: Sexual and reproductive health. World Health Organization; 2004. 2248 p.
55. GBD 2015 Obesity Collaborators, Afshin A, Forouzanfar MH, Reitsma MB, Sur P, Estep K, et al. Health effects of overweight and obesity in 195 countries over 25 years. N Engl J Med. 2017 Jul 6;377(1):13–27.
56. Prasad KN. Micronutrients in Health and Disease [Internet]. 2016. Available from: http://dx.doi.org/10.1201/ebk1439821060
57. Allen LH, Peerson JM, Olney DK. Provision of multiple rather than two or fewer micronutrients more effectively improves growth and other outcomes in micronutrient-deficient children and adults. J Nutr. 2009 May;139(5):1022–30.
58. De Benoist B, McLean E, Andersson M, Rogers L. Iodine deficiency in 2007: global progress since 2003. Food Nutr Bull. 2008;29(3):195–202.
59. Bhutta ZA, Das JK, Rizvi A, Gaffey MF, Walker N, Horton S, et al. Evidence-based interventions for improvement of maternal and child nutrition: what can be done and at what cost? Lancet. 2013 Aug 3;382(9890):452–77.
60. Sommer A, West KP, Olson JA, Catharine Ross A. Vitamin A Deficiency: Health, Survival, and Vision. Oxford University Press; 1996. 438 p.
61. Lopez A, Cacoub P, Macdougall IC, Peyrin-Biroulet L. Iron deficiency anaemia. Lancet. 2016 Feb 27;387(10021):907–16.
62. Das JK, Salam RA, Thornburg KL, Prentice AM, Campisi S, Lassi ZS, et al. Nutrition in adolescents: physiology, metabolism, and nutritional needs. Ann NY Acad Sci. 2017 Apr;1393(1):21–33.
63. Hoddinott J, Maluccio JA, Behrman JR, Flores R, Martorell R. Effect of a nutrition intervention during early childhood on economic productivity in Guatemalan adults. Lancet. 2008 Feb 2;371(9610):411–16.
64. Yeates K, Lohfeld L, Sleeth J, Morales F, Rajkotia Y, Ogedegbe O. A global perspective on cardiovascular disease in vulnerable populations. Can J Cardiol. 2015 Sep;31(9):1081–93.
65. Bateson P, Barker D, Clutton-Brock T, Deb D, D'Udine B, Foley RA, et al. Developmental plasticity and human health. Nature. 2004 Jul 22;430(6998):419–21.
66. Barker DJ. The fetal and infant origins of disease. Eur J Clin Invest. 1995 Jul;25(7):457–63.
67. Barker DJ, Osmond C. Infant mortality, childhood nutrition, and ischaemic heart disease in England and Wales. Lancet. 1986 May 10;1(8489):1077–81.
68. Almond D, Currie J. Killing me softly: The fetal origins hypothesis. J Econ Perspect. 2011 Summer;25(3):153–72.
69. Barker DJ, Osmond C. Inequalities in health in Britain: specific explanations in three Lancashire towns. Br Med J. 1987 Mar 21;294(6574):749–52.
70. Arlinghaus KR, Truong C, Johnston CA, Hernandez DC. An intergenerational approach to break the cycle of malnutrition. Curr Nutr Rep. 2018 Dec;7(4):259–67.
71. United Nations Administrative Committee on Coordination Sub-Committee on Nutrition (ACC/SCN). 4th Report—The World Nutrition Situation: Nutrition throughout the Life Cycle. United Nations; 2000.
72. Roseboom TJ. The effects of prenatal exposure to the Dutch famine 1944–1945 on health across the lifecourse. In: Victor Preedy VBP, editor. Handbook of Famine, Starvation, and Nutrient Deprivation. Springer International Publishing; 2019.

References

73. Yarde F, Broekmans FJM, van der Pal-de Bruin KM, Schönbeck Y, te Velde ER, Stein AD, et al. Prenatal famine, birthweight, reproductive performance and age at menopause: the Dutch hunger winter families study. Hum Reprod. 2013 Dec;28(12):3328–36.
74. Stein AD, Pierik FH, Verrips GHW, Susser ES, Lumey LH. Maternal exposure to the Dutch famine before conception and during pregnancy: quality of life and depressive symptoms in adult offspring. Epidemiology. 2009 Nov;20(6):909–15.
75. Roseboom T, de Rooij S, Painter R. The Dutch famine and its long-term consequences for adult health. Early Hum Dev. 2006 Aug;82(8):485–91.
76. Roseboom TJ, Painter RC, van Abeelen AFM, Veenendaal MVE, de Rooij SR. Hungry in the womb: what are the consequences? Lessons from the Dutch famine. Maturitas. 2011 Oct 1;70(2):141–45.
77. Painter RC, Roseboom TJ, Bleker OP. Prenatal exposure to the Dutch famine and disease in later life: an overview. Reprod Toxicol. 2005 Sep;20(3):345–52.
78. Prentice AM, Ward KA, Goldberg GR, Jarjou LM, Moore SE, Fulford AJ, et al. Critical windows for nutritional interventions against stunting. Am J Clin Nutr. 2013 May;97(5):911–18.
79. Barker DJP, Bergmann RL, Ogra PL. The Window of Opportunity: Pre-pregnancy to 24 Months of Age. Karger Medical and Scientific Publishers; 2008. 266 p.

Chapter 6
Transformations Across Diets and Food Systems

Introduction

This chapter explains how our changing world has shaped food systems and diets. Although healthy diets and nutritious foods are essential to health, current global dietary patterns are suboptimal. Over time, changes to global food systems have led to less healthy diets. The "nutrition transition" refers to the significant dietary, lifestyle, and epidemiological shifts that occur as global incomes rise. Changes to global food supplies, environments, and prices have expanded access to both healthy and unhealthy food options for consumers. The transformation of diets and food systems is driven by globalization, trade, urbanization, and consumer preference.

Changing Diets

In the last three decades, dietary patterns have changed significantly around the world. These changes affect the health of people in low-, middle-, and high-income countries. Some dietary changes have positively affected health outcomes, while other changes have impaired health. Although some positive changes have occurred, global diets remain suboptimal.

Around the world, some dietary patterns have changed in positive ways. Since 1990, fruit consumption has increased in all regions and vegetable consumption has increased in some areas. The consumption of trans fats has declined in all regions, while red meat consumption has declined in most areas [1]. Income growth and a more interconnected food supply have helped to improve dietary diversity and facilitate these positive changes in consumption.

Despite these positive changes, the consumption of less healthy foods has also increased. Processed meat consumption has increased in all regions of the world. In East Asia, the consumption of red meat rose by nearly 40%. Sugar-sweetened beverage (SSB) consumption has risen in most regions, with the largest increase in North America [2]. In some parts of the world, the consumption of highly-processed packaged foods has also increased. As Fig. 6.1 shows, global per capita sales of packaged foods rose more than 13% between 2005 and 2017. Although consumers in Europe, North America, and Oceania purchase the highest volumes of packaged foods, sales growth is currently stagnant or declining in these regions. Africa and Asia experience a smaller volume of packaged food sales, but sales have steadily increased since 2005 [1].

In addition to shifts in dietary patterns, people around the world have also changed *how* they eat. The number of calories consumed increased 24% since 1960, while the amount of protein consumed rose by 25% and fat by 46% [4]. Since the 1970s, portion sizes have grown larger, especially in the United States, United Kingdom, and Latin America [5, 6]. Large portions are the "new normal," as consuming excessive calories has become prevalent regardless of a person's age, sex, socioeconomic status, or body mass index (BMI). Increases in portion size are especially common among energy-dense, high-calorie food products [7].

More and more, people obtain food from restaurants, fast-food chains, cafeterias, street vendors, and other places away from their homes. In the United States, food eaten away from home accounts for more than 50% of total food expenditures [8]. Snacks eaten "on the go" have increasingly replaced main lunches and dinners [9]. Eating outside the home has also become more common in Asia, Africa, Latin America, and the Caribbean, where the proportion of overall income spent on foods eaten away from home has risen significantly [10, 11]. In low-and middle-income countries (LMICs), between 13 and 50% of total energy intake comes from ready-to-eat food sold by street vendors [12]. The demand for foods eaten away from home is likely to increase in the next decade as an estimated 3 billion people enter the global middle class [13].

The Nutrition Transition

The nutrition transition is a specific type of dietary shift that occurs as people move to urban places and their lifestyles change. The term "nutrition transition" refers to the demographic and epidemiological shifts that take place among populations along with dietary and lifestyle changes [14, 15]. Urbanization, migration, economic development, globalization, and trade have significantly influenced the nutrition transition [16, 17].

As countries become wealthier and more urbanized, people increasingly live in different environments, as Fig. 6.2 shows. As part of this transition, low-income countries begin to adopt the patterns of more industrialized, high-income nations. Rural subsistence farming becomes less common and populations become less reliant on agriculture for their livelihoods. Food supply chains, markets, and environments become more varied and, sometimes, more sophisticated and longer [18].

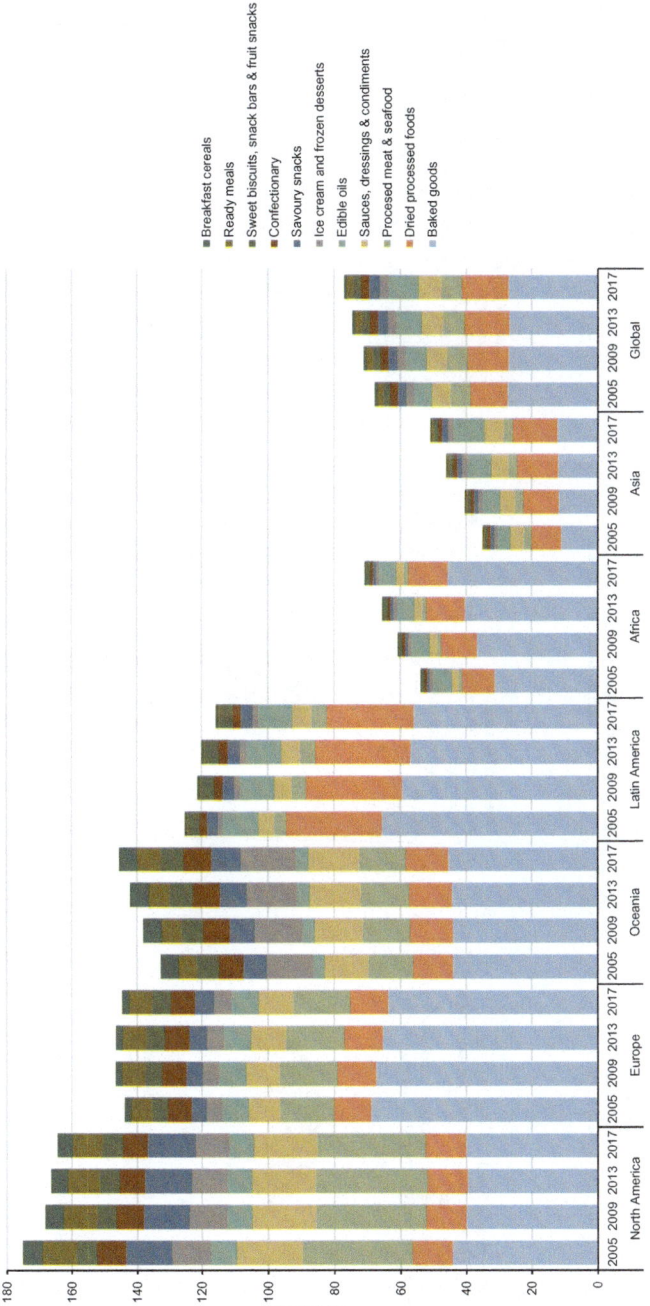

Fig. 6.1 Trends and patterns in per capita packaged food category sales by region, 2005–2017 [3]

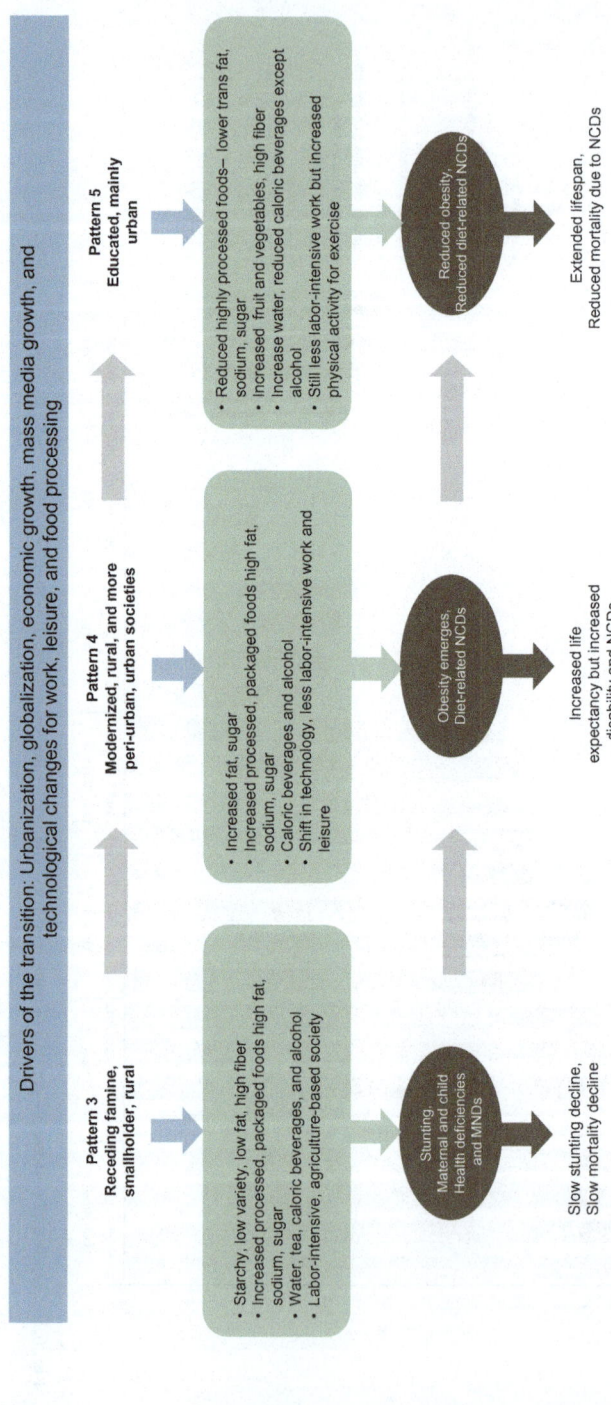

Fig. 6.2 The nutrition transition and patterns [15]

These changes to economies and food systems directly affect diets and nutrition. As economies transition, diets change from simple, less diverse ones to those with a range of options. Populations that previously relied on staple grains and seasonal, local foods are able to access more diverse and nutrient-rich foods, including animal source foods (ASF). While these changes can help people access healthy foods, there is also more access to processed and fast foods [19].

The changes associated with the nutrition transition also affect health outcomes. In addition to dietary shifts, physical activity often decreases as lifestyles, employment types, and transportation change [19]. As a result of these changes, disease burdens can shift: populations that were previously vulnerable to undernutrition, communicable diseases, and maternal and child mortality may instead experience higher levels of overweight, obesity, and noncommunicable diseases (NCDs) [20]. LMICs may be able to avoid negative health outcomes associated with the nutrition transition but doing so requires significant effort.

Food System Transformation

In recent decades, food systems around the world have changed significantly. Food systems are more interconnected at both global and local levels, with longer, more complex food supply chains. A range of different actors produce, process, transport, and sell food through those chains [21–23]. As a result of globalization, urbanization, and increased wealth, people's food preferences and behaviors have shifted toward diets that are cheaper, less healthy, and more convenient [24, 25]. Changing lifestyles, technological developments, and public policy are also important drivers of food system transformation [4]. Sudden shocks, such as the COVID-19 pandemic, can also radically change food systems, at least temporarily, as Box 6.1 illustrates.

> **Box 6.1 Effects of the COVID-19 pandemic on food systems**
> In December 2019, the SARS-CoV-2 virus was traced back to a seafood wet market in Wuhan, China. These markets are food environments where wildlife and other animals are bought and sold for fur, medicine, and food [26]. The SARS-CoV-2 virus causes COVID-19, a zoonotic disease, which led to a full-blown global pandemic. The origins of COVID-19 lie in animals; a "spillover event" likely caused the infectious disease to spread to humans. In the case of SARS-CoV-2, the spillover event was shown to be catastrophic for global world order, creating significant morbidity and death among the world's human population and long-term economic upheaval [27].
>
> The COVID-19 pandemic clearly illustrated how a health system shock can have profound impacts on every other system, including food systems [28]. Within the global food system, the middle of the food supply chain—including the processing, packaging, and distribution stages—was the hardest hit [29].

COVID-19 also impacted people's movements, making physical access to food more challenging [30–32]. Lockdowns, curfews, and restrictions on border movement constrained food access and made it difficult for food retail and food service facilities to operate in a normal capacity [31]. As a result, more people suffered from or became at risk of food insecurity, child undernutrition, and variable increases in food price [33–35].

As the pandemic continued to grip the world, emerging case studies showed how COVID-19 affected food security at the national and regional levels. In Italy, strict lockdowns disrupted people's eating behaviors, which contributed to an increase in stress-induced unhealthy food consumption (emotional eating) and eating anxiety [36]. In Spain, consumption of calories increased while the nutritional quality of diets decreased during lockdown [37]. Among adolescents in Pakistan, home confinement and school closures led to a decline in physical activity, while overall food consumption, intake of unhealthy foods, and weight gain increased [38]. In Saudi Arabia, online grocery buying, home-cooked meals, and takeout food orders all increased during the restrictions. Families also consumed more food, especially less healthy snacks [39]. While strong measures were not put in place to limit movement in the United States, food establishment operating hours and capacities were restricted. In the Asia and South Pacific region, quarantines and the ensuing loss of incomes constrained food access and consumption at the household level. Export bans on basic foods also increased food insecurity [40].

Changing Food Supplies

The food supply refers to the number of crops and animal products that contribute to energy, protein, fat, and food weight. Over time, the production, movement, and trade of vast amounts of food within food supplies has become incredibly proficient. In the past 50 years, most countries' food supplies have increased on average. The proportion of calories from energy-dense foods in these food supplies has increased as well [41].

At the same time that national food supplies have increased, they have also become more similar. On average, variation between food supplies has declined by more than 68%. While the availability of energy, protein, and fat has increased in most countries' food supplies, the global population, as a whole, increasingly relies on a relatively short list of major food crops. The most important crops in this group are wheat, rice, sugar, maize, and soybeans [41]. Crops like wheat, rice, and soy have become more widespread in the food supply, while crops like sorghum, millet, rye, cassava, and sweet potato have become marginalized and less important [41, 42].

The global dependence on a limited number of major crops carries implications for human health and the environment. The production of these foods requires expansive monocultural systems of agriculture [43, 44]. These production systems are supported by agricultural supply policies and are highly productive per unit area, which increases the affordability of these foods worldwide [45]. However, the cheaply available macronutrients sourced from these crops contribute negatively to health outcomes by increasing the risk of obesity, heart disease, and diabetes [46, 47]. Fruit and vegetable consumption can contribute positively to dietary diversity and health outcomes, yet the supply of these foods is currently insufficient to achieve healthy diets for all [45, 48].

Trade policy can make national food supplies and diets more diverse. Trade increases the availability of different types of foods and extends the season in which products are available [49, 50]. International food trade is essential to nutrient access: it allows lower-income countries to feed and nourish huge numbers of people [51]. While trade influences the range of available and affordable foods, it also introduces less healthy foods that are cheaper and could be harmful to health [52–56]. To achieve positive health outcomes through trade, policymakers must focus on the nutrition imperative. Without this focus, trade can manifest as either a positive stimulus or an obstacle to health [57, 58].

Changing Food Environments

Around the world, food environments are changing rapidly as a result of increasing globalization, urbanization, and income growth. Globalization affects distribution and retail models, which can rapidly change the organization of the entire food supply chain [59, 60]. Globalization contributes to the expansion of supermarkets and hypermarkets in LMICs. While these retail outlets provide larger population centers with more choice and higher-quality food, they can also exclude or marginalize small-scale producers from certain supply chains [21, 59, 61–65]. Box 6.2 describes in detail how globalization affects food environments with specific cases from Mexico, Brazil, and Ghana.

> **Box 6.2 The globalization of food environments**
>
> Food environments are evolving around the world. Much of this evolution is driven by demand, as the food retail sector responds to the changing tastes and rising incomes of its consumers. Food environments also influence the demand for new foods and diets through the density and proximity of retail outlets, and the price, promotion, placement, and provision of different types of food [66].
>
> Globalization also affects food environments as large-scale multinational companies expand across the world [14, 25]. Many governments struggle to govern the public health impacts of food systems when powerful companies

arrive and dominate the direction of food systems in their countries. Multinational food and beverage companies exert their influence by introducing "Westernized" foods and dietary patterns. The introduction of new foods and eating habits contribute to rapid dietary shifts away from traditional foods and diets [67, 68].

The influence of multinational food companies is especially strong in Latin America, sub-Saharan Africa, and Asia, where fast-food chains and food companies have rapidly transformed diets [69, 70]. In Mexico, SSBs and processed foods became more accessible after the North American Free Trade Agreement led to increased investment by U.S. companies like Coca-Cola [71]. On average, Mexicans purchase 1,928 calories of packaged foods and beverages per day [72]. In the Brazilian Amazon, Nestle recruited local women to sell their food products door-to-door across the favelas, a highly successful venture reaching 700,000 low-income customers per month [73]. In Ghana, the rapidly expanding Kentucky Fried Chicken (KFC) chain introduced a menu that blends local culture with "aspirational" American food. To change the perception that fast food is a "special treat" rather than an everyday routine, KFC also reduced its prices and targeted its advertising to newly middle-class customers [74].

The cases of Mexico, Brazil, and Ghana are just a few examples of countries experiencing the effects of globalization on their food environments. Worldwide, global sales of fast food grew 30% from 2011 to 2016 [74]. From 2002 to 2016, sales of ultra-processed foods by global companies increased by 20–90% in lower-income countries [75]. These transformations lead to both benefits and negative consequences. A larger proportion of people's diets consist of foods that are cheap, convenient, and tasty. However, these foods are largely unhealthy, and this cheap food paradigm comes at a significant cost as rates of obesity and NCDs rise around the world [76].

Changing food environments also affect consumer preferences and demand. The "supermarket revolution," or rapid spread of formal supermarkets and fast-food chains, has increased the availability and affordability of a wide range of products [77, 78]. This expansion is associated with the increased consumption of processed foods, which is also linked to rising obesity and less healthy diets. As consumer preferences change due to urbanization and income growth, consumers can also shape the food environment through their buying power [64].

Changing Affordability of Healthy Diets

For many people around the world, nutritious foods and healthy diets are unaffordable. Healthy diets cost 60% more than diets that meet basic nutrient needs and nearly five times more than diets that meet basic energy needs. Globally, 1.9 billion people in Asia, 965 million in Africa, and 104.2 million in Latin America and the Caribbean cannot afford healthy diets [79]. Of the healthy diets proposed by the Eat-*Lancet* Commission, the most affordable one exceeded household per capita income for more than 1.58 billion people [80].

Food prices are a major driver of consumption patterns. Price-induced dietary changes can impair dietary diversity and quality, contribute to malnutrition, and adversely affect health [81–83]. Since 2003, the real price of food has risen around the world [83]. Rising prices can have tangible and dramatic effects: in 2008, the global increase in cereal prices drove an additional 40 million people to hunger [81].

Changes to global food prices most directly affect people in low-income countries. Local productivity and value chain efficiency can make perishable nutritious foods more expensive and difficult to trade [82]. Populations in low-income countries spend a large proportion of their income—up to 62%—on food expenditures [84]. Poor households are especially vulnerable, as they may spend 50–80% of their income on food [80, 85]. Poor populations primarily rely on cereals and have less access to ASF, fruits, and vegetables [86]. To cope with rising prices, poor populations may consume cheaper staple foods or energy-dense, low-nutrient foods; limit consumption of nutrient-rich foods; and reduce overall food intake [81–83].

Increases in global food prices have smaller impacts on consumers in middle- and high-income countries. People in these countries spend less of their income—between 6 and 30%—on food purchases. As the prevalence of diet-related noncommunicable diseases (DR-NCDs) rise in these countries, governments are increasingly using food price as a means to encourage healthier eating [83]. These interventions require further research, but initial evidence suggests that taxing unhealthy foods and subsidizing healthy products can improve diets [87].

Income and diet quality are interconnected. As incomes rise in low-income countries, households typically tend to buy more expensive, perishable foods, such as ASF, fruits, and vegetables [19, 88]. However, rising income is also associated with substantial increases in the consumption of less nutritious foods [89, 90]. With more disposable income, people tend to consume more foods high in sugar, salt, and saturated and trans fats, such as highly-processed and packaged foods, SSBs, and red and processed meats [91]. Snacking and eating away from home also tend to increase, with less cooking taking place at home [92, 93].

Incomes are projected to increase over time, which will influence global diets. As an additional 3 billion people enter the global middle class by 2030, there will be more demand for ASF, edible vegetable oils, and processed foods. The demand for ASF is expected to double, while demand for starchy staples will slow. The demand for takeaway foods will also likely increase [13]. Some countries, such as China and Brazil, have already experienced increased demand for ASF as incomes rise. This trend reflects the situation in developed countries with already higher incomes per capita, where demand for these foods is higher compared to less affluent nations [94].

Key Messages and Conclusions

Global dietary patterns are not in alignment with optimal human health. People's food choices and diets present a considerable risk for disease and mortality. Despite these risks, projections of future dietary patterns indicate that the trend of eating less healthy foods will continue.

Dietary changes occur because of shifts in globalization, urbanization, and other global economic drivers. These drivers have contributed to a "nutrition transition," in which changes in dietary consumption and energy expenditure have coincided with economic, demographic, and epidemiological changes.

Changes to the food system also affect diets. Food supplies are highly efficient but risk becoming overly dependent on a limited number of crops. Food environments are evolving toward super-and hypermarkets that provide both diverse, safe foods and less healthy, energy-dense ones.

Food affordability remains a massive challenge around the world. Perishable, nutritious foods tend to be unaffordable for a significant number of people, particularly the extremely poor. As incomes rise, people are often able to afford more foods, which include both healthier and less nutritious foods.

References

1. Development Initiatives. 2018 Global Nutrition Report: Shining a light to spur action on nutrition. Development Initiatives; 2018.
2. Haddad L, Hawkes C, Waage J, Webb P, Godfray C, Toulmin C. Food systems and diets: facing the challenges of the 21st century. London, UK: Global Panel on Agriculture and Food Systems for Nutrition; 2016.
3. Baker P, Machado P, Santos T, Sievert K, Backholer K, Hadjikakou M, et al. Ultra-processed foods and the nutrition transition: global, regional and national trends, food systems transformations and political economy drivers. Obes Rev. 2020 Dec;21(12):e13126.
4. Vermeulen SJ, Park T, Khoury CK, Béné C. Changing diets and the transformation of the global food system. Ann NY Acad Sci [Internet]. 2020 Jul 26. Available from: http://dx.doi.org/10.1111/nyas.14446
5. Marteau TM, Hollands GJ, Shemilt I, Jebb SA. Downsizing: policy options to reduce portion sizes to help tackle obesity. BMJ. 2015 Dec 2;351:h5863.
6. Poti JM, Popkin BM. Trends in energy intake among US children by eating location and food source, 1977-2006. J Am Diet Assoc. 2011 Aug;111(8):1156–64.
7. Livingstone MBE, Pourshahidi LK. Portion size and obesity. Adv Nutr. 2014 Nov;5(6):829–34.
8. Saksena MJ, Okrent AM, Anekwe TD, Cho C, Dicken C, Effland A et al. America's Eating Habits: Food Away From Home. USDA ERS; 2018.
9. Kant AK, Graubard BI. 40-year trends in meal and snack eating behaviors of American adults. J Acad Nutr Diet. 2015 Jan;115(1):50–63.
10. Tian X, Zhong L, von Cramon-Taubadel S, Tu H, Wang H. Restaurants in the neighborhood, eating away from home and BMI in China. PLoS One. 2016 Dec 13;11(12):e0167721.
11. Popkin BM, Reardon T. Obesity and the food system transformation in Latin America. Obes Rev. 2018 Aug;19(8):1028–64.
12. Steyn NP, McHiza ZJ. Obesity and the nutrition transition in Sub-Saharan Africa. Ann N Y Acad Sci. 2014 Apr;1311:88–101.

13. Ranganathan J, Vennard D, Waite R. Shifting diets for a sustainable food future. World Resources [Internet]. 2016. Available from: https://www.researchgate.net/profile/Janet_Ranganathan/publication/301541772_Shifting_Diets_for_a_Sustainable_Food_Future/links/5717b3dd08ae986b8b79e1a8/Shifting-Diets-for-a-Sustainable-Food-Future.pdf
14. Popkin BM. Technology, transport, globalization and the nutrition transition food policy. Food Policy. 2006 Dec 1;31(6):554–69.
15. Drewnowski A, Popkin BM. The nutrition transition: new trends in the global diet. Nutr Rev. 1997 Feb;55(2):31–43.
16. Popkin BM. Relationship between shifts in food system dynamics and acceleration of the global nutrition transition. Nutr Rev. 2017 Feb 1;75(2):73–82.
17. Popkin BM, Adair LS, Ng SW. Global nutrition transition and the pandemic of obesity in developing countries. Nutr Rev. 2012 Jan;70(1):3–21.
18. Seto KC, Ramankutty N. Hidden linkages between urbanization and food systems. Science. 2016 May 20;352(6288):943–45.
19. Kearney J. Food consumption trends and drivers. Philos Trans R Soc Lond B Biol Sci. 2010 Sep 27;365(1554):2793–807.
20. Haddad LJ, Achadi E, Ag Bendech M, Ahuja A, Bhatia K, Bhutta Z, et al. Global Nutrition Report [Internet]. International Food Policy Research Institute; 2015. Available from: http://dx.doi.org/10.2499/9780896295643
21. Reardon T, Timmer CP. The economics of the food system revolution. Annu Rev Resour Econ. 2012 Aug 1;4(1):225–64.
22. Kiminami L, Furuzawa S. Dynamic changes in China's food system. Studies in Regional Science. 2014;44(1):41–62.
23. Gliessman S. Transforming our food systems. Agroecology and Sustainable Food Systems. 2018;42(5):475–76.
24. Hawkes C, Popkin BM. Can the sustainable development goals reduce the burden of nutrition-related non-communicable diseases without truly addressing major food system reforms? BMC Med. 2015 Jun 16;13:143.
25. Brunelle T, Dumas P, Souty F. The impact of globalization on food and agriculture: the case of the diet convergence. J Environ Dev. 2014 Mar 1;23(1):41–65.
26. Wu Y-C, Chen C-S, Chan Y-J. The outbreak of COVID-19: an overview. J Chin Med Assoc. 2020 Mar;83(3):217–20.
27. Fanzo J, Covic N, Dobermann A, Henson S, Herrero M, Pingali P, et al. A research vision for food systems in the 2020s: defying the status quo. Global Food Security. 2020 Sep;26:100397.
28. Barrett CB. Actions now can curb food systems fallout from COVID-19. Nature Food [Internet]. 2020. Available from: http://dx.doi.org/10.1038/s43016-020-0085-y
29. Hobbs JE. Food supply chains during the COVID-19 pandemic. Can J Agric Econ. 2020 Jun;68(2):171–76.
30. Akter S. The impact of COVID-19 related "stay-at-home" restrictions on food prices in Europe: findings from a preliminary analysis. Food Secur. 2020 Jul 8;12(4):1–7.
31. Arndt C, Davies R, Gabriel S, Harris L, Makrelov K, Robinson S, et al. Covid-19 lockdowns, income distribution, and food security: an analysis for South Africa. Glob Food Sec. 2020 Sep;26:100410.
32. Townsend L. The professional wild food community and Covid-19: the use of online platforms in supporting people to access alternative food sources. Local Development & Society. 2020 Aug 24;1–6.
33. Headey D, Heidkamp R, Osendarp S, Ruel M, Scott N, Black R, et al. Impacts of COVID-19 on childhood malnutrition and nutrition-related mortality. Lancet. thelancet.com; 2020 Aug 22;396(10250):519–21.
34. Pereira M, Oliveira AM. Poverty and food insecurity may increase as the threat of COVID-19 spreads. Public Health Nutr. 2020 Dec;23(17):3236–40.
35. Wolfson JA, Leung CW. Food insecurity during COVID-19: an acute crisis with long-term health implications. Am J Public Health. 2020 Dec;110(12):1763–65.

36. Di Renzo L, Gualtieri P, Cinelli G, Bigioni G, Soldati L, Attinà A, et al. Psychological aspects and eating habits during COVID-19 home confinement: results of EHLC-COVID-19 Italian online survey. Nutrients [Internet]. 2020 Jul 19;12(7). Available from: http://dx.doi.org/10.3390/nu12072152
37. Batlle-Bayer L, Aldaco R, Bala A, Puig R, Laso J, Margallo M, et al. Environmental and nutritional impacts of dietary changes in Spain during the COVID-19 lockdown. Sci Total Environ. 2020 Dec 15;748:141410.
38. Allabadi H, Dabis J, Aghabekian V, Khader A, Khammash U. Impact of COVID-19 lockdown on dietary and lifestyle behaviours among adolescents in Palestine. Dynam Human Health. 2020;7:2170.
39. Alhusseini N, Alqahtani A. COVID-19 pandemic's impact on eating habits in Saudi Arabia. J Public Health Res. 2020 Jul 28;9(3):1868.
40. Kim K, Kim S, Park C-Y. Food Security in Asia and the Pacific amid the COVID-19 Pandemic [Internet]. Asian Development Bank; 2020. Available from: https://think-asia.org/handle/11540/12119
41. Khoury CK, Bjorkman AD, Dempewolf H, Ramirez-Villegas J, Guarino L, Jarvis A, et al. Increasing homogeneity in global food supplies and the implications for food security. Proc Natl Acad Sci USA. 2014 Mar 18;111(11):4001–4006.
42. High Level Panel of Experts. Sustainable agricultural development for FSN: what roles for livestock? 2016.
43. Herrero M, Thornton PK, Power B, Bogard JR, Remans R, Fritz S, et al. Farming and the geography of nutrient production for human use: a transdisciplinary analysis. Lancet Planet Health. 2017 Apr;1(1):e33–42.
44. Nelson G, Bogard J, Lividini K, Arsenault J, Riley M, Sulser TB, et al. Income growth and climate change effects on global nutrition security to mid-century. Nature Sustainability. 2018;1(12):773–81.
45. Pingali P. Agricultural policy and nutrition outcomes—getting beyond the preoccupation with staple grains. Food Security. 2015;7(3):583–91.
46. Du SF, Wang HJ, Zhang B, Zhai FY, Popkin BM. China in the period of transition from scarcity and extensive undernutrition to emerging nutrition-related non-communicable diseases, 1949-1992. Obes Rev. 2014;15:8–15.
47. Popkin BM. Nutrition Transition, Diet Change, and Its Implications. Reference Module in Biomedical Sciences [Internet]. 2019. Available from: http://dx.doi.org/10.1016/b978-0-12-801238-3.11153-5
48. Berners-Lee M, Kennelly C, Watson R, Hewitt CN. Current global food production is sufficient to meet human nutritional needs in 2050 provided there is radical societal adaptation [Internet]. 2018. Available from: https://www.elementascience.org/article/10.1525/elementa.310/
49. Friel S, Schram A, Townsend B. The nexus between international trade, food systems, malnutrition and climate change. Nature Food. 2020;1(1):51–58.
50. Hawkes C, Grace D, Thow AM. Trade liberalization, food, nutrition and health. Trade and Health: Towards building a National Strategy Geneva, WHO. 2015;92–116.
51. Wood SA, Smith MR, Fanzo J, Remans R, DeFries RS. Trade and the equitability of global food nutrient distribution. Nature Sustainability. 2018 Jan 1;1(1):34–37.
52. Friel S, Gleeson D, Thow A-M, Labonte R, Stuckler D, Kay A, et al. A new generation of trade policy: potential risks to diet-related health from the trans pacific partnership agreement. Global Health. 2013 Oct 16;9(1):46.
53. Schram A, Labonte R, Baker P, Friel S, Reeves A, Stuckler D. The role of trade and investment liberalization in the sugar-sweetened carbonated beverages market: a natural experiment contrasting Vietnam and the Philippines. Global Health. 2015 Oct 12;11(1):41.
54. Thow AM. Trade liberalisation and the nutrition transition: mapping the pathways for public health nutritionists. Public Health Nutr. 2009 Nov;12(11):2150–58.
55. Hawkes C. Uneven dietary development: linking the policies and processes of globalization with the nutrition transition, obesity and diet-related chronic diseases. Global Health. 2006 Mar 28;2:4.

References

56. Stuckler D, McKee M, Ebrahim S, Basu S. Manufacturing epidemics: the role of global producers in increased consumption of unhealthy commodities including processed foods, alcohol, and tobacco. PLoS Med. 2012 Jun 26;9(6):e1001235.
57. Thow AM, Nisbett N. Trade, nutrition, and sustainable food systems. Lancet. 2019 Aug 31;394(10200):716–18.
58. Baker P, Brown AD, Wingrove K, Allender S, Walls H, Cullerton K, et al. Generating political commitment for ending malnutrition in all its forms: A system dynamics approach for strengthening nutrition actor networks. Obes Rev [Internet]. 2019 Jun 27. Available from: http://dx.doi.org/10.1111/obr.12871
59. Reardon T, Hopkins R. The supermarket revolution in developing countries: policies to address emerging tensions among supermarkets, suppliers and traditional retailers. The European Journal of Development Research. 2006 Dec 1;18(4):522–45.
60. Reardon T, Timmer CP, Minten B. Supermarket revolution in Asia and emerging development strategies to include small farmers. Proc Natl Acad Sci USA. 2012 Jul 31;109(31):12332–37.
61. Reardon T, Berdegué JA. The rapid rise of supermarkets in Latin America: challenges and opportunities for development. Dev Policy Rev. 2002 Sep 28;20(4):371–88.
62. Reardon T, Dillon M. Crossfire: "Is the growth of supermarkets in developing countries to the detriment of small-scale producers?" Food Chain. 2011;1(1):7–10.
63. Fongar A, Gödecke T, Qaim M. Various forms of double burden of malnutrition problems exist in rural Kenya. BMC Public Health. 2019 Nov 21;19(1):1543.
64. Khonje MG, Qaim M. Modernization of African food retailing and (un)healthy food consumption. Sustain Sci Pract Policy. 2019 Aug 9;11(16):4306.
65. Wanyama R, Gödecke T, Chege CGK, Qaim M. How important are supermarkets for the diets of the urban poor in Africa? Food Security. 2019;11(6):1339–53.
66. Vandevijvere S, Swinburn B. Creating healthy food environments through global benchmarking of government nutrition policies and food industry practices. Arch Public Health. 2014 Mar 5;72(1):7.
67. Popkin BM. The implications of the nutrition transition for obesity in the developing world. Oxford University Press New York; 2010.
68. Popkin BM, Mendez M. The rapid shifts in stages of the nutrition transition: the global obesity epidemic. Global Health. 2007;68–80.
69. Christian M, Gereffi G. Fast-Food Value Chains and Childhood Obesity: A Global Perspective. In: Freemark MS, editor. Pediatric Obesity: Etiology, Pathogenesis and Treatment. Cham: Springer International Publishing; 2018. pp. 717–30.
70. da Silva GF, da Rocha A, Pacheco H. The Internationalization of Brazilian Fast-Food Chains: A Marketing Failure? In: Liberman L, Newburry W, editors. Internationalization, Innovation and Sustainability of MNCs in Latin America. London: Palgrave Macmillan UK; 2013. pp. 124–46.
71. Clark SE, Hawkes C, Murphy SME, Hansen-Kuhn KA, Wallinga D. Exporting obesity: US farm and trade policy and the transformation of the Mexican consumer food environment. Int J Occup Environ Health. 2012 Jan;18(1):53–65.
72. Bandy L. New Nutrition Data Shows Global Calorie Consumption [Internet]. Euromonitor International. 2015. Available from: https://blog.euromonitor.com/new-nutrition-data-shows-global-calorie-consumption/
73. Jacobs A, Richtel M. How big business got Brazil hooked on junk food. New York Times. 2017.
74. Searcey, D, Richtel, M. Obesity was rising as Ghana embraced fast food. Then came KFC. The New York Times. 2017.
75. Adams J, Hofman K, Moubarac J-C, Thow AM. Public health response to ultra-processed food and drinks. BMJ. 2020 Jun 26;369:m2391.
76. Popkin BM, Corvalan C, Grummer-Strawn LM. Dynamics of the double burden of malnutrition and the changing nutrition reality. Lancet. 2020 Jan 4;395(10217):65–74.
77. Lu L, Reardon T. An economic model of the evolution of food retail and supply chains from traditional shops to supermarkets to e-commerce. Am J Agric Econ. 2018 Oct 1;100(5):1320–35.

78. Luck M, Benkenstein M. Consumers between supermarket shelves: the influence of interpersonal distance on consumer behavior. Journal of Retailing and Consumer Services. 2015;26:104–14.
79. FAO, IFAD, UNICEF, WFP. The State of Food Security and Nutrition in the World 2020 [Internet]. 2020. Available from: http://www.fao.org/3/ca9692en/CA9692EN.pdf
80. Hirvonen K, Bai Y, Headey D, Masters WA. Affordability of the EAT–Lancet reference diet: a global analysis. The Lancet Global Health. 2020 Jan 1;8(1):e59–66.
81. Green R, Cornelsen L, Dangour AD, Turner R, Shankar B, Mazzocchi M, et al. The effect of rising food prices on food consumption: systematic review with meta-regression. BMJ. 2013 Jun 17;346:f3703.
82. Dizon F, Herforth A, Wang Z. The cost of a nutritious diet in Afghanistan, Bangladesh, Pakistan, and Sri Lanka. Global Food Security. 2019 Jun 1;21:38–51.
83. Cornelsen L, Green R, Turner R, Dangour AD, Shankar B, Mazzocchi M, et al. What happens to patterns of food consumption when food prices change? Evidence from a systematic review and meta-analysis of food price elasticities globally. Health Econ. 2015;24(12):1548–59.
84. Gao G. World food demand. Am J Agric Econ. 2012 Jan;94(1):25–51.
85. Banerjee AV, Duflo E. The economic lives of the poor. J Econ Perspect. 2007;21(1):141–67.
86. Headey DD, Alderman HH. The Relative Caloric Prices of Healthy and Unhealthy Foods Differ Systematically across Income Levels and Continents. J Nutr [Internet]. 2019 Jul 23 [cited 2019 Jul 23]. Available from: https://academic.oup.com/jn/advance-article-pdf/doi/10.1093/jn/nxz 158/28951648/nxz158.pdf
87. Afshin A, Micha R, Webb M, Capewell S, Whitsel L, Rubinstein A, et al. Effectiveness of Dietary Policies to Reduce Noncommunicable Diseases. In: Dorairaj Prabhakaran, Shuchi Anand, Thomas A. Gaziano, Jean-Claude Mbanya, Yangfeng Wu, editor. Disease Control Priorities, Third Edition (Volume 5): Cardiovascular, Respiratory, and Related Disorders. 2017. pp. 101–15.
88. Alexandratos N, Bruinsma J. World agriculture towards 2030/2050: the 2012 revision [Internet]. Food and Agriculture Organization of the United Nations; 2012 Jun. Available from: https://ageconsearch.umn.edu/record/288998/
89. Imamura F, Micha R, Khatibzadeh S, Fahimi S, Shi P, Powles J, et al. Dietary quality among men and women in 187 countries in 1990 and 2010: a systematic assessment. The Lancet Global health. 2015 Mar;3(3):e142.
90. Tong TYN, Imamura F, Monsivais P, Brage S, Griffin SJ, Wareham NJ, et al. Dietary cost associated with adherence to the Mediterranean diet, and its variation by socio-economic factors in the UK Fenland Study. Br J Nutr. 2018 Mar;119(6):685–94.
91. Drewnowski A, Darmon N. The economics of obesity: dietary energy density and energy cost–. Am J Clin Nutr. 2005;82(1):265S–273S.
92. Miller V, Mente A, Dehghan M, Rangarajan S, Zhang X, Swaminathan S, et al. Fruit, vegetable, and legume intake, and cardiovascular disease and deaths in 18 countries (PURE): a prospective cohort study. Lancet. 2017 Nov 4;390(10107):2037–49.
93. Teo K, Lear S, Islam S, Mony P, Dehghan M, Li W, et al. Prevalence of a healthy lifestyle among individuals with cardiovascular disease in high-, middle- and low-income countries: The Prospective Urban Rural Epidemiology (PURE) study. JAMA. 2013 Apr 17;309(15):1613–21.
94. Tilman D, Clark M. Global diets link environmental sustainability and human health. Nature. 2014 Nov 27;515(7528):518–22.

Chapter 7
Drivers Shaping Food Systems

Introduction

Food systems are affected by many different factors in complex ways. These influential factors are considered "drivers" when their impacts occur consistently over a period of time and thus durably alter food system activities and outcomes [1]. Drivers may be endogenous to food systems, but many are independent and exogenous. Food system drivers may be governed or shaped by external actors, and impacts may be deliberate or unintentional. Drivers can affect every component of the food system, from food supply and environment to consumer demand. This chapter focuses on major macro-level drivers, which include environmental, sociocultural, political and economic, and demographic drivers. The chapter also discusses the present-day challenges and future opportunities presented by innovation, technology, and infrastructure.

Biophysical and Environmental Drivers

The natural resource base provides the foundation for the food system. Through the mediating influence of the food system, diets and nutrition outcomes are also inextricably linked to natural resources and ecosystems. Natural resources include land, water, nutrients, soil, sunlight, energy, and biodiversity, all of which are critical inputs needed to produce food [2]. The natural resource base supports the diversity of landscapes and ecosystems, which have multiple benefits for people and the environment.

Climate change and variability affect the productivity and resilience of ecosystems and landscapes that produce food. The effects of climate change also carry repercussions for the health and nutritional status of communities and households.

Ecosystems and Biodiversity

The food system is heavily dependent on ecosystems and biodiversity. Ecosystems include areas that are managed by people, such as farms, as well as wild areas, such as forests and waterways. Biodiversity refers to the number and inter-species variety of plant and animal species [3]. Food systems rely on "ecosystem services" that provide benefits for the overall nutrient recycling system and human health [4] (see Box 7.1).

> **Box 7.1 What are ecosystem services?**
> Ecosystem services are the benefits people derive from ecosystems. Ecosystems provide services and goods, such as food, wood and other raw materials, plants, animals, fungi and microorganisms. They also provide essential regulating services, such as crop pollination, water purification, and soil stabilization, and cultural services, such as recreation and a sense of place [4].

The relationship between food systems and ecosystems is highly complex, because environmental changes are both a driver and outcome of food systems. Agriculture and food systems can only be sustained if natural resources, including soil, water, land, and biodiversity, are well managed through sustainable use and conservation. If soil lacks key nutrients or is contaminated with heavy metals, for example, crop yields and livestock production can be impaired. Decreases in food production can subsequently affect food security, dietary quality, and human health [3].

As part of this bidirectional relationship, food system activities can impair the health of ecosystems and natural resources. As Chapter 9 discusses in detail, food production is the largest cause of environmental change [5]. Production activities contribute 11–24% of the planet's greenhouse gas emissions, use 40% of available land, and use 70% of available freshwater [5, 6]. Agriculture and food production are major drivers of biodiversity loss, deforestation, species extinction, and natural resource degradation [5, 7]. If not properly managed, certain agricultural methods can increase environmental degradation. For example, industrialized methods that extensively use chemical inputs, such as fertilizers, pesticides, and antibiotics, can negatively affect ecosystems [8, 9].

Food security, diets, and nutrition all depend on biodiversity [3], much of which can be found in wild landscapes, such as forests and waterways, as well as farms. "Agrobiodiversity" refers to the types of foods and the vast varieties of species used for food and agriculture. Farm size is closely linked to agrobiodiversity: smaller farms and landscapes produce more diverse crops and thus provide more nutrients, particularly micronutrients, as compared to large-scale farms [10]. Around the world, agriculture systems of different countries have become increasingly similar. The food supply has followed suit, as populations rely on the same major food crops, such as wheat, rice, sugar, palm oil, maize, and soy [11]. Other foods such as sorghum, millet, sweet potato, and yam have been marginalized. At the same time, food system activities and the demand for certain foods negatively affect global biodiversity. The growing demand for animal source foods (ASF), such as meat and dairy, has significantly impaired the world's biodiversity "hotspots." To expand agricultural land, these hotspots, which contain 44% of the world's plants and 35% of its terrestrial vertebrates, have been reduced by nearly 90% of their original size [12, 13].

Climate Change

Climate change refers to significant changes in global weather patterns and sea levels that have occurred over a significant period of time. Human activity is the primary cause of planetary warming and, regardless of any mitigation efforts, global surface temperature change is projected to exceed 1.5 °C by the end of the twenty-first century [14, 15]. Projections of climate variability suggest that less predictable, shifting seasons and climate-related natural disasters, such as severe floods and droughts, will affect food systems and human health. At the present and in the future, the effects of climate change negatively affect environmental ecosystems and human well-being.

Climate change affects the entire food system, as shown in Fig. 7.1. Increased planetary warming is expected to reduce crop productivity in some low-resource settings. Countries in tropical regions will experience the greatest declines in crop productivity and fish populations [16]. At the storage and distribution stages of the food system, climate change is projected to cause food losses from fungal contamination and extreme weather events that disrupt supply chains, among other factors [17–19].

Climate-mediated changes to food systems will ultimately affect diets and nutrition. As climate change leads to declines in agricultural productivity and increases in food losses, food prices will likely rise, and nutritious foods will become even less affordable. Research on food prices indicates that when prices rise, people consume fewer nutritious foods and more inexpensive, ultra-processed foods [19, 21, 22]. The effects of climate change may also affect nutritional quality: increases in carbon dioxide have been shown to reduce the zinc, iron, and protein content of some staple crops, such as grains and legumes [21, 23–25].

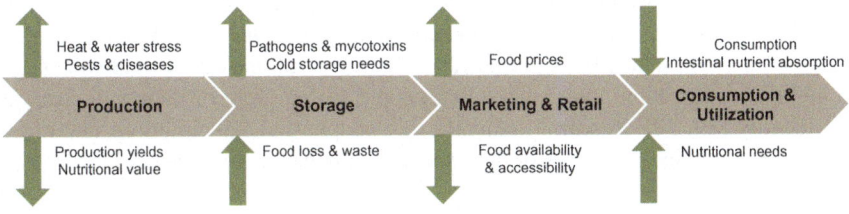

Fig. 7.1 Effects of climate change on the food supply chain [20]

Left unmitigated, the effects of climate change on the food system will likely cause increased food insecurity. Low-income populations are at a heightened risk of food insecurity and limited access to an adequate supply of nutrient-dense foods [26, 27]. The effects of climate change on food security and nutritional status may also result in lower incomes, reduced resilience, and, on a broader scale, more displacement, migration, and prolonged poverty [14].

Sociocultural Drivers

Food choices reflect personal identity, culture, and social traditions. Food is an important part of culture: the types of foods we consume, the way we prepare and eat them, the people with whom we share food, and the places where we eat are repositories of tradition. Individual choices and food systems both shape and reflect cultural identity. Cultural tradition and gender norms are major drivers of food environments and diets.

Social Norms, Culture, and Traditions

Cultural traditions and social norms influence food habits and dietary patterns. These habits may be variously called "cuisines," "foodways," "food heritage," or "food cultures" [28, 29]. Culture underpins every aspect of food and eating: it influences food acquisition, ingredients and preparation methods, meal composition, food presentation, number and timing of meals eaten each day, portion size, and fasting cycles, among others [29, 30].

A culture's food habits provide value and meaning that extend beyond physical nourishment. The act of sharing food is a social experience that reflects cultural values and represents a collective association [28, 29, 31]. Food behaviors and habits may be practical or symbolically meaningful in a given culture [29, 30]. Cultural values and traditions influence perceptions of acceptability: the "cultural relativism" of eating helps explain why foods like foie gras, chitterlings, chicken nuggets, bushmeat, genetically modified (GM) foods, and insects are alternately embraced or abhorred around the world [28].

Food choice is essential to individual identity, as it can shape a person's sense of self and standing in the world. Food can signify a person's economic or social status, religion, or ethnic background [29, 32]. Many cultural beliefs and values are so highly ingrained and internalized that people are unaware of their influence on self-identity [29, 30]. Research indicates that people make assumptions about the values, lifestyle, and behaviors of others based on their dietary patterns [29].

Women's Status and Empowerment

Around the world, women play a major role in shaping food systems and diets. In their biological and social roles as mothers and caregivers, women give birth, breastfeed, and tend to the needs of children. In most societies, women also prepare the food that the entire household eats. As workers and laborers, women represent a significant proportion of the agricultural workforce [33].

Despite their importance, the contributions made by women often remain undervalued. Women bear more responsibility for unpaid household and childcare labor than men, which affects their involvement in other activities, such as paid work. In some regions, rising migration and changing livelihoods have led women to become increasingly responsible for agricultural production. This "feminization" of agriculture is most common in South Asia, especially in countries like Nepal and Bangladesh where the male heads of households have migrated to other countries or regions that have a surplus of low-wage labor. Even as women take on more work, their access to agricultural inputs, tools, information and extension services, land, and other resources remains limited. These obstacles can limit women's agricultural productivity, reinforce existing gender norms, and perpetuate poverty [34–37]. The added responsibility of agricultural labor can also carry negative repercussions for health and nutrition outcomes [38, 39].

Women's empowerment can directly affect household-level diets and nutrition. "Empowerment" refers to a woman's ability to make life choices for herself and others [40]. A woman's status and level of empowerment affect her ability to manage her time, make decisions, utilize health services, and control household income and other resources [40–45]. Empowerment influences the nutritional status of women and children: higher levels of empowerment are associated with an increased share of income spent on food, improved food security, and increased dietary diversity [43, 45–49]. A comparative study of low-and middle-income countries (LMICs) showed that improved educational attainment and societal status for women played a major role in reducing hunger between 1970 and 1995 [50–52].

Political and Economic Drivers

A country's political landscape can significantly influence the functionality of food systems through agricultural, health, and trade policies. In many countries, policies such as agricultural subsidies and trade can influence the availability and affordability of certain types of food. In turn, this can affect what foods are available in the food supply [53, 54]. Governments can also implement food-based dietary guidelines, which can shape policies and promote a healthy diet. For example, tax policies can be used to de-incentivize the consumption of less healthy foods, such as sodas and junk food. Investment is needed to ensure sufficient resources are devoted to creating a sustainable food system [55].

Leadership and Governance

At both the global and local level, governments shape food systems through policies and investments. Governance involves the use of economic, political, and administrative powers to manage a country's affairs. Global nutrition governance involves improving nutrition outcomes through decision-making, implementation, accountability, and other processes and mechanisms. Effective governance requires political commitment, leadership, policy coherence, knowledge and data, and capacity [56].

Policymakers consider many factors and strive to balance the needs of many stakeholders as they make decisions that influence food systems. These decisions involve the design and implementation of policies, as well as investments in programs that strengthen public health and food systems. Policy decisions can contribute to an "enabling environment" that yields positive outcomes for food and nutrition goals, or a "disabling environment" that results in negative outcomes [57]. Food and nutrition governance may be influenced by civil society groups, international and regional organizations, donors, research organizations, academia, and private sector companies. Power dynamics play an important role in decision-making: more prominent, powerful groups may exert undue influence on decision-making and leave less powerful groups marginalized. Disagreement between influential actors can also lead to power struggles and imbalances that shape food systems in unsustainable ways [55, 58].

Globalization and Trade

Globalization and trade play a major role in shaping food systems. Globalization is a dynamic process that increases the interconnectedness of populations around the world [59]. Globalization and trade have helped facilitate the integration of global markets, direct investment by foreign companies, expansion of transnational food companies, and cross-cultural food marketing [60]. These drivers affect the type, quantity, quality, cost, and desirability of foods that are available to consumers, as Fig. 7.2 shows [60, 61].

Globalization and trade are a significant influence on diets and nutrition. Through trade, globalization has increased the diversity of the food supply, particularly micronutrient-rich foods, and reduced the cost of food [62]. Trade has allowed for greater access to seasonal foods year-round [63]. However, globalization is also considered a major driver of the nutrition transition: it has helped shift diets toward more energy-dense processed and prepared foods and led to more sedentary lifestyles [64–67]. In low-income countries, trade has incentivized the production of energy-dense foods, led to higher prices for more nutritious foods, and contributed to the increased popularity of "Westernized" diets [68, 69]. Box 7.2 describes how free trade has increased consumption of fatty meats in Pacific Island nations, and how these countries have used policy action to address the health impacts of these foods. While

Political and Economic Drivers

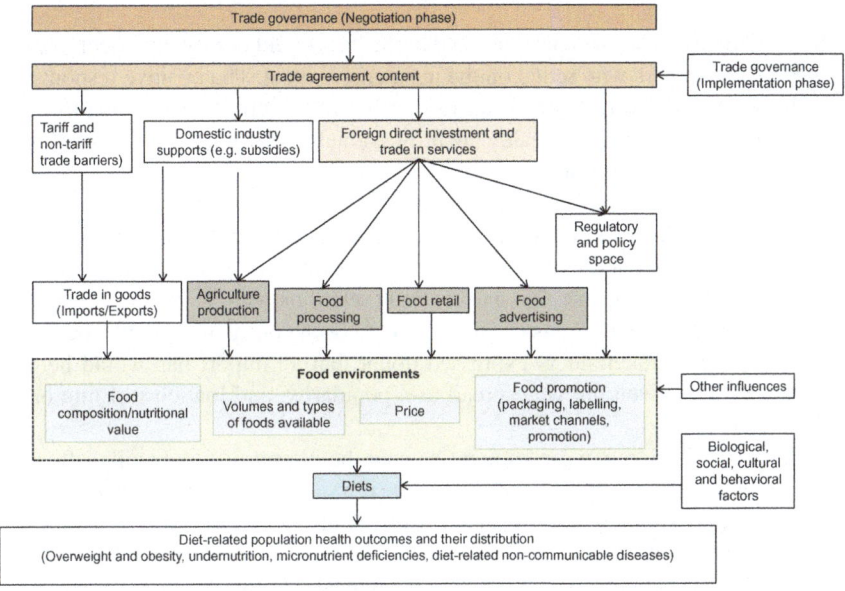

Fig. 7.2 Impacts of trade on food systems and diets [61]

globalization and trade can improve dietary diversity and mitigate undernutrition, these drivers can alternately increase the risks of overconsumption and exacerbate inequality [60–62, 70].

> **Box 7.2 Trade policies to reduce unhealthy meat consumption in Fiji, Samoa, and Tonga**
>
> In Pacific Island countries, policymakers have used trade policies to address unhealthy food environments with varying success. In these countries, globalization and trade liberalization have contributed to the increased availability of imported foods high in sugar, salt, and fat [71]. Free trade has also led to the "dumping" of low-quality, inexpensive food [72]. These foods have contributed to a rapid nutrition transition and significant increase in the prevalence of obesity, cardiovascular disease, diabetes, and other diet-related noncommunicable diseases (DR-NCDs) [72, 73].
>
> In 2000, the government of Fiji banned the sale of mutton flaps, which resulted in an immediate decline in the product's availability. Prior to the ban, the country imported more than 220 tons of mutton flaps from New Zealand alone. Although the policy allowed mutton flaps to be imported for processing rather than direct sale, it effectively halved the number of imports. The ban was widely supported by consumers and retailers, though many policymakers doubted the measure would improve the overall healthfulness of

diets. Some stakeholders also feared that the ban would negatively affect low-income consumers who relied on the inexpensive meat. The positive response to the policy was likely driven by prevailing public concerns about the quality of mutton flaps, advocacy by healthcare professionals, and a consumer awareness campaign about the product's health risks [71, 72].

In 2004, Tongan policymakers drafted a proposal to restrict the import of mutton flaps. However, the draft measure was not ultimately advanced to the legislature over concerns that it would complicate the country's entry into the World Trade Organization and its trade relations with neighboring countries. While mutton flap consumption had long been considered a public health concern, some stakeholders expressed doubt that an import ban would help improve diets, given the widespread use, popularity, and low cost of mutton flap meat [72].

In 2007, the Samoan government banned the import of turkey tails, effectively ceasing their supply. A government health survey found that, as a result of the ban, approximately half of survey respondents shifted to consuming other cheap meats, such as sausage or mutton, while one-quarter shifted to lower-fat meat and seafood products. When Samoa ascended to the World Trade Organization in 2011, however, the ban on turkey tails was reversed. The measure was considered a barrier to free trade and subsequently replaced by a 300% import duty [72, 74].

The cases of these three Pacific Island nations illustrate the complexities of trying to align nutrition and trade goals. Though it is difficult to ascertain whether these policy measures directly led to declines in fatty meat consumption, these measures helped to alter the food supply and raise consumer awareness of the linkage between unhealthy foods and adverse health outcomes. Even less successful measures represent an important attempt to expand policy dialogue in order to integrate food systems and health into the trade agenda [72].

Conflicts and Humanitarian Crises

The stress of violent conflict and humanitarian crisis affects every aspect of food systems. At the production stage, crops, livestock, land, and water systems may be destroyed. Disruptions to infrastructure can impair the processing, distribution, and sale of food products [75, 76]. As a result, food supply chains that were previously stable may become unpredictable. These disruptions contribute to food shortages and limit food access and overall food security. Crises can also affect people's livelihoods and lead to lower incomes [77].

The relationship between crisis, food insecurity, and malnutrition is highly complex. Violent conflict and/or natural events, such as droughts or floods, are often the primary drivers of crises. However, food insecurity can also contribute to conflict through rising food prices, price volatility, and food shortages [78–81]. Crises also act as drivers of food insecurity and malnutrition. Box 7.3 describes how South Sudan's ongoing conflict situation has affected food insecurity and childhood undernutrition. Globally, the prevalence of chronic undernutrition is increasingly concentrated in conflict-affected countries [82, 83]. The effects of conflict carry adverse consequences for nutrition and health throughout an individual's life and into future generations [79]. Given the persistent effects of conflict on hunger, countries that experience long-standing crises may struggle to escape the cycle of poor nutrition and poverty [83, 84].

Box 7.3 The effects of war on nutrition and food security in South Sudan

In 2011, South Sudan gained independence from the Republic of Sudan to become the world's newest sovereign nation. The country's victory was hard-fought following decades of violent conflict and associated poverty, famine, and disease. The triumph of independence was short-lived, however, as political struggles between the country's two largest ethnic groups led to the onset of civil war in 2013. By 2018, the war had displaced approximately 4.5 million people and led to the deaths of an estimated 380,000 people, either through direct conflict or disease, hunger, and other causes exacerbated by the fighting [85, 86]. Peace agreements signed in 2018 and 2020 have brought hope for the resolution of conflict, though the security situation remains highly fragile and complex [87].

The war in South Sudan has culminated in a massive humanitarian crisis that has destroyed livelihoods and deepened poverty. The conflict has decimated the country's already-limited infrastructure and disrupted access to healthcare, education, water and sanitation, markets, and humanitarian aid. An estimated 40% of the country's population has access to safe water, while only 10% can access basic sanitation [88]. Economic decline and instability have led to high inflation rates and currency depreciation [69, 84]. Rural areas, where most of the country's population lives and works in subsistence farming, have been hardest hit. The fighting has targeted agricultural assets, limited access to livestock products, and resulted in shortages of staple foods [77, 89].

The country's protracted humanitarian crisis has also intensified food insecurity and malnutrition. In 2017, famine was declared amidst record-high food prices and inflation [77, 84]. As in many conflict settings, it is difficult to ascertain accurate, up-to-date food security and nutrition data, but estimates suggest that 5.5 million people currently face acute food insecurity, a figure that may rise to 7.3 million by 2021 [88, 90]. Among children under the age of five, between 31–58% experience stunting and between 10–22.7% experience wasting [91, 92].

> Key drivers of food insecurity and undernutrition in South Sudan include poor macroeconomic conditions and limited access to basic services. Widespread disease, such as the severe cholera outbreak in 2017, and suboptimal young child feeding practices, such as low rates of exclusive breastfeeding, also contribute [84, 91]. Low agricultural yields, limited food imports, and high transportation costs have led to rising food prices, limiting access and availability [77, 84]. Food insecurity and poverty have also been exacerbated by cyclical flooding and droughts, as well as the more recent threat of COVID-19 [89, 93].

Demographic Drivers

Population change, urbanization, and migration influence the trajectory of food systems around the world. These demographic drivers affect food consumption and demand, which carry ramifications for food production and the environment. Changing population dynamics affect hunger and food security and are intensified by climate change and conflict. These drivers are especially relevant in LMICs.

Population Growth

By 2050, the global population is projected to grow to 9.8 billion people. This massive expansion represents an increase of approximately two billion people from the global population in 2020, as shown in Fig. 7.3. Population growth will primarily be driven by rising birth rates in Africa and Asia. Some regions, such as Africa, will experience a growing population of young people, while others, like Europe and Asia, will face a significant aging population [94, 95].

Population growth and changing dynamics place tremendous strains on food systems. Shifts in population dynamics coincide with changes in global dietary patterns. These changing diets increasingly feature ASF, which are highly resource-intensive and environmentally impactful. Population growth and dietary change act as major drivers of global land use change [97]. The world's growing population will require more food to sustain itself, but the demand for certain resource-intensive foods, such as some ASF, will place undue pressure on an overburdened system. While land use efficiency may lead to higher yields, these production methods require external inputs, such as pesticides and fertilizers, that negatively affect the environment [98]. As the global population grows, changes to dietary patterns and food demand will be necessary to ensure the sustainable production of sufficient nutritious food for all [95, 99, 100].

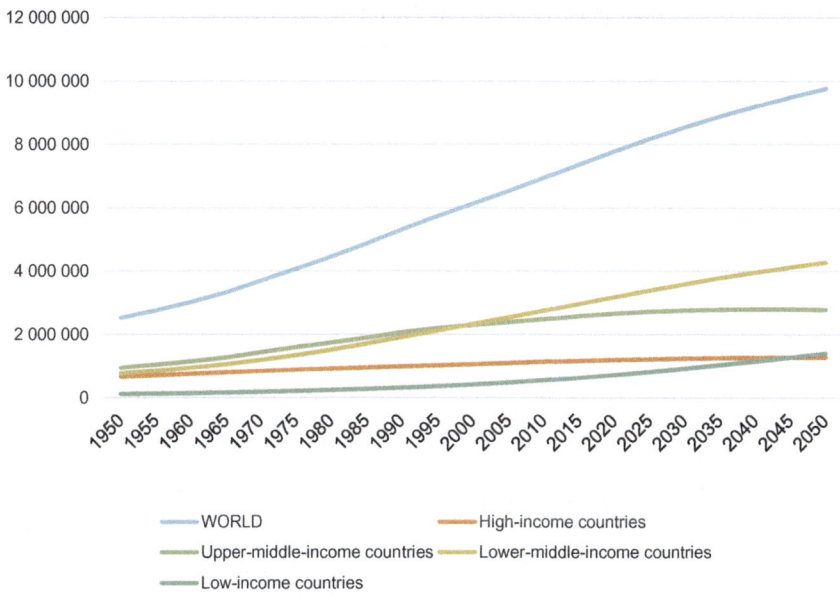

Fig. 7.3 Global population growth, 1950–2050 [96]

Urbanization

The global population is increasingly becoming urbanized. By 2050, more than 6 billion people, or approximately two-thirds of the world's population, will live in urban areas (Fig. 7.4). The vast majority of this growth will occur in Africa and Asia, where 56% and 64% of the respective populations will be urbanized [101–103]. These changes have major ramifications for food systems and natural resources, as urban areas currently account for 60% of global energy consumption, 70% of global waste, and 70% of greenhouse gas emissions [102].

Urbanization changes people's relationship with food and shapes their food systems. Rising urbanization is associated with an increase in energy-dense diets and greater demand for ASF, fats and oils, refined grains, and fruits and vegetables. Many urban dwellers prefer processed and prepared foods, which can be less healthy than fresh foods but more convenient [55, 104]. Urbanization changes the food environment by increasing the number of supermarkets, which can provide a safer, more varied array of foods. However, low-income populations may not have physical or economic access to healthy, fresh foods from these retailers [105–107]. For these populations, the "built" environment in urban areas helps determine nutritional status, food security, and food safety [108, 109].

The effects of urbanization on food consumption and demand will likely present additional challenges for food systems. Urban demand influences the types of foods grown in agricultural areas and how these foods are processed, distributed, and

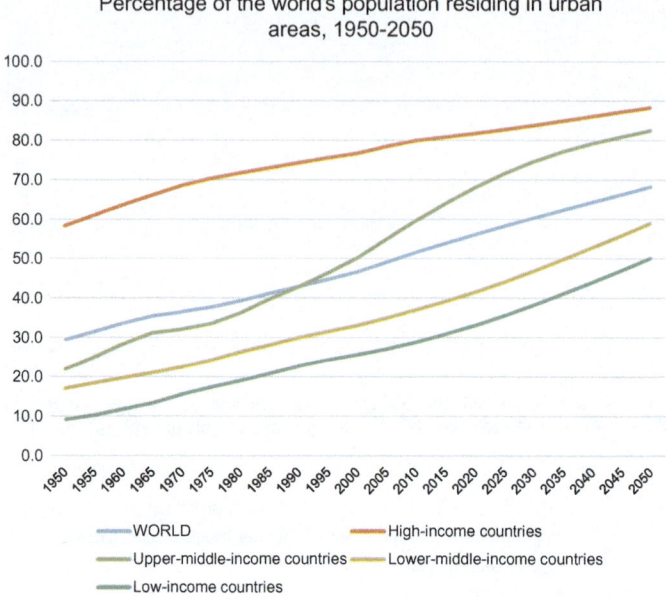

Fig. 7.4 Percentage of the world's population residing in urban areas, 1950–2050 [96]

marketed. Urban spaces require longer food chains and more processing, packaging, and refrigeration [55, 102, 104]. Urbanization is also a major driver of land use change: the expansion of urban areas displaces agricultural production from fertile croplands and contributes to biodiversity loss [110, 111].

Migration and Forced Displacement

Around the world, people leave their homes for many different reasons. Migrants may move to find new jobs, reunite with family, or pursue educational opportunities, among other reasons. Others experience forced displacement as internally displaced persons, asylum seekers, or refugees. War or conflict, natural disasters, extreme environmental events, or different forms of persecution can force people to relocate. International migration is on the rise: in 2019, there were approximately 272 million migrants, an increase of more than 40% since 2000 [112].

Migration, food systems, and rural development are highly interconnected. Economic growth in non-agricultural sectors has historically been a major driver of rural-to-urban migration: poverty and lack of opportunity can act as "push factors" that compel people to leave low-paying agricultural work, while job availability in urban areas can likewise act as a "pull factor" for migration. Young people are most likely to leave the agricultural sector in rural areas and migrate for better employment opportunities [113]. Rural areas are also disproportionately affected by violent conflicts that damage or destroy agricultural assets and lead to forced displacement [114]. Migration flows will likely increase as the effects of climate change on agriculture intensify the competition for natural resources [113].

Forced migration, hunger, and food insecurity intersect as part of a complex cycle. Violent conflicts and climate shocks underpin food insecurity and displacement: conflicts are a major driver of the rise in global hunger and forced migration, while climate shocks exacerbate fragility and food insecurity [114]. Food insecurity acts as a driver for migration, especially when caused by conflict or climate-mediated impacts on agriculture [114, 115]. People may migrate to escape hunger or famine, or they may relocate for employment opportunities that increase their household's resilience to food insecurity and other shocks [113]. Migration can also increase vulnerability, which can contribute to higher levels of food insecurity among migrant populations in their destinations [116].

Innovation, Technology, and Infrastructure

In past decades, innovation and infrastructure have been a major influence on food system transformation. These drivers will continue to be critical as the world's societies address the needs of a rapidly growing population in the context of climate change and natural resource scarcity. Building more efficient, sustainable food systems will require new research and technologies, as well as better access to and use of existing technologies and infrastructure.

Innovation and Technology

Innovation and technology are major drivers of food system transformation. The Industrial Revolution modernized agricultural production through mechanization, breeding methods, and fertilizers. Technologies in food processing and preservation have changed the way food can be stored, cooked, and transported [117]. Modern innovations in agricultural technology, product development, processing, packaging, and logistics can stimulate change at other stages of the food supply chain. Demand or supply at one stage in the food supply chain can generate new developments that reverberate throughout the food system. University research centers, applied research institutions, and private sector companies may work independently or collaborate through public–private partnerships to research and develop food system technologies [118].

The effects of innovation and technology on the food supply chain can positively shape diets and nutrition. Farm technologies help support agricultural intensification, improve productivity, and enhance efficiency. These innovations have generated non-farmemployment opportunities that are especially beneficial for women and youth [118]. Longer supply chains connect rural farmers to markets and provide them with opportunities to produce more diversified, high-value crops. Technology can improve access to information, reduce costs, protect food safety, and create alternative networks throughout the food supply chain. These innovations have primarily affected nutrition outcomes by lowering food costs and making seasonal foods more widely available. Time-saving technologies have positively altered women's responsibilities, allowing them more time to engage in the labor market, education, or childcare [118–120].

Technological innovations also carry negative repercussions for food systems. The opportunities presented by farm technologies do not extend to all food producers, especially small-scale farmers. Long supply chains are often more vulnerable to climate shocks, food safety risks, disease, conflict and unrest, and energy costs. These chains have also introduced more processed and packaged foods into the food supply. While these convenience foods may contribute to economic development and women's empowerment by freeing up time that would otherwise be spent on food preparation, they negatively affect health and nutrition outcomes. High costs, limited capacity, and lack of connectivity also present challenges to technological adoption. As Chapter 10 discusses in more detail, the impacts of new, potentially "disruptive" food system innovations, such as gene editing, automation, and big data, on sustainability and food system goals remain hypothetical.

Infrastructure and the Built Environment

Infrastructure is a critical component of food systems, as it facilitates the transportation of food from the place of production to the places where it will be processed, distributed, sold, and consumed. Transportation requires road, railway, and shipping infrastructure to move food by motor vehicle, train, ship, plane, or animal. Infrastructure has improved significantly over the last 50 years: in the last 15 years alone, travel times between cities in sub-Saharan Africa have radically declined. Trips that once required three to five hours can now be accomplished in one hour or less [121]. However, infrastructure quality and access vary considerably, and many of the world's politically marginalized and poor, rural populations remain disconnected from markets [20, 55, 122, 123].

Infrastructure directly affects food environments. Food must be transported over long distances to areas of food shortage in order to improve security and stabilize prices. Efficient, quick transport protects against food waste and foodborne disease. Evidence suggests the quality and availability of infrastructure can affect nutrition outcomes in young children [124]. Infrastructure also influences people's ability to access food through the built environment: it helps determine the distance to food entry points and the transportation needed to access these points [55]. "Obesogenic" environments lack access to healthy, affordable foods, and feature an overabundance of fast-food and takeout restaurants that foster unhealthy dietary patterns [125, 126].

Key Messages and Conclusions

Food systems, diets, and nutrition are shaped by many different, highly complex drivers. Environmental, sociocultural, political, economic, and demographic factors all play a role in food system transformation. The global population is continuously changing as people migrate to urban areas, birth rates increase in some areas and stagnate elsewhere, and lifestyles shift. Globalization heightens the connections between countries and facilitates international trade. Population growth and changing diets require more resources to produce food, yet the effects of climate change present a monumental challenge.

These dynamic food system drivers intersect and evolve in complex ways. As the world's population rapidly grows and evolves, the food system will need to sustainably produce enough nutritious food for all. Agricultural productivity is bound by the natural resource base, but food system activities can also degrade these foundational resources. Globalization, migration, and urbanization shape food supply chains and dietary patterns. These drivers can improve access to nutrient-rich foods, but they also contribute to the overconsumption of highly-processed, energy-dense foods. They also affect sociodemographic patterns and household structures in ways that influence broader cultural and societal traditions. Policy governance can help mediate these evolving trends, mitigate challenges, and create enabling environments for diets and nutrition. Technology and infrastructure are also critical, though these innovations must be developed and implemented in ways that protect the health of both people and the planet.

References

1. Béné C, Prager SD, Achicanoy HAE, Toro PA, Lamotte L, Cedrez CB, et al. Understanding food systems drivers: A critical review of the literature. Global Food Security. 2019 Dec 1;23:149–59.
2. National Research Council, Institute of Medicine, Board on Agriculture and Natural Resources, Food and Nutrition Board, Committee on a Framework for Assessing the Health, Environmental, and Social Effects of the Food System. A Framework for Assessing Effects of the Food System. National Academies Press; 2015. 444 p.
3. DeClerck FAJ, Fanzo J, Palm C, Remans R. Ecological approaches to human nutrition. Food Nutr Bull. 2011 Mar;32(1 Suppl):S41–50.
4. Duraiappah AK, Naeem S, Agardy T, Ash NJ, Cooper HD, Diaz S, et al. Ecosystems and human well-being: biodiversity synthesis; a report of the Millennium Ecosystem Assessment. 2005; Available from: https://experts.umn.edu/en/publications/ecosystems-and-human-well-being-biodiversity-synthesis-a-report-o
5. Willett W, Rockström J, Loken B, Springmann M. Food in the Anthropocene: the EAT–Lancet Commission on healthy diets from sustainable food systems. Lancet [Internet]. 2019; Available from: https://www.thelancet.com/journals/lancet/article/PIIS0140-6736(18)31788-4/fulltext?fbclid=IwAR2ftk_lpUKlVbQ-B93qUXmWnm6bA4dfFA5paVFCG0vExt5c516oikYOCsk
6. Springmann M, Wiebe K, Mason-D'Croz D, Sulser TB, Rayner M, Scarborough P. Health and nutritional aspects of sustainable diet strategies and their association with environmental

impacts: a global modelling analysis with country-level detail. Lancet Planet Health. 2018 Oct;2(10):e451–61.
7. Tilman D, Clark M. Global diets link environmental sustainability and human health. Nature. 2014 Nov 27;515(7528):518–22.
8. Gore AC, Chappell VA, Fenton SE, Flaws JA, Nadal A, Prins GS, et al. EDC-2: The Endocrine Society's Second Scientific Statement on Endocrine-Disrupting Chemicals. Endocr Rev. 2015 Dec;36(6):E1–150.
9. Alder J, Barling D, Dugan P, Herren HR, Josupeit H, Lang T, et al. Avoiding future famines: strengthening the ecological foundation of food security through sustainable food systems. A UNEP synthesis report Nairobi (Kenya): United Nations Environment Programme [Internet]. 2012; Available from: https://openaccess.city.ac.uk/2576/1/
10. Herrero M, Thornton PK, Power B, Bogard JR, Remans R, Fritz S, et al. Farming and the geography of nutrient production for human use: a transdisciplinary analysis. Lancet Planet Health. 2017 Apr;1(1):e33–42.
11. Khoury CK, Bjorkman AD, Dempewolf H, Ramirez-Villegas J, Guarino L, Jarvis A, et al. Increasing homogeneity in global food supplies and the implications for food security. Proc Natl Acad Sci U S A. 2014 Mar 18;111(11):4001–6.
12. Machovina B, Feeley KJ, Ripple WJ. Biodiversity conservation: The key is reducing meat consumption. Sci Total Environ. 2015 Dec 1;536:419–31.
13. Myers N, Mittermeier RA, Mittermeier CG, da Fonseca GA, Kent J. Biodiversity hotspots for conservation priorities. Nature. 2000 Feb 24;403(6772):853–8.
14. Intergovernmental Panel On Climate Change. Climate Change 2014: Synthesis Report. Contribution of Working Groups I, II and III to the Fifth Assessment Report of the Intergovernmental Panel on Climate Change [Internet]. 2014. Available from: http://energyeficiency.clima.md/files/1_Cadrul_International/2_Documente/8_IPCC/Eng/IPCC_Who_is_who.pdf
15. Hoegh-Guldberg O, Jacob D, Bindi M, Brown S, Camilloni I, Diedhiou A, et al. Impacts of 1.5 C global warming on natural and human systems. Global warming of 1 5° C An IPCC Special Report [Internet]. 2018; Available from: https://helda.helsinki.fi/handle/10138/311749
16. Mbow C, Rosenzweig C, Barioni LG, Benton TG, Herrero M, Krishnapillai M, et al. Food security. In: Climate Change and Land: an IPCC special report on climate change, desertification, land degradation, sustainable land management, food security and greenhouse gas fluxes in terrestrial ecosystems. IPCC; 2019.
17. Medina A, Rodriguez A, Magan N. Effect of climate change on Aspergillus flavus and aflatoxin B1 production [Internet]. Vol. 5, Frontiers in Microbiology. 2014. Available from: http://dx.doi.org/10.3389/fmicb.2014.00348
18. Arndt C, Strzepeck K, Tarp F, Thurlow J, Fant C 4th, Wright L. Adapting to climate change: an integrated biophysical and economic assessment for Mozambique. Sustainability Sci. 2011;6(1):7–20.
19. Vermeulen SJ, Campbell BM, Ingram J. Climate change and food systems. 2012.
20. Fanzo J, McLaren R, Davis C, Choufani J. Climate change and variability: What are the risks for nutrition, diets, and food systems? [Internet]. Intl Food Policy Res Inst; 2017 Jun. Available from: https://play.google.com/store/books/details?id=IiMmDwAAQBAJ
21. Lake IR, Hooper L, Abdelhamid A, Bentham G, Boxall ABA, Draper A, et al. Climate change and food security: health impacts in developed countries. Environ Health Perspect. 2012 Nov;120(11):1520–6.
22. Lock K, Stuckler D, Charlesworth K, McKee M. Potential causes and health effects of rising global food prices. BMJ. 2009 Jul 13;339:b2403.
23. Beach RH, Sulser TB, Crimmins A, Cenacchi N, Cole J, Fukagawa NK, et al. Combining the effects of increased atmospheric carbon dioxide on protein, iron, and zinc availability and projected climate change on global diets: a modelling study. The Lancet Planetary Health. 2019 Jul 1;3(7):e307–17.
24. Myers SS, Zanobetti A, Kloog I, Huybers P, Leakey ADB, Bloom AJ, et al. Increasing CO_2 threatens human nutrition. Nature. 2014 Jun 5;510(7503):139–42.
25. Vermeulen SJ, Campbell BM, Ingram J. Climate change and food systems. 2012.

26. Fanzo J, Davis C, McLaren R, Choufani J. The effect of climate change across food systems: Implications for nutrition outcomes. Global food security [Internet]. 2018; Available from: https://www.sciencedirect.com/science/article/pii/S2211912418300063
27. United Nations System Standing Committee on Nutrition. Sixth report on the world nutrition situation: Progress in nutrition. United Nations System Standing Committee on Nutrition; 2010.
28. Crowther G. Eating Culture: An Anthropological Guide to Food. University of Toronto Press, Higher Education Division; 2018.
29. Kittler PG, Sucher KP and Nelms M. Food and Culture. Cengage Learning; 2011.
30. Fieldhouse P. Food and Nutrition: Customs and Culture. Springer; 2013.
31. Allison A, Counihan C, Van Esterik P. Food and Culture: A Reader. Carole Counihan PVE, editor. Routledge; 2013.
32. Fischler C. Food, self and identity. Information. 1988 Jun 1;27(2):275–92.
33. Johnston LM, Finegood DT. Cross-sector partnerships and public health: challenges and opportunities for addressing obesity and noncommunicable diseases through engagement with the private sector. Annu Rev Public Health. 2015 Mar 18;36:255–71.
34. Slavchevska V, Kaaria S, Taivalmaa SL. The Feminization of Agriculture. In: Allan T, Bromwich B, Keulertz M, Colman A, editors. The Oxford Handbook of Food, Water and Society. Oxford University Press; 2019.
35. Slavchevska V, Kaaria S, Taivalmaa S-L. Feminization of agriculture in the context of rural transformations: What is the evidence? World Bank; 2016.
36. Sahed K, Flora B, Islam MM, Others. A review on feminization of agriculture and women empowerment in Bangladesh. Fundamental and Applied Agriculture. 2017;2(1):183–8.
37. Tamang S, Paudel KP, Shrestha KK. Feminization of agriculture and its implications for food security in rural Nepal. Journal of Forest and Livelihood. 2014;12(1):20–32.
38. Gillespie S, Kadiyala S. Exploring the agriculture-nutrition disconnect in India. Reshaping agriculture for nutrition and health Washington DC, International Food Policy Research Institute. 2012;173–82.
39. Pattnaik I, Lahiri-Dutt K, Lockie S, Pritchard B. The feminization of agriculture or the feminization of agrarian distress? Tracking the trajectory of women in agriculture in India. Journal of the Asia Pacific Economy. 2018;23(1):138–55.
40. Pratley P. Associations between quantitative measures of women's empowerment and access to care and health status for mothers and their children: A systematic review of evidence from the developing world. Soc Sci Med. 2016 Nov;169:119–31.
41. Smith LC, Haddad L. Reducing Child Undernutrition: Past Drivers and Priorities for the Post-MDG Era. World Dev. 2015 Apr 1;68:180–204.
42. Bhagowalia P, Menon P, Quisumbing AR, Vidhya Soundararajan J. What dimensions of women's empowerment matter most for child nutrition. Evidence Using Nationally Representative Data from Bangladesh Washington DC: International Food Policy Research Institute [Internet]. 2012; Available from: https://pdfs.semanticscholar.org/8959/68005daa003762089a98232fd345bd98e778.pdf
43. Ruel MT, Alderman H. Maternal and Child Nutrition Study Group Nutrition-sensitive interventions and programmes: how can they help to accelerate progress in improving maternal and child nutrition. Lancet. 2013;382(9891):536–51.
44. Herforth A, Ballard TJ. Nutrition indicators in agriculture projects: Current measurement, priorities, and gaps. Global Food Security. 2016 Sep 1;10:1–10.
45. Talukder A, Haselow NJ, Osei AK, Villate E, Reario D, Kroeun H, et al. Homestead food production model contributes to improved household food security and nutrition status of young children and women in poor populations. Field Actions Science Reports, Special Issue 1 | 2000 Urban Agriculture [Internet]. 2010 Feb 15 [cited 2020 Oct 26];(Special1). Available from: http://journals.openedition.org/factsreports/404
46. van den Bold M, Quisumbing AR, Gillespie S. Womens Empowerment and Nutrition: An Evidence Review. Intl Food Policy Res Inst; 2013. 80 p.

47. Fox EL, Davis C, Downs SM, Schultink W, Fanzo J. Who is the Woman in Women's Nutrition? A Narrative Review of Evidence and Actions to Support Women's Nutrition throughout Life. Curr Dev Nutr. 2019 Jan;3(1):nzy076.
48. Weinhardt LS, Galvao LW, Yan AF, Stevens P, Mwenyekonde TN, Ngui E, et al. Mixed-Method Quasi-Experimental Study of Outcomes of a Large-Scale Multilevel Economic and Food Security Intervention on HIV Vulnerability in Rural Malawi. AIDS Behav. 2017 Mar;21(3):712–23.
49. Malapit HJL, Quisumbing AR. What dimensions of women's empowerment in agriculture matter for nutrition in Ghana? Food Policy. 2015 Apr;52:54–63.
50. Asian Development Bank. Gender equality and food security—women's empowerment as a tool against hunger. Asian Development Bank; 2013.
51. Smith L and Haddad L. Exploring Child Malnutrition in Developing Countries: A Cross-Country Analysis. IFPRI; 1999.
52. World Bank. Improving nutrition through multisectoral approaches: agriculture and rural development. World Bank; 2013.
53. Food and Agriculture Organization of the United Nations, International Fund for Agricultural Development, World Food Programme, World Health Organization, United Nations Children's Fund. The State of Food Security and Nutrition in the World 2019: Safeguarding against economic slowdowns and downturns. Food & Agriculture Org.; 2019. 239 p.
54. O'Neill K. Traditional beneficiaries: trade bans, exemptions, and morality embodied in diets [Internet]. Vol. 35, Agriculture and Human Values. 2018. p. 515–27. Available from: http://dx.doi.org/10.1007/s10460-017-9846-0
55. High Level Panel of Experts. Nutrition and Food Systems. 2017 p. 152.
56. Gillespie S, van den Bold M, Hodge J. Nutrition and the governance of agri-food systems in South Asia: A systematic review. Food Policy. 2019 Jan 1;82:13–27.
57. Gillespie S, Nisbett N. Governance and leadership in agri-food systems and nutrition [Internet]. Agriculture for improved nutrition: seizing the momentum. 2019. p. 122–33. Available from: http://dx.doi.org/10.1079/9781786399311.0122
58. Harris J, Anderson M, Clément C, Nisbett N. The Political Economy of Food. IDS Bull [Internet]. 2019 Aug 5 [cited 2020 Aug 17];50(2). Available from: https://bulletin.ids.ac.uk/index.php/idsbo/article/view/3031
59. Patterns of Interconnectedness, Interdependence and Globalisation – the Empirical Picture. In: Globalisation and Interdependence in the International Political Economy: Rhetoric and Reality. Bloomsbury Academic; 2013.
60. Hawkes C. Uneven dietary development: linking the policies and processes of globalization with the nutrition transition, obesity and diet-related chronic diseases. Global Health. 2006 Mar 28;2:4.
61. Friel S, Gleeson D, Thow A-M, Labonte R, Stuckler D, Kay A, et al. A new generation of trade policy: potential risks to diet-related health from the trans pacific partnership agreement. Global Health. 2013 Oct 16;9(1):46.
62. Wood SA, Smith MR, Fanzo J, Remans R, DeFries RS. Trade and the equitability of global food nutrient distribution. Nature Sustainability. 2018 Jan 1;1(1):34–7.
63. Popkin BM. Technology, transport, globalization and the nutrition transition food policy. Food Policy. 2006 Dec 1;31(6):554–69.
64. Friel S, Gleeson D, Thow A-M, Labonte R, Stuckler D, Kay A, et al. A new generation of trade policy: potential risks to diet-related health from the trans pacific partnership agreement. Global Health. 2013 Oct 16;9(1):46.
65. Baker P, Kay A, Walls H. Trade and investment liberalization and Asia's noncommunicable disease epidemic: a synthesis of data and existing literature. Global Health. 2014 Sep 12;10:66.
66. Schram A, Labonte R, Baker P, Friel S, Reeves A, Stuckler D. The role of trade and investment liberalization in the sugar-sweetened carbonated beverages market: a natural experiment contrasting Vietnam and the Philippines. Global Health. 2015 Oct 12;11(1):41.
67. Turner C, Aggarwal A, Walls H, Herforth A, Drewnowski A, Coates J, et al. Concepts and critical perspectives for food environment research: A global framework with implications for action in low- and middle-income countries. Global Food Security. 2018 Sep 1;18:93–101.

References

68. Baker P, Friel S, Schram A, Labonte R. Trade and investment liberalization, food systems change and highly processed food consumption: a natural experiment contrasting the soft-drink markets of Peru and Bolivia. Global Health. 2016 Jun 2;12(1):24.
69. FAO, IFAD, UNICEF, WFP. The State of Food Security and Nutrition in the World 2020 [Internet]. 2020. Available from: http://www.fao.org/3/ca9692en/CA9692EN.pdf
70. Thow AM, Nisbett N. Trade, nutrition, and sustainable food systems. Lancet. 2019 Aug 31;394(10200):716–8.
71. Ravuvu A, Friel S, Thow A-M, Snowdon W, Wate J. Monitoring the impact of trade agreements on national food environments: trade imports and population nutrition risks in Fiji. Global Health. 2017 Jun 13;13(1):33.
72. Thow AM, Swinburn B, Colagiuri S, Diligolevu M, Quested C, Vivili P, et al. Trade and food policy: Case studies from three Pacific Island countries. Food Policy. 2010 Dec 1;35(6):556–64.
73. Thow AM, Reeve E, Naseri T, Martyn T, Bollars C. Food supply, nutrition and trade policy: reversal of an import ban on turkey tails. Bull World Health Organ. 2017 Oct 1;95(10):723–5.
74. Thow AM, Downs S, Jan S. A systematic review of the effectiveness of food taxes and subsidies to improve diets: understanding the recent evidence. Nutr Rev. 2014 Sep;72(9):551–65.
75. Pingali P. Agricultural policy and nutrition outcomes–getting beyond the preoccupation with staple grains. Food Security. 2015;7(3):583–91.
76. Gordon IJ, Prins HHT, Squire GR. Food Production and Nature Conservation: Conflicts and Solutions. Routledge; 2016. 348 p.
77. FAO, IFAD, WFP. The State of Food Insecurity in the World 2018. Building climate resilience for food security and nutrition. FAO; 2018.
78. Brück T, d'Errico M. Food security and violent conflict: Introduction to the special issue. World Dev. 2019 Jul 1;119:145–9.
79. Martin-Shields CP, Stojetz W. Food security and conflict: Empirical challenges and future opportunities for research and policy making on food security and conflict. World Dev. 2019 Jul 1;119:150–64.
80. Hendrix C, Brinkman H-J. Food insecurity and conflict dynamics: Causal linkages and complex feedbacks. Stability: International Journal of Security and Development [Internet]. 2013;2(2).
81. F. Shenggen, R. Pandya-Lorch, S. Yosef, L. Zseleczky, editor. Resilience for food and nutrition security. IFPRI; 2014.
82. Delbiso TD, Rodriguez-Llanes JM, Donneau A-F, Speybroeck N, Guha-Sapir D. Drought, conflict and children's undernutrition in Ethiopia 2000–2013: a meta-analysis. Bull World Health Organ. 2017;95(2):94.
83. von Grebmer K, Bernstein J, de Waal A, Prasai N, Yin S, Yohannes Y. 2015 Global Hunger Index: Armed conflict and the challenge of hunger. Intl Food Policy Res Inst; 2015. 46 p.
84. Food Security Information Network. 2018 Global Report on Food Crises. FSIN; 2018.
85. Blanchard LP. The Crisis in South Sudan. Congressional Research Service; 2014.
86. Checchi F, Testa A, Warsame A, Quach L, Burns R. Estimates of crisis-attributable mortality in South Sudan, December 2013–April 2018: a statistical analysis. London School of Tropical Medicine and Hygiene. 2018;
87. United Nations High Commissioner for Refugees (UNHCR). South Sudan Situation: Regional Update [Internet]. 2020. Available from: file:///Users/csd/Downloads/UNHCR%20Regional%20Update%20-%20SSD%20Situation%20Jan-Feb%202020%20(1).pdf
88. Crisis in South Sudan [Internet]. UNICEF. 2020. Available from: https://www.unicefusa.org/mission/emergencies/conflict/south-sudan
89. USAID. Food Assistance Fact Sheet - South Sudan [Internet]. USAID. 2020. Available from: https://www.usaid.gov/south-sudan/food-assistance
90. UNICEF. An estimated 10.4 million children in the Democratic Republic of the Congo, northeast Nigeria, the Central Sahel, South Sudan and Yemen will suffer from acute malnutrition in 2021 [Internet]. 2020. Available from: https://www.unicef.org/press-releases/estimated-104-million-children-democratic-republic-congo-northeast-nigeria-central

91. Global Nutrition Report. 2020 Global Nutrition Report: Action on equity to end malnutrition. 2020.
92. World Food Programme. Synthesis report of WFP's country portfolio evaluations in Africa (2016–2018). WFP; 2019.
93. UNICEF. COVID-19 and conflict: A deadly combination [Internet]. UNICEF. 2020. Available from: https://www.unicef.org/coronavirus/covid-19-and-conflict-deadly-combination
94. UN Department of Economic and Social Affairs, Population division. World Population Prospects: The 2017 Revision. UNDESA; 2017.
95. WHO, National Institute on Aging, National Institutes of Health, U.S. Department of Health and Human Services. Global Health and Aging. 2015.
96. UN Department of Economic and Social Affairs. World Population Prospects: The 2018 Revision. UNDESA; 2018.
97. Alexander P, Rounsevell MDA, Dislich C, Dodson JR, Engström K, Moran D. Drivers for global agricultural land use change: The nexus of diet, population, yield and bioenergy. Glob Environ Change. 2015 Nov 1;35:138–47.
98. Kastner T, Rivas MJI, Koch W, Nonhebel S. Global changes in diets and the consequences for land requirements for food. Proc Natl Acad Sci U S A. 2012 May 1;109(18):6868–72.
99. Crist E, Mora C, Engelman R. The interaction of human population, food production, and biodiversity protection. Science. 2017 Apr 21;356(6335):260–4.
100. Ehrlich PR, Harte J. Opinion: To feed the world in 2050 will require a global revolution. Proc Natl Acad Sci U S A. 2015 Dec 1;112(48):14743–4.
101. United Nations of Economic and Social Affairs. World Urbanization Prospects 2018. UNDESA; 2018.
102. Bloem S, de Pee S. Developing approaches to achieve adequate nutrition among urban populations requires an understanding of urban development. Global Food Security. 2017 Mar 1;12:80–8.
103. Bloem S, de Pee S. How Urbanization Patterns Can Guide Strategies for Achieving Adequate Nutrition. In: de Pee Douglas Taren Martin W. Bloem S, editor. Nutrition and Health in a Developing World. 3rd ed. New York: Humana Press; 2017. p. 685–703.
104. Fan S, Cho EE, Rue C. Food security and nutrition in an urbanizing world. China Agricultural Economic Review [Internet]. 2017; Available from: https://www.emerald.com/insight/content/doi/10.1108/CAER-02-2017-0034/full/html
105. Demmler KM, Ecker O, Qaim M. Supermarket Shopping and Nutritional Outcomes: A Panel Data Analysis for Urban Kenya [Internet]. Vol. 102, World Development. 2018. p. 292–303. Available from: http://dx.doi.org/10.1016/j.worlddev.2017.07.018
106. Wanyama R, Gödecke T, Chege CGK, Qaim M. How important are supermarkets for the diets of the urban poor in Africa? Food Security. 2019;11(6):1339–53.
107. Qaim M. Globalisation of agrifood systems and sustainable nutrition. Proc Nutr Soc. 2017 Feb;76(1):12–21.
108. Ruel MT, Garrett J, Yosef S, Olivier M. Urbanization, Food Security and Nutrition. In: de Pee S, Taren D, Bloem MW, editors. Nutrition and Health in a Developing World. Cham: Springer International Publishing; 2017. p. 705–35.
109. Oppert J-M, Charreire H. The importance of the food and physical activity environments. Nestle Nutr Inst Workshop Ser. 2012 Oct 29;73:113–21.
110. Barthel S, Isendahl C, Vis BN, Drescher A, Evans DL, van Timmeren A. Global urbanization and food production in direct competition for land: Leverage places to mitigate impacts on SDG2 and on the Earth System. The Anthropocene Review. 2019 Apr 1;6(1–2):71–97.
111. Seto KC, Ramankutty N. Hidden linkages between urbanization and food systems. Science. 2016 May 20;352(6288):943–5.
112. UN Department of Economic and Social Affairs. World Population Prospects: The 2019 Revision. UNDESA; 2019.
113. Food and Agriculture Organization of the United Nations, International Fund for Agricultural Development, and International Organization for Migration and the World Food Programme. The Linkages Between Migration, Agriculture, Food Security and Rural Development [Internet]. WFP; 2018. Available from: http://www.fao.org/3/CA0922EN/CA0922EN.pdf

References

114. Food and Agriculture Organization of the United Nations and International Food Policy Research Institute. Conflict, migration, and food security: the role of agriculture and rural development. FAO and IFPRI; 2017.
115. Sadiddin A, Cattaneo A, Cirillo M, Miller M. Food insecurity as a determinant of international migration: evidence from Sub-Saharan Africa. Food Security. 2019 Jun 1;11(3):515–30.
116. Crush J. Linking Food Security, Migration and Development. Int Migr. 2013 Oct 16;51(5):61–75.
117. Hueston W, McLeod A. Overview of the global food system: changes over time/space and lessons for future food safety. Improving food safety through a one health approach: workshop summary. Washington (DC): National Academies Press (US); 2012.
118. Reardon T, Echeverria R, Berdegué J, Minten B, Liverpool-Tasie S, Tschirley D, et al. Rapid transformation of food systems in developing regions: Highlighting the role of agricultural research & innovations. Agric Syst. 2019 Jun 1;172:47–59.
119. El Bilali H, Allahyari MS. Transition towards sustainability in agriculture and food systems: Role of information and communication technologies. Information Processing in Agriculture. 2018 Dec 1;5(4):456–64.
120. National Academies of Sciences, Engineering, and Medicine; Health and Medicine Division; Food and Nutrition Board; Food Forum. Innovations in the Food System: Exploring the Future of Food: Proceedings of a Workshop. Maitin-Shepard M, editor. Washington (DC): National Academies Press (US); 2020.
121. International Food Policy Research Institute. 2019 Global food policy report. IFPRI; 2019.
122. Blimpo MP, Harding R, Wantchekon L. Public Investment in Rural Infrastructure: Some Political Economy Considerations. J Afr Econ. 2013 Aug 1;22(suppl_2):ii57–83.
123. Fanzo JC, Downs S, Marshall QE, de Pee S, Bloem MW. Value Chain Focus on Food and Nutrition Security. In: de Pee S, Taren D, Bloem MW, editors. Nutrition and Health in a Developing World. Cham: Springer International Publishing; 2017. p. 753–70.
124. Thapa G, Shively G. A dose-response model of road development and child nutrition in Nepal. Research in Transportation Economics. 2018 Oct 1;70:112–24.
125. Townshend T, Lake A. Obesogenic environments: current evidence of the built and food environments. Perspect Public Health. 2017 Jan;137(1):38–44.
126. Lake AA. Neighbourhood food environments: food choice, foodscapes and planning for health. Proc Nutr Soc. 2018 Aug;77(3):239–46.

Part III
The Influence of Food Policy on Diets and Nutrition

Part III

Chapter 8
Policies Affecting Food Supply Chains

Introduction

Food and agricultural policies shape what types of food are produced and their movement through the food supply chain at the global, regional, and local levels. As Chapters 2 and 3 describe, the supply chain involves all the activities needed to bring food from farm to fork, including production, trade, transportation, processing, packaging, and markets. Many different actors create, enact, and oversee policies that govern these activities and processes, with governments being the primary player in enforcing policies. Yet there are many other actors that implement these policies, which in turn, take food supply chains into different purposes and directions, including the private sector of food and beverage industry and traders.

Well-functioning, ideal food supply chains provide sufficient safe, nutritious food for everyone around the world. This chapter discusses the many different types of food supply policies relevant to diets and nutrition, as well as the role that different actors play in shaping these policies. Policies that affect food production and trade; processing and packaging; and markets, distribution, and public procurement represent opportunities to improve supply chains and leverage them for nutrition and health goals.

Ideal Food Supply Chains for Diets and Nutrition

Ideal food supply chains ensure that safe and nutritious foods are available, accessible, affordable, and safe for all people. In recent decades, food supply chains have changed dramatically to become longer, with more actors interacting across the chain, and more complex. This transformation reflects increased globalization and urbanization, income growth, supply chain modernization, and dietary demand shifts [1]. Although changes to global supply chains have improved access to diverse, nutritious foods for some, they have also expanded the availability of less healthy processed and packaged foods. Changes to the supply chain also influence the availability, safety, price, and marketing of food within the food environment [2]. Policy interventions that govern different activities along the supply chain can help leverage and reorient these chains for positive nutrition and health outcomes. Ideal supply chains can increase access to nutrient-rich foods and increase the nutritional value of products as they move along the chain [3].

Value chain analysis can help to leverage nutrition throughout the supply chain. As described in Chapter 2, food value chains represent the ways in which value is added to food products within the supply chain. "Value" may refer to economic worth, product features, and/or the product price relative to its benefits [4, 5]. Value chain analysis helps identify points within the supply chain that can be leveraged, or changed, to achieve nutrition goals. These leverage points include nutrition "entry points," where nutritional value can be enhanced, and "exit points," where nutrients are removed as a food product passes through the chain [1, 6]. Figure 8.1 depicts the ways in which nutrition can enter and exit the supply chain [1]. Through value chain analysis, nutrition entry points can be optimized and exit points minimized.

Agricultural production, the initial stage of the food supply chain, is fundamental to nutrition and health. Agricultural productivity can ensure food security and sustain the nutritional and health status of billions of people [7]. Policy support and interventions that improve harvest techniques and training, connect farmers with markets, and develop infrastructure can help reduce food and nutrient waste at the production stage. Limiting losses of fruits, vegetables, and nuts is especially important, given their nutritional value and potential for value addition [8]. Investments that support farm systems growing a diversity of crops and livestock can potentially contribute positively to dietary quality, diversity, micronutrient status, and reductions in maternal and child undernutrition. However, achieving the greatest benefits from farm diversification may require addressing other causal factors, such as access to markets, behavior change, and education [9–23]. Biofortification and genetic strategies, such as genetically modified organism (GMO) technology, can also improve nutrient density and quality, as well as the resilience of crops and livestock to environmental challenges and efficiency of production [24]. Diversity contributes to ecosystems, which can be mutually beneficial to agricultural productivity [24, 25].

Once food is produced and passes through the "farm gate," its nutritional value can be improved at the processing stage. Processing and packaging methods can optimize food quality and nutrient availability, improve safety, reduce waste, and increase a product's shelf life [24]. These methods may include milling, cooling, heating, canning, fermentation, and drying, among others. Some of these methods can range from low- to high-tech. Food fortification adds either one or multiple micronutrient(s) to food products. Products that are fortified are often staples—flours, oils, milk, and salt. Food product reformulation, often done by the food industry, removes or reduces less healthy ingredients, such as sodium and trans fats, from foods [26]. These processing methods are especially valuable for populations with higher nutritional needs and requirements, such as young children and pregnant women.

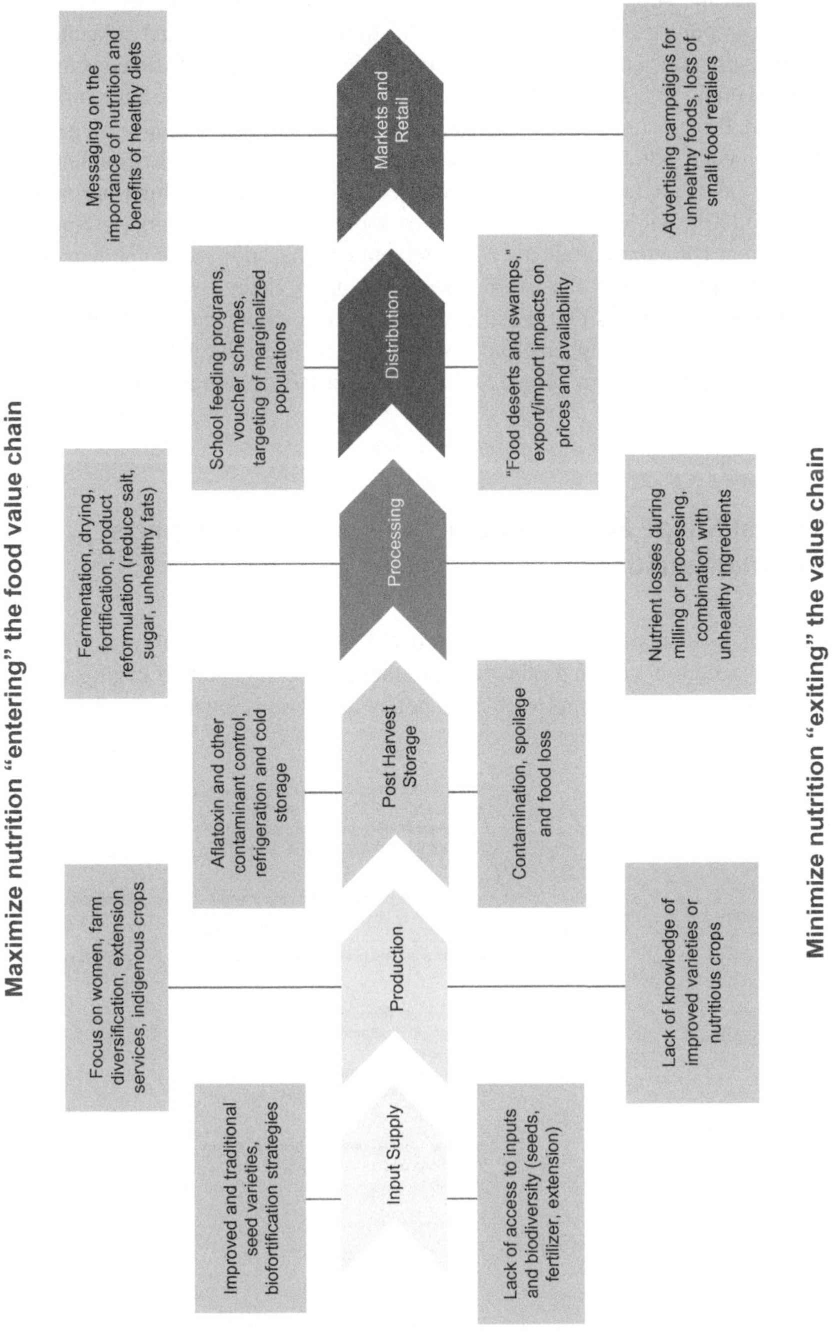

Fig. 8.1 Entry and exit points for nutrition along food supply chains [1]

Post-production interventions that target quality, sustainability, logistics, and processes along the supply chain can also be leveraged for nutrition. In low-and middle-income countries (LMICs), interventions to improve storage and cold chain capacity can help reduce post-farm food losses. In high-income countries, consumer education and retail-level interventions are the most effective leverage points to minimize waste [8]. Private standards and certifications, which may be voluntary or legally mandated, can contribute to improvements in food safety, health [2], environmental sustainability, and fair labor [27]. Emerging technologies, such as high-pressure processing and Ultraviolet irradiation, provide more sustainable, energy-efficient methods of processing food products [24]. Interventions that shift consumer demand toward healthier food options can reverberate across supply chains to affect processes and outputs at earlier stages [1]. Raising awareness of the importance of nutrition and providing technology capacity and assistance to increase the nutritional value of foods among supply chain actors can also help influence demand for healthy, nutritious foods.

Policies that Shape Food Supply Chains and Their Impacts on Diets and Nutrition

Many types of food supply policies can improve the diversity and quality of foods. These policies tend to focus on production and trade, processing and packaging, and distribution and markets. Examples of these policy levers are shown in Fig. 8.2.

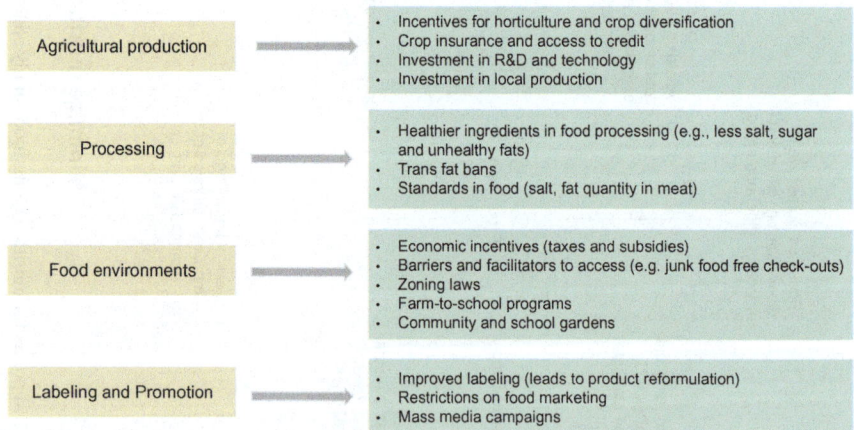

Fig. 8.2 Food supply policy levers [28]

Policies that Affect Food Production and Trade

Subsidy policies

An agricultural subsidy is an incentive paid by governments to farmers or agribusinesses. Subsidies help to supplement income earned through agriculture, manage the supply of agricultural commodities, and influence the cost of those commodities. Typical subsidized commodities are staple foods, such as rice, maize, wheat, feed grains, cotton, dairy, sugar, and oilseeds like soybeans, as well as some meat products.

Many countries have enacted agricultural subsidy policies. In Europe, the Common Agricultural Policy, launched in 1962, aims to improve agricultural productivity, ensure a reasonable standard of living and income for farmers, and maintain rural life. As part of the EU's Green Deal, their 2020 Farm to Fork initiative takes a strong stance on introducing sustainability and resilience into food production and trade policies. In the United States, the Farm Bill provides subsidies for major crops, such as corn, sugar, dairy, cotton, and other major cash crops. In China, more than $150 billion USD is directed toward agricultural subsidies, with significant funding for soybeans [29, 30].

Subsidies benefit food producers and governments, but they also present challenges. These policies provide farmers with a consistent income and insurance during times of hardship. However, they penalize agricultural businesses that grow produce not included in subsidy coverage. In the United States, for example, fruit and vegetable crops are not eligible for subsidies, which lessens the incentive for farmers to grow these important, nutritious crops [31]. Subsidies help countries manage their food supply and reduce the need to import food. However, these policies require government intervention and impact other markets. Subsidies also strengthen the market control of big agribusiness companies and environmentally harmful production methods favored by such companies, such as monoculture cropping and concentrated animal feeding operations (CAFOs).

Historically, subsidy programs have helped ensure the provision of staple grains for the world's population. These policies have focused on improving the agricultural productivity of staple grains and cereals. Subsidies have contributed positively to food security goals, but these programs rarely align with what is considered a healthy diet (Fig. 8.3). In many countries, subsidy policies do not incorporate nutrient-rich crops or align with the recommendations of dietary guidelines [32].

Evaluating the impacts of agricultural subsidies on diets and nutrition remains a major challenge. Subsidy programs are typically designed around political and economic goals rather than health aims [34]. As such, further research is needed to understand how subsidies can affect diets and nutrition. Establishing causal connections and disentangling the effects of subsidies from other factors is also difficult. Research that definitively determines the effects of subsidies on diets and nutrition would be highly complex and possibly infeasible [35]. However, existing research suggests that subsidies can positively affect diets and nutrition in some contexts.

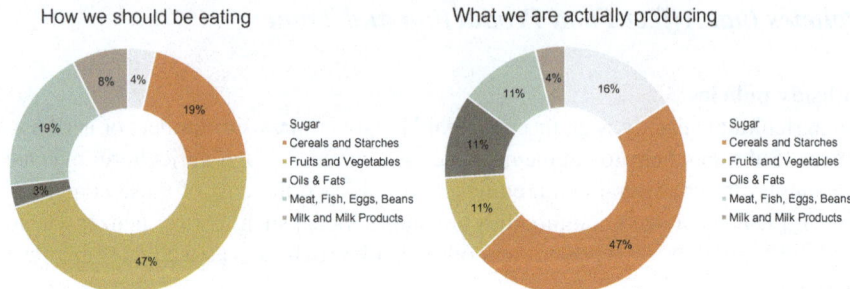

Fig. 8.3 What we produce to what we eat [33]

In LMICs, subsidies contribute to positive outcomes through agricultural production, household income, household behavior, and changes in food consumption [36]. Box 8.1 illustrates the challenges of linking subsidies to nutrition outcomes in the United States and Malawi.

> **Box 8.1 Impact of agricultural subsidies on nutrition in the United States and Malawi**
> Subsidies have long been a major component of agricultural policy. Subsidy programs can affect agricultural intensification and diversification, as well as nutrition outcomes. Despite the importance of subsidy policies, their effects on nutrition and health remain difficult to ascertain. In some cases, the evidence may be unclear, while in others, it may be challenging to disentangle the effects of subsidies from other causal factors.
>
> In the United States, agricultural subsidies finance the production of commodity crops, such as corn, soy, and wheat. The effect of these subsidies on nutrition and health outcomes is highly debated. Several research studies suggest that the overconsumption of calories from subsidized crops like corn and soy is associated with heightened cardiometabolic risks and obesity [37–39]. While some researchers have called for agricultural and nutrition policies to be better aligned for the sake of health outcomes, others argue that subsidies have low or negligible impacts on dietary patterns and obesity [37, 40, 41].
>
> In Malawi, tobacco has long been the focus of agricultural commercialization, despite the crop's high production costs, uncertain yields, and inconsistent profit margins. In 2005, the government implemented the Farm Input Subsidy Policy with the goal of increasing maize production, improving household food security, and enhancing the autonomy of the country's food supply. Research on the impacts of agricultural subsidies identified meaningful benefits for diets and nutrition. The provision of these subsidies was associated with increased crop diversification, household dietary diversity, and improvements in child undernutrition [42, 43]. However, input subsidies were not the sole cause of improved dietary diversity, as diversity of livestock production and women's

empowerment and education also significantly affected food consumption [44]. In addition, the prevalence of childhood stunting was lower among maize-producing households than those that produced cash crops and limited staple food production [45].

Price and income support policies

Price and income support policies affect activities throughout the food supply chain. Given the interconnected nature of the food supply chain, interventions that target specific processes or activities can have broader impacts on pricing and costs throughout the chain. Over time, changes to the food supply chain have altered the distribution of cost and profit within the supply chain. The balance of cost and profit, or the "value" of a product, has shifted away from food producers to processors, manufacturers, and retailers [46, 47]. Innovations throughout the food system, such as agricultural efficiencies and cold chain technologies, and economic drivers, such as globalization, have contributed significantly to these value shifts [46]. Costs, profits, and value within the supply chain are also shaped by many other factors, such as the availability and cost of agricultural inputs, logistics and transportation costs, labor, environmental regulations, trade tariffs and bans, and consumer demand [46–48].

Historically, price and income support policies have focused on the production stage of the supply chain. These interventions aimed to reduce volatility in producer incomes and food prices, help producers manage risks, and subsidize the production and pricing of select commodities [46, 47]. Although price and value shifts within the supply chain have resulted in lower food prices for consumers, concerns remain about the consolidation of power by processors and retailers [46–48]. More recent policy interventions have focused on expanding opportunities for small-scale farmers, optimizing the potential for competition amidst increasing vertical and horizontal integration, and ensuring fair contracting agreements [47–53]. However, some argue that concerns of market abuse are exaggerated, and policy interventions could affect the transmission of costs within the supply chain, resulting in higher food prices for consumers [48, 54].

Pricing and income support policies influence diets and nutrition through their effects on food prices at the consumer level. Food prices directly affect food affordability, consumption patterns, and diet quality. Populations in LMICs tend to spend a larger proportion of their income on food than do people in high-income countries, though there is significant variation within wealthy countries [55]. For many poor households, increases in food prices often reduce the quantity and nutritional quality of food consumed, which can lead to reductions in diet quality [56–59]. Increases in food prices are associated with a higher prevalence of stunting in children, impaired growth in infants, and decreased micronutrient status in mothers [60–66].

Trade policies

Trade policies influence global food availability, as well as food production and imports at the global and national levels. Trade can affect both producers' profits and consumers' costs, primarily through its effects on food prices. Trade policies can also shift production patterns, leading to improvements in the way food is produced and traded. Policies governing trade also affect many other aspects of the food system, as Chapter 6 describes.

International trade is critically important to the food supply chain because it facilitates the movement and distribution of different types of foods and the nutrients contained within foods around the world. Without trade, far fewer people would be able to meet their nutritional needs. For example, 934 million would be deprived of protein and 146 million would not be able to fulfill vitamin A requirements. As a result of free trade, it is estimated that an additional 70 million people have access to folate and 16.79 billion more can access vitamin B12 [67].

Demands at the consumer level can have important implications for trade patterns. Although individual consumers in lower-income countries—where the impact of trade could be most beneficial—do not have global market influence, their aggregate demands can be important [68]. For example, low-income countries in West Africa that have a strong national demand for rice can be important rice importers, despite having a low per-capita income. If efforts to shift consumer preferences to nutrient-rich food products were successful at an aggregate scale, they could potentially help create a substantial market demand [69]. This type of dietary shift is reflected in the growing demand for diets rich in sugar, oil, and meat, though this particular demand shift has led to negative nutrition outcomes [2, 70, 71].

Despite the benefits of international trade for food supply chains, it also presents many challenges for diets and nutrition. Globalization has increased the choice and year-round accessibility of many fresh foods in more affluent markets around the world. While open trade is generally associated with lower food prices, its effects on food cost and availability can also make healthy options inaccessible for those most in need. The distribution of imported food items—and associated nutrients—often depends on the ability to pay. Globalization and trade liberalization are also associated with an increase in access to energy-dense, highly-processed foods of little to no nutritional value, especially in urban areas of LMICs where there is significant market infiltration [72]. Trade agreements that focus on food as an economic commodity contribute to food environments where the most affordable, accessible foods are less healthy ones [73].

International trade does not always ensure that populations in need of nutrients have access to them. Many countries need to augment the micronutrient composition of their food supplies, yet the foods that are most easily traded, such as staple grains, are often low in these micronutrients. This deficit can be mitigated, however, by encouraging the demand and regional trade of high-nutrient foods. Food aid, which is linked to trade, likewise prioritizes staple grains due mainly to cost efficiencies and easy transport: these grains provide energy but are not enriched with micronutrients that are needed in recipient countries. For instance, the provision of rice to northern Niger may meet a short-term caloric deficit and thus help stave off acute malnutrition, but it will not fulfill the long-term nutrient needs of the target population. Policy actions that increase the nutritional diversity of food aid could help augment the availability of food nutrients in national food supplies, however the logistics of doing this is incredibly challenging amidst humanitarian response constraints [74–77].

The effects of trade policies also reverberate beyond diets and nutrition. Trade specialization that focuses on environmentally harmful crops, such as large-scale oil palm plantations, can lead to deforestation. Countries may be vulnerable to sudden changes in global trade patterns, whether due to price shocks; political polarizations, shifts and priorities; or environmental disasters or other disruptions [78, 79].

Policies that Target the Processing and Packaging of Foods

Reformulation and bans on food ingredients

Reformulation is a change to a food or beverage's processing or composition that is intended to either reduce or remove harmful ingredients and nutrients or increase beneficial ones. Harmful ingredients and nutrients affected by reformulation include salt, added sugar, saturated and trans fats, and energy density. Beneficial ingredients and nutrients include fiber and protein. Nutrient profiling, which is the classification or ranking of foods based on their nutrient composition, is often used in reformulation [80–82].

From a public health standpoint, reformulation is intended to improve diets, nutrition, and health by decreasing the intake of unhealthy ingredients or nutrients without requiring much in the way of consumer behavior change. Processed foods are usually the target for reformulation strategies as the increased global consumption of these products has been linked with overweight and obesity and NCDs [83–87]. Minimally processed foods can be reformulated as well, such as by reducing salt in canned vegetables and reducing added sugar in dried fruit. Box 8.2 provides examples of how foods can be reformulated to improve health outcomes.

> **Box 8.2 How reformulation improves the nutrient content of different food products**
> - Reduces salt in chips, crackers, breads, processed meats, canned soups, and sauces
> - Reduces sugar in breakfast cereals, cookies, cakes, candy, and other confectionery
> - Reduces saturated and trans fats in dairy products, crackers, cookies, and cakes
> - Adds whole grains or other fiber to snacks, breakfast cereals, and breads
> - Alters livestock diets to improve the fatty acid profiles of milk, butter, and other dairy products
> - Adds healthy oils to butter spreads
> - Adds herb extracts to cooking oils, which delay degradation and improve health properties
> - Adds vegetables to chips, breads, and other products to increase their fiber, vitamins, and phytochemicals

- Adds phytochemicals, such as betalains (found in beets, for example), that have strong antioxidant properties

Most reformulation efforts have been undertaken voluntarily by food and beverage companies, which has led to an inconsistent approach with little accountability. Voluntary reformulation has allowed the food industry to set their own targets, including the number of affected products and timeframe. There is little accountability, as the industry monitors and evaluates its own progress. As a result, products have been reformulated in an inconsistent way: foods that have not been reformulated are available on store shelves alongside reformulated ones. Although this approach has had the benefit of occurring without political intervention, it has allowed the food industry to avoid direct mandatory regulation [88, 89].

Food labeling and taxes can also encourage the food industry to reformulate foods. Labels range from informational front-of-package labels to warning labels. Food companies may voluntarily reformulate products to receive a better label rating or avoid a warning label. Increasing consumer demands for healthy and sustainable foods may also compel the food industry to undertake reformulation. Companies may voluntarily reformulate to avoid or pay less in taxes on foods that have been deemed unhealthy. In response to taxes on sugar-sweetened beverages (SSBs) in several countries, food companies reformulated their products to reduce sugar content [88].

While most reformulation efforts have been voluntary, mandatory limits and bans on ingredients or nutrients, such as those on salt and trans fats, have stimulated product reformulation. Mandatory reformulation allows the public health sector to set meaningful targets and timelines. This approach is based on nutrition and health research instead of industry profits, and it combines independent monitoring and evaluation with meaningful consequences for noncompliance [90]. Box 8.3 describes the United Kingdom's campaign to reformulate foods high in sodium.

Box 8.3 Sodium reformulation in the United Kingdom

High sodium consumption can lead to high blood pressure, which is a major risk factor for heart disease and stroke. Prepared and processed foods can contain high amounts of "hidden" salt, which consumers may not be aware of [91]. Reducing salt intake is one of the most cost-effective means of improving health outcomes [92].

In 2003, the United Kingdom implemented a voluntary program in collaboration with industry to reduce sodium consumption. Key components of the program included measuring salt intake in a random population sample and setting targets for salt intake. The government's strategy plan established progressively lower voluntary salt targets for different foods and clear time frames for industry to reformulate food products. The threat of regulatory action helped to ensure that products were reformulated. The government also used nutrition labels and educational campaigns to inform consumers and raise awareness of the health effects of excess sodium intake. During the first seven years of the program, the sodium content of food products declined significantly (up to 70%) and sodium levels in the UK population declined by 15% [93, 94].

Many other countries have since followed the UK's population-based approach to reduce salt intake. In 2013, the World Health Assembly agreed to a 30% relative reduction in salt intake by 2025 as part of its target goal to prevent and control NCDs [92]. As of 2015, 75 countries had developed national salt reduction policies. In some countries, sodium consumption has declined due to improvements in knowledge, attitudes, and behavior [95]. Existing evidence indicates that comprehensive, multicomponent strategies that include mandatory reformulation, food labeling, and educational campaigns are more effective in reducing population-level salt intake than interventions that focus on individual choice [96].

Fortification

Food fortification is the process of adding essential vitamins and minerals to commonly consumed foods. The most commonly fortified foods include maize flour, wheat flour, oils, rice, and salt, because these are commonly consumed everyday foods and are ubiquitous in the food system. Examples include iodized salt, vitamin A- and D-enriched oils, and B-vitamin fortified flours. Foods may be fortified to replace micronutrients that are lost during processing, such as with cereals, or to address micronutrient deficiencies in the population [97, 98].

Fortification policies and standards vary around the world, as Fig. 8.4 shows. Some countries mandate the fortification of a food with one or more vitamins or minerals. Mandatory fortification does not require any consumer-level behavior change, meaning that consumers can continue to buy and eat their usual foods. This approach is more likely to lead to a public health benefit, because the consumer does not need to actively identify and purchase fortified food [99]. Other countries rely on voluntary fortification by publishing official documentation and/or a food standard that provides guidance or regulations for fortification [100]. This type of fortification is undertaken at the discretion of the private sector, although it should be based on governmental standards [97].

Food fortification interventions can directly lead to positive health and nutrition outcomes. Fortification is one of the most cost-effective, proven interventions to address vitamin and mineral deficiencies [101]. Within the last two decades, large-scale fortification programs have been more widely implemented in LMICs to address deficiency diseases [102]. In countries worldwide, salt iodization programs have reduced the risk of goiter, cretinism, low cognitive function, and iodine deficiency [103, 104]. Fortifying various foods with iron has improved the hemoglobin and iron status of women and children in many countries [98, 105–107]. Other food fortification programs have been shown to reduce anemia, vitamin A deficiency,

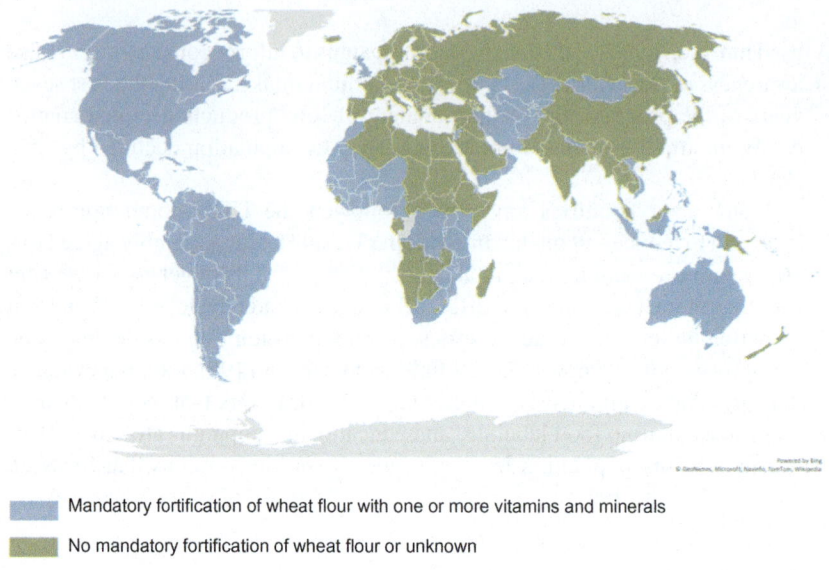

Mandatory fortification of wheat flour with one or more vitamins and minerals

No mandatory fortification of wheat flour or unknown

Fig. 8.4 Fortification legislation around the world [100]

and neural tube defects [103]. In addition to these health benefits, fortification also spreads the cost and burden of intervention between consumers and the public and private sectors [100].

Policies that Impact Markets, Distribution, and Public Procurement

Marketplace policies

Food markets, grocery stores, and other retail outlets represent some of the many physical spaces where people obtain their food. Markets can be formal, such as stores, or informal, such as street vending. They can operate at a local, regional, and/or international scale. Globally, 80% of smallholder farmers operate in local and domestic food markets, many of which are informal [108]. Markets provide the "value" at the end stages of the food chain, which makes them critical for actors in the food supply. The marketing and retail stages of the food supply chain carry great importance for consumers, as changes to these sectors have a greater impact on food prices than changes at the production stage [47]. Chapter 9 delves further into the environmental design and triggers of markets that shape consumer decisions.

Market and trade incentive policies can protect nutrition and health outcomes by ensuring equal access for smallholder farmers. Many barriers prevent these producers from accessing and benefiting from domestic and international markets. Policies and investment that improve transportation and road infrastructure would allow producers to reach markets. Interventions that improve storage, including cold storage, would help farmers preserve their harvests to sell at a later time [109]. Existing policies have led to gains for both livelihoods and nutrition. In East Africa, for example, female farmers supply nutritious crops, such as pumpkin and cowpea greens, to supermarket chains [110]. Smallholder farmers in the Andes, West Africa, and Ethiopia have likewise benefited from the popularity of nutritious traditional foods, such as quinoa, millet, and teff, in North America and Europe [111].

Policies that govern modern markets and retailers along with free markets and open trade have also influenced diets and nutrition. In high-income countries, the consolidation of food marketing and retail has generally benefited consumers by lowering food prices [53]. LMICs have increasingly experienced free and open markets, which have resulted in a "supermarket revolution," where modern retail outlets have rapidly expanded at the expense of more traditional markets. In these settings, supermarkets have increased access to diverse, affordable foods and contributed to improvements in childhood undernutrition. However, modern markets can also contribute to overweight and obesity by increasing access to highly-processed foods [112–114]. Africa is also seeing an increase in processed food consumption, which is associated with a double burden of malnutrition (DBM) [115]. While policies should incentivize supermarkets to supply more nutritious food items at affordable prices, the dynamics of supermarket shopping could change rapidly over the next decade as online shopping becomes more prevalent in developing countries.

Zoning laws
Physical access to food influences what people can purchase and consume. "Food deserts" are places without markets or stores to buy food, while "food swamps" are places with many food retailers but few, if any, healthy food options. Both food deserts and swamps are an increasing problem around the world. Zoning policies are needed to encourage healthy retail outlets and combat the spread of food deserts. Regulations can restrict "unhealthy" food retail outlets, such as fast-food restaurants, in order to address food swamps. These interventions can involve the provision and promotion of healthy beverages, fruits and vegetables, and other nutritious foods in supermarkets, small food retailers, and rest stops [116]. Zoning regulations can also help limit the advertising of unhealthy foods. These policy actions affect both the retail stage of the food supply chain and food environments, which are discussed in Chapter 9.

Zoning policies can improve access to healthy foods, which can lead to better outcomes for diets and nutrition. In households that experience food insecurity, barriers to food access are associated with lowered consumption of fruits and vegetables [117]. Mobile markets, food carts, and other easily accessible retail outlets that provide fruits and vegetables have contributed to healthier diets and nutritional benefits in numerous high-, middle-, and low-income countries [118–121]. Fast-food and other retailers can incorporate more nutritious options into their menus to improve diets. In Mexico, fast-food restaurants offer healthy options like fruits, salads, and rotisserie chicken [122]. However, the long-term effectiveness of these policy interventions depends on consumer demand, food retail competition, and retailer profitability [123].

Public procurement policies

Public procurement policies shape programs that provide social protection and "safety nets." These programs are meant to reduce poverty by "catching" low-income populations undergoing hardships in a "safety net" that provides assistance until they can sustain themselves. Safety net interventions include a wide range of programs with different impacts—from cash to vouchers targeting food purchases and food itself. The largest safety net programs operate on a national scale, such as those in India and Ethiopia, though there are many informal programs woven into a community's social structure that operate on a smaller, local level.

Public procurement policies also affect the provision of food in public places, such as schools, hospitals, workplaces, and government buildings. These policies contribute to improved diets and nutrition outcomes, as well as educational status and livelihoods, in many different contexts [124–126]. These policies, and their effects on nutrition and health, are discussed in detail in Chapter 9.

Common social protection interventions include cash and in-kind transfer programs, which provide a substitute for income, and food assistance programs, which enhance access to food. The terms and parameters of these programs vary. Cash transfer programs may be unconditional, meaning income is given without any obligations, or conditional, meaning that participants are required to participate in work, training, education, health, nutrition, or other activities. Eligibility for income or food assistance may be determined by income or inclusion in a marginalized community.

Safety net programs can positively affect diets, nutrition, and health. In certain countries, cash and food transfer programs have been shown to improve diet quality, food insecurity, and undernutrition [127]. In cash transfer programs in Africa and Latin America, households spent the majority of their cash on food, which led to improvements in food security and dietary diversity [128–139]. These programs also contribute to increases in livestock ownership, farm and non-farm assets, and savings [140]. Well-designed evaluations can also improve nutrition outcomes [141, 142]. Conditional cash transfer programs contribute to better health outcomes, as children from households that participate in these programs are more likely to receive preventive health checkups, and, in some countries, experience improved growth outcomes [141–144].

Although safety net programs can positively affect diet and nutrition outcomes, their impacts have not always been significant or beneficial. In India, the Public Distribution System positively affected calorie consumption and select nutrients but did not affect nutrition in poor households [145, 146]. Evaluations of different safety net programs showed insignificant impacts on child growth [143, 144], mixed impacts on children's diets [144], and insignificant impacts on nutrition outcomes [147]. These programs can also result in unintended negative outcomes for diets and nutrition. Some interventions have provided or subsidized foods and beverages high in energy, sugar, fat, and salt. In other contexts, cash transfer assistance has been used by households to purchase unhealthy foods [127].

Key Messages and Conclusions

By bringing food from farm to fork, food supply chains function as the "nervous system" of the food system. Supply chains are critical to the overall functionality of food systems, and activities throughout the chain carry meaningful implications for diets, nutrition, and health. The importance of food supply chains was starkly demonstrated by the stresses of the COVID-19 pandemic. Disruptions to farm labor, processing, and transportation contributed to supply chain pressure that affected food availability around the world [148]. In both times of peace and crisis, policies governing food production, trade, processing, and retail are essential to maintaining an efficient food supply chain.

Food supply chains also present opportunities to improve the diets, nutrition, and health of people around the world. While subsidy, income support, and trade programs can ensure food security, low consumer prices, and access to healthy foods, they may also expand the availability of less healthy foods. Policies that support food reformulation and fortification can reduce harmful nutrients and improve nutrient value without requiring consumer behavior change. Marketplace, zoning, and public procurement policies can enhance diets and nutrition by supporting diverse agricultural production, limiting sales of unhealthy foods, and protecting low-income populations. Through policy interventions, food supply chains can be leveraged for nutrition in order to increase nutrients and reduce losses as foods pass along the chain. Integrating nutrition into the food supply chain can lead to changes that resonate throughout the food system in order to further benefit diets and health.

References

1. Fanzo JC, Downs S, Marshall QE, de Pee S, Bloem MW. Value Chain Focus on Food and Nutrition Security. In: de Pee S, Taren D, Bloem MW, editors. Nutrition and Health in a Developing World. Cham: Springer International Publishing; 2017. p. 753–70.
2. Hawkes C, Grace D, Thow AM. Trade liberalization, food, nutrition and health. Trade and Health: Towards building a National Strategy Geneva, WHO. 2015;92–116.
3. Morgan EH, Hawkes C, Dangour AD, Lock K. Analyzing food value chains for nutrition goals. J Hunger Environ Nutr. 2018 Feb 20;1–19.
4. Haq ZU. Food Value chain analysis: A review of selected studies for Pakistan and Guidelines for Further Research [Internet]. Working Paper; 2012. Available from: http://www.academia.edu/download/46134728/FVA.pdf
5. Adam Diamond, Debra Tropp, James Barham, Michelle Frain Muldoon, Stacia Kiraly, and Patty Cantrell. Food Value Chains: Creating Shared Value to Enhance Marketing Success. U.S. Dept. of Agriculture, Agricultural Marketing Service; 2014.

6. Downs S, Fanzo J. Managing value chains for improved nutrition. good nutrition: perspectives for the 21st century. Karger, Basel, Switzerland; 2016.
7. Bank W, World Bank. From Agriculture to Nutrition [Internet]. 2007. Available from: http://dx.doi.org/10.1596/28183
8. Rezaei M, Liu B. Food loss and waste in the food supply chain. International Nut and Dried Fruit Council: Reus, Spain. 2017;26–7.
9. Webb P, Block S. Support for agriculture during economic transformation: Impacts on poverty and undernutrition. PNAS. Proceedings of the National Academy of Sciences. 2012;109(31):12309–14.
10. Ruel MT, Alderman H, Maternal and Child Nutrition Study Group. Nutrition-sensitive interventions and programmes: how can they help to accelerate progress in improving maternal and child nutrition? Lancet. 2013 Aug 10;382(9891):536–51.
11. Ruel MT, Quisumbing AR, Balagamwala M. Nutrition-sensitive agriculture: What have we learned so far? Global Food Security. 2018 Jun 1;17:128–53.
12. Olney DK, Leroy JL, Ruel MT. Evaluation of Nutrition-sensitive Programs. In: de Pee S., Taren D., Bloem M., editor. Nutrition and Health in a Developing World. Humana Press; 2017. p. 603–24.
13. Headey D, Chiu A, Kadiyala S. Agriculture's role in the Indian enigma: help or hindrance to the crisis of undernutrition? Food Security. 2012;4(1):87–102.
14. Sibhatu KT, Krishna VV, Qaim M. Production diversity and dietary diversity in smallholder farm households. Proc Natl Acad Sci U S A. 2015 Aug 25;112(34):10657–62.
15. Carletto G, Ruel M, Winters P, Zezza A. Farm-level pathways to improved nutritional status. The Journal of Development Studies [Internet]. 2015;51(8). Available from: https://openknowledge.worldbank.org/handle/10986/23514
16. Koppmair S, Kassie M, Qaim M. Farm input subsidies and the adoption of natural resource management technologies [Internet]. 2016. Available from: https://ageconsearch.umn.edu/record/235313/
17. Aberman N-L, Meerman J, Benson T. Agriculture, food security, and nutrition in Malawi: Leveraging the links. Intl Food Policy Res Inst; 2018. 82 p.
18. Dulal B, Mundy G, Sawal R, Rana PP, Cunningham K. Homestead Food Production and Maternal and Child Dietary Diversity in Nepal: Variations in Association by Season and Agroecological Zone. Food Nutr Bull. 2017 Sep;38(3):338–53.
19. Murendo C, Nhau B, Mazvimavi K, Khanye T, Gwara S. Nutrition education, farm production diversity, and commercialization on household and individual dietary diversity in Zimbabwe. Food Nutr Res [Internet]. 2018;62(0). Available from: http://dx.doi.org/10.29219/fnr.v62.1276
20. Zanello G, Shankar B, Poole N. Buy or make? Agricultural production diversity, markets and dietary diversity in Afghanistan. Food Policy. 2019;87:101731.
21. Olney DK, Talukder A, Iannotti LL, Ruel MT, Quinn V. Assessing impact and impact pathways of a homestead food production program on household and child nutrition in Cambodia. Food Nutr Bull. 2009 Dec;30(4):355–69.
22. Sibhatu KT, Qaim M. Review: Meta-analysis of the association between production diversity, diets, and nutrition in smallholder farm households. Food Policy. 2018 May 1;77:1–18.
23. Ruel MT, Quisumbing AR, Balagamwala M. Nutrition-sensitive agriculture: What have we learned and where do we go from here? Intl Food Policy Res Inst; 2017. 80 p.
24. Augustin MA, Riley M, Stockmann R, Bennett L, Kahl A, Lockett T, et al. Role of food processing in food and nutrition security. Trends Food Sci Technol. 2016 Oct 1;56:115–25.
25. Hawkes C, Ruel M. The links between agriculture and health: an intersectoral opportunity to improve the health and livelihoods of the poor. Bull World Health Organ. 2006 Dec;84(12):984–90.
26. Downs S, Fanzo J. Managing value chains for improved nutrition. good nutrition: perspectives for the 21st century. Karger, Basel, Switzerland; 2016.
27. Bartley, T., Koos, S., Samel, H., Setrini, G., and Summers, N. Looking behind the Label: Global Industries and the Conscientious Consumer. Indiana University Press; 2015.

28. Haddad L, Hawkes C, Waage J, Webb P, Godfray C, Toulmin C. Food systems and diets: Facing the challenges of the 21st century. London, UK: Global Panel on Agriculture and Food Systems for Nutrition; 2016.
29. Lopez RA, He X, De Falcis E. What Drives China's New Agricultural Subsidies? World Dev. 2017 May 1;93:279–92.
30. Gale F. Growth and Evolution in China's Agricultural Support Policies. U.S. Department of Agriculture, Economic Research Service; 2013.
31. Wallinga D. Agricultural policy and childhood obesity: a food systems and public health commentary. Health Aff. 2010 Mar;29(3):405–10.
32. Pingali P. Agricultural policy and nutrition outcomes – getting beyond the preoccupation with staple grains [Internet]. Vol. 7, Food Security. 2015. p. 583–91. Available from: http://dx.doi.org/10.1007/s12571-015-0461-x
33. Global Panel on Agriculture and Food Systems for Nutrition. Future Food Systems: For people, our planet, and prosperity [Internet]. 2020. Available from: https://www.glopan.org/wp-content/uploads/2020/11/Foresight-2_WEB_2Nov.pdf
34. Kennedy, ET and Alderman, H. Comparative analyses of nutritional effectiveness of food subsidies and other food-related interventions. International Food Policy Research Institute; 1987.
35. Faulkner GEJ, Grootendorst P, Nguyen VH, Andreyeva T, Arbour-Nicitopoulos K, Auld MC, et al. Economic instruments for obesity prevention: results of a scoping review and modified Delphi survey. Int J Behav Nutr Phys Act. 2011 Oct 6;8:109.
36. Walls HL, Johnston D, Tak M, Dixon J, Hanefeld J, Hull E, et al. The impact of agricultural input subsidies on food and nutrition security: a systematic review. Food Security. 2018;10(6):1425–36.
37. Siegel KR, McKeever Bullard K, Imperatore G, Kahn HS, Stein AD, Ali MK, et al. Association of Higher Consumption of Foods Derived From Subsidized Commodities With Adverse Cardiometabolic Risk Among US Adults. JAMA Intern Med. 2016 Aug 1;176(8):1124–32.
38. Silventoinen K, Sans S, Tolonen H, Monterde D, Kuulasmaa K, Kesteloot H, et al. Trends in obesity and energy supply in the WHO MONICA Project. Int J Obes Relat Metab Disord. 2004 May;28(5):710–8.
39. Putnam J, Allshouse J, Kantor LS, Others. US per capita food supply trends: more calories, refined carbohydrates, and fats. Food Rev. 2002;25(3):2–15.
40. Franck C, Grandi SM, Eisenberg MJ. Agricultural subsidies and the American obesity epidemic. Am J Prev Med. 2013 Sep;45(3):327–33.
41. Alston JM, Okrent AM, Rickard BJ. Impact of agricultural policies on caloric consumption. Trends Endocrinol Metab. 2013 Jun;24(6):269–71.
42. Harou AP. Unraveling the effect of targeted input subsidies on dietary diversity in household consumption and child nutrition: The case of Malawi. World Dev. 2018 Jun 1;106:124–35.
43. Michelson H, Galford G, Michelson H, Galford G. Agricultural production subsidies and child health: Evidence from Malawi [Internet]. Unknown; 2016 [cited 2021 Jan 12]. Available from: https://ageconsearch.umn.edu/record/236815/
44. Snapp SS, Fisher M. "Filling the maize basket" supports crop diversity and quality of household diet in Malawi. Food Security. 2015 Feb 1;7(1):83–96.
45. Wood B, Nelson C, Kilic T, Murray S. Up in smoke? Agricultural commercialization, rising food prices and stunting in Malawi. The World Bank; 2013.
46. Hawkes C. Identifying Innovative Interventions to Promote Healthy Eating Using Consumption-Oriented Food Supply Chain Analysis. J Hunger Environ Nutr. 2009 Jul;4(3–4):336–56.
47. Committee on a Framework for Assessing the Health, Environmental, and Social Effects of the Food System, Food and Nutrition Board, Board on Agriculture and Natural Resources, Institute of Medicine, National Research Council, Nesheim MC, Oria M, Yih PT, editors. Framework for Assessing the Health, Environmental, and Social Effects of the Food System. National Academies Press; 2015.

48. Saitone TL, Sexton RJ. Concentration and consolidation in the US food supply chain: the latest evidence and implications for consumers, farmers, and policymakers. Econ Rev [Internet]. 2017; Available from: https://www.cabdirect.org/cabdirect/abstract/20173384668
49. Bukeviciute L, Dierx A, Ilzkovitz F. The functioning of the food supply chain and its effect on food prices in the European Union. Office for infrastructures and logistics of the European Communities; 2009.
50. Bukeviciute L, Dierx A, Ilzkovitz F, Roty G, Bukeviciute L, Dierx A, et al. Price transmission along the food supply chain in the European Union [Internet]. Unknown; 2009 [cited 2021 Jan 12]. Available from: https://ageconsearch.umn.edu/record/57987/
51. Cacchiarelli L, Lass D, Sorrentino A. CAP reform and price transmission in the Italian pasta chain. Agribusiness. 2016;32(4):482–97.
52. Pokrivcak J, Rajcaniova M. Price transmission along the food supply chain in Slovakia [Internet]. Vol. 26, Post-Communist Economies. 2014. p. 555–68. Available from: http://dx.doi.org/10.1080/14631377.2014.937111
53. Saitone TL, Sexton RJ. Agri-food supply chain: evolution and performance with conflicting consumer and societal demands. Eur Rev Agric Econ. 2017 Sep 1;44(4):634–57.
54. Bunte FHJ. Pricing and performance in agri-food supply chains. Quantifying the agri-food supply chain: proceedings of [Internet]. 2006; Available from: https://library.wur.nl/WebQuery/wurpubs/fulltext/21090
55. USDA ERS Food Expenditure Series. Percent of consumer expenditures spent on food, alcoholic beverages, and tobacco that were consumed at home, by selected countries, 2015. USDA ERS; 2016.
56. Herforth A, Ahmed S. The food environment, its effects on dietary consumption, and potential for measurement within agriculture-nutrition interventions. Food Security. 2015 Jun 1;7(3):505–20.
57. FAO, IFAD, UNICEF, WFP. The State of Food Security and Nutrition in the World 2020 [Internet]. 2020. Available from: http://www.fao.org/3/ca9692en/CA9692EN.pdf
58. Sanogo I. Global food price crisis and household hunger: a review of recent food security assessments findings. 2009.[WWW document]. URL http://www.odihpn.org/report.asp.
59. Swan SH, Hadley S, Cichon B. Crisis behind closed doors: Global food crisis and local hunger. J Agrar Chang. 2010 Jan;10(1):107–18.
60. Arndt C, Hussain MA, Salvucci V, Østerdal LP. Effects of food price shocks on child malnutrition: The Mozambican experience 2008/2009. Econ Hum Biol. 2016 Sep;22:1–13.
61. Headey DD, Alderman HH. The Relative Caloric Prices of Healthy and Unhealthy Foods Differ Systematically across Income Levels and Continents. J Nutr [Internet]. 2019 Jul 23 [cited 2019 Jul 23]; Available from: https://academic.oup.com/jn/advance-article-pdf/doi/10.1093/jn/nxz158/28951648/nxz158.pdf
62. Christian P. Impact of the economic crisis and increase in food prices on child mortality: exploring nutritional pathways. J Nutr. 2010 Jan;140(1):177S – 81S.
63. Martin-Prevel Y, Delpeuch F, Traissac P, Massamba JP, Adoua-Oyila G, Coudert K, et al. Deterioration in nutritional status of young children and their mothers in young children and their mothers in Brassaville, Congo, following the 1994 devaluation of the CFA franc. Bull World Health Organ. 2000;78:108–18.
64. Thorne-Lyman AL, Valpiani N, Sun K, Semba RD, Klotz CL, Kraemer K, et al. Household dietary diversity and food expenditures are closely linked in rural Bangladesh, increasing the risk of malnutrition due to the financial crisis. J Nutr. 2010 Jan;140(1):182S–8S.
65. Campbell AA, de Pee S, Sun K, Kraemer K, Thorne-Lyman A, Moench-Pfanner R, et al. Household rice expenditure and maternal and child nutritional status in Bangladesh. J Nutr. 2010 Jan;140(1):189S–94S.
66. Gitau R, Makasa M, Kasonka L, Sinkala M, Chintu C, Tomkins A, et al. Maternal micronutrient status and decreased growth of Zambian infants born during and after the maize price increases resulting from the southern African drought of 2001–2002. Public Health Nutr. 2005;8(7):837–43.

67. Wood SA, Smith MR, Fanzo J, Remans R, DeFries RS. Trade and the equitability of global food nutrient distribution. Nature Sustainability. 2018 Jan 1;1(1):34–7.
68. Cirera X, Masset E. Income distribution trends and future food demand. Philos Trans R Soc Lond B Biol Sci. 2010 Sep 27;365(1554):2821–34.
69. USDA ERS. New Directions in Global Food Markets. USDA ERS; 2005.
70. Hawkes C, Chopra M, Friel S. 10Globalization, Trade, andtheNutrition Transition. Globalization and health: Pathways, evidence and policy [Internet]. 2009; Available from: https://books.google.com/books?hl=en&lr=&id=eQ2RAgAAQBAJ&oi=fnd&pg=PT234&dq=Globalization+trade+and+the+nutrition+transition&ots=Pp_nfar2LA&sig=c8l_EGSvpK8mozhVkwfhuEqGNrI
71. Hawkes C. The role of foreign direct investment in the nutrition transition. Public Health Nutr. 2005 Jun;8(4):357–65.
72. de Soysa I, de Soysa AK. Do Globalization and Free Markets Drive Obesity among Children and Youth? An Empirical Analysis, 1990–2013. International Interactions. 2018 Jan 2;44(1):88–106.
73. Thow AM. Trade liberalisation and the nutrition transition: mapping the pathways for public health nutritionists. Public Health Nutr. 2009 Nov;12(11):2150–8.
74. Awokuse TO. Food aid impacts on recipient developing countries: A review of empirical methods and evidence. J Int Dev. 2011 May 1;23(4):493–514.
75. Clay E. Trade policy options for enhancing food aid effectiveness. Issue Paper [Internet]. 2012;41. Available from: https://www.icnl.org/wp-content/uploads/North-Korea_trade.pdf
76. Zakari S, Ying L, Song B. Factors Influencing Household Food Security in West Africa: The Case of Southern Niger. Sustain Sci Pract Policy. 2014 Mar 5;6(3):1191–202.
77. Zakari S, Ying L, Song B. Market integration and spatial price transmission in Niger grain markets: Market integration and spatial price transmission. Afr Dev Rev. 2014 Jun;26(2):264–73.
78. Meyfroidt P. Trade-offs between environment and livelihoods: Bridging the global land use and food security discussions. Global Food Security. 2018 Mar 1;16:9–16.
79. Copeland BR. Trade and the Environment. In: Bernhofen D, Falvey R, Greenaway D, Kreickemeier U, editors. Palgrave Handbook of International Trade. London: Palgrave Macmillan UK; 2013. p. 423–96.
80. Scott P. Global panel on agriculture and food systems for nutrition: food systems and diets: facing the challenges of the 21st century. Food Security. 2017;9(3):653–4.
81. Drewnowski A. Uses of nutrient profiling to address public health needs: from regulation to reformulation. Proc Nutr Soc. 2017 Aug;76(3):220–9.
82. Nutrient Profiling: Report of a WHO/IASO Technical Meeting. WHO; 2010.
83. Monteiro CA, Cannon G, Levy RB, Moubarac J-C, Louzada ML, Rauber F, et al. Ultra-processed foods: what they are and how to identify them. Public Health Nutr. 2019 Apr;22(5):936–41.
84. Fardet A. Characterization of the Degree of Food Processing in Relation With Its Health Potential and Effects. Adv Food Nutr Res. 2018 May 3;85:79–129.
85. Steele EM, Baraldi LG, da Costa Louzada ML, Moubarac J-C, Mozaffarian D, Monteiro CA. Ultra-processed foods and added sugars in the US diet: evidence from a nationally representative cross-sectional study [Internet]. Vol. 6, BMJ Open. 2016. p. e009892. Available from: http://dx.doi.org/10.1136/bmjopen-2015-009892
86. Poti JM, Mendez MA, Ng SW, Popkin BM. Is the degree of food processing and convenience linked with the nutritional quality of foods purchased by US households? Am J Clin Nutr. 2015 Jun;101(6):1251–62.
87. Baker P, Friel S. Processed foods and the nutrition transition: evidence from Asia. Obes Rev. 2014 Jul;15(7):564–77.
88. Vandevijvere S, Vanderlee L. Effect of Formulation, Labelling, and Taxation Policies on the Nutritional Quality of the Food Supply. Curr Nutr Rep. 2019 Sep;8(3):240–9.
89. Campbell N, Reilly K, Claudy M, Finucane F. Reformulating reformulation: A technical appraisal and policy context for the 2019 FDI report on the impact of ultra-processed food

reformulation in Ireland [Internet]. TRiSS Working Paper Series; 2019 [cited 2021 Jan 12]. Report No.: TRiSS-WPS-05-2019. Available from: https://www.econstor.eu/handle/10419/226790
90. van Gunst A, Roodenburg AJC, Steenhuis IHM. Reformulation as an Integrated Approach of Four Disciplines: A Qualitative Study with Food Companies. Foods [Internet]. 2018 Apr 20;7(4). Available from: http://dx.doi.org/10.3390/foods7040064
91. He FJ, Campbell NRC, MacGregor GA. Reducing salt intake to prevent hypertension and cardiovascular disease. Rev Panam Salud Publica. 2012 Oct;32(4):293–300.
92. Salt reduction [Internet]. WHO. 2020. Available from: https://www.who.int/news-room/fact-sheets/detail/salt-reduction
93. Wyness LA, Butriss JL, Stanner SA. Reducing the population's sodium intake: the UK Food Standards Agency's salt reduction programme. Public Health Nutr [Internet]. 2012; Available from: https://www.cambridge.org/core/journals/public-health-nutrition/article/reducing-the-populations-sodium-intake-the-uk-food-standards-agencys-salt-reduction-programme/9289C9978849B50578E974F1F6BEA01E
94. He FJ, Brinsden HC, MacGregor GA. Salt reduction in the United Kingdom: a successful experiment in public health. J Hum Hypertens. 2014 Jun;28(6):345–52.
95. Trieu K, Neal B, Hawkes C, Dunford E, Campbell N, Rodriguez-Fernandez R, et al. Salt reduction initiatives around the world – A systematic review of progress towards the global target. PLoS One. 2015 Jul 22;10(7):e0130247.
96. Hyseni L, Elliot-Green A, Lloyd-Williams F, Kypridemos C, O'Flaherty M, McGill R, et al. Systematic review of dietary salt reduction policies: Evidence for an effectiveness hierarchy? PLoS One. 2017 May 18;12(5):e0177535.
97. de Benoist B, Dary O, Hurrell R AL. Guidelines on food fortification with micronutrients. WHO; 2006.
98. Das JK, Salam RA, Kumar R, Bhutta ZA. Micronutrient fortification of food and its impact on woman and child health: a systematic review. Syst Rev. 2013 Aug 23;2:67.
99. WHO. Guidelines on food fortification with micronutrients. WHO; 2015.
100. Global Fortification Data Exchange [Internet]. Global Fortification Data Exchange. 2020. Available from: https://fortificationdata.org/
101. Lomborg B. How to Spend $75 Billion to Make the World a Better Place. Copenhagen Consensus Center; 2014.
102. Osendarp SJM, Martinez H, Garrett GS, Neufeld LM, De-Regil LM, Vossenaar M, et al. Large-Scale Food Fortification and Biofortification in Low- and Middle-Income Countries: A Review of Programs, Trends, Challenges, and Evidence Gaps. Food Nutr Bull. 2018 Jun;39(2):315–31.
103. Keats EC, Neufeld LM, Garrett GS, Mbuya MNN, Bhutta ZA. Improved micronutrient status and health outcomes in low-and middle-income countries following large-scale fortification: Evidence from a systematic review and meta-analysis. Am J Clin Nutr. 2019;109(6):1696–708.
104. Aburto, N, Abudou, M, Candeias V, Wu T. Effect and safety of salt iodization to prevent iodine deficiency disorders: a systematic review with meta-analyses. WHO; 2014.
105. Gera T, Sachdev HS, Boy E. Effect of iron-fortified foods on hematologic and biological outcomes: systematic review of randomized controlled trials. Am J Clin Nutr. 2012 Aug;96(2):309–24.
106. Chen J, Zhao X, Zhang X, Yin S, Piao J, Huo J, et al. Studies on the effectiveness of NaFeEDTA-fortified soy sauce in controlling iron deficiency: a population-based intervention trial. Food Nutr Bull. 2005 Jun;26(2):177–86; discussion 187–9.
107. Mannar V, Gallego EB. Iron fortification: country level experiences and lessons learned. J Nutr. 2002 Apr;132(4 Suppl):856S – 8S.
108. CFS (Committee on World Food Security). Connecting smallholders to markets. Policy recommendations. CFS; 2016.
109. High Level Panel of Experts. Investing in smallholder agriculture for food security. HLPE; 2013.
110. Cernansky R. The rise of Africa's super vegetables. Nature. 2015 Jun 11;522(7555):146–8.

111. Bellemare MF, Fajardo-Gonzalez J, Gitter SR. Foods and fads: The welfare impacts of rising quinoa prices in Peru. World Dev. 2018 Dec 1;112:163–79.
112. Reardon T, Timmer CP, Minten B. Supermarket revolution in Asia and emerging development strategies to include small farmers. Proc Natl Acad Sci U S A. 2012 Jul 31;109(31):12332–7.
113. Legesse Debela B, Demmler KM, Klasen S, Qaim M. Supermarket food purchases and child nutritional outcomes in Kenya [Internet]. GlobalFood Discussion Papers; 2018 [cited 2020 Dec 2]. Report No.: 120. Available from: https://www.econstor.eu/handle/10419/179500
114. Wanyama R, Gödecke T, Chege CGK, Qaim M. How important are supermarkets for the diets of the urban poor in Africa? Food Security. 2019;11(6):1339–53.
115. Reardon T, Tschirley D, Liverpool-Tasie LSO, Awokuse T, Fanzo J, Minten B, et al. The processed food revolution in African food systems and the double burden of malnutrition. Global Food Security. 2021 Mar 1;28:100466.
116. Peeters A. Obesity and the future of food policies that promote healthy diets. Nat Rev Endocrinol. 2018 Jul;14(7):430–7.
117. Drisdelle C, Kestens Y, Hamelin A-M, Mercille G. Disparities in Access to Healthy Diets: How Food Security and Food Shopping Behaviors Relate to Fruit and Vegetable Intake. J Acad Nutr Diet [Internet]. 2020 Jun 24; Available from: http://dx.doi.org/10.1016/j.jand.2020.03.020
118. Tinker I. Street Foods: Urban Food and Employment in Developing Countries. Oxford University Press; 1997. 256 p.
119. Acho-Chi C. The mobile street food service practice in the urban economy of Kumba, Cameroon. Singap J Trop Geogr [Internet]. 2002; Available from: https://onlinelibrary.wiley.com/doi/abs/10.1111/1467-9493.00122
120. Dannefer R, Williams DA, Baronberg S, Silver L. Healthy bodegas: increasing and promoting healthy foods at corner stores in New York City. Am J Public Health. 2012 Oct;102(10):e27–31.
121. Zepeda L, Reznickova A. Measuring effects of mobile markets on healthy food choices. University of Wisconsin, Madison [Internet]. 2013; Available from: https://icma.org/sites/default/files/306028_Measuring%20Effects%20of%20Mobile%20Markets%20on%20Health%20Food%20Choices%20PPT.pdf
122. Bridle-Fitzpatrick S. Food deserts or food swamps?: A mixed-methods study of local food environments in a Mexican city. Soc Sci Med. 2015 Oct;142:202–13.
123. Cleary R, Bonanno A, Chenarides L, Goetz SJ. Store profitability and public policies to improve food access in non-metro U.S. counties. Food Policy. 2018 Feb 1;75:158–70.
124. Sumberg J, Sabates-Wheeler R. Linking agricultural development to school feeding in sub-Saharan Africa: Theoretical perspectives. Food Policy. 2011;36(3):341–9.
125. Kazianga H, De Walque D, Alderman H, Others. School feeding Programs and the nutrition of siblings: evidence from a randomized trial in rural Burkina Faso. Economics Working Paper Series [Internet]. 2009;908. Available from: http://business.okstate.edu/site-files/docs/ecls-working-papers/0908_Kazianga_SchoolFeeding.pdf
126. Hawkes C, Jaime PC, Rugani IC, Brasil BG. How to engage across sectors: Lessons on leveraging agriculture for nutrition from the Brazilian school meal program. Revista de Saúde Pública [Internet]. 2016 Aug 11 [cited 2021 Jan 12];50. Available from: https://openaccess.city.ac.uk/id/eprint/18781/
127. Hawkes C, Ruel MT, Salm L, Sinclair B, Branca F. Double-duty actions: seizing programme and policy opportunities to address malnutrition in all its forms. Lancet. 2020 Jan 11;395(10218):142–55.
128. Handa S, Seidenfeld D, Tembo G, Prencipe L, Peterman A. Zambia's Child Grant Program: 24-month impact report. Washington DC, USA: American Institutes for Research. 2013.
129. Miller C, Tsoka M, Reichert K. Impact evaluation report external evaluation of the Mchinji Social Cash Transfer pilot. 2008.
130. Berhane K, Kumie A, Afullo A, Bazeyo W, Rugigana E, Samet J. Establishing an environmental and occupational health hub for research and training in Eastern Africa: Lessons learned and next steps. Ann Glob Health. 2015 Mar 12;81(1):216.

131. Veras Soares CT. Impact Evaluation of the Expansion of the Food Subsidy Programme in Mozambique. 2010 [cited 2021 Jan 12]; Available from: http://citeseerx.ist.psu.edu/viewdoc/summary?doi=10.1.1.408.6192
132. Attanasio O, Gómez LC, Heredia P, Vera-Hernández M. The short-term impact of a conditional cash subsidy on child health and nutrition in Colombia. 2005; Available from: https://pdfs.semanticscholar.org/7958/13a42d749250bb61abc927e44c77ee9e740c.pdf
133. Olinto P, Flores R, Morris S, Veiga A. The impact of the Bolsa Alimentação Program on food consumption. In: annual meetings of the International Association of Agricultural Economists [Internet]. academia.edu; 2003. Available from: https://www.academia.edu/download/48551132/Impact_20of_20BA_20on_20food_20consumption_v2_8_2003_20OlintoFloresMorr.pdf
134. Fernald LCH, Gertler PJ, Neufeld LM. Role of cash in conditional cash transfer programmes for child health, growth, and development: an analysis of Mexico's Oportunidades. Lancet. 2008 Mar 8;371(9615):828–37.
135. Macours K, Schady N, Vakis R. Cash Transfers, Behavorial Changes and Cognitive Development in Early Childhood: Evidence from a Randomized Control Experiment. IDB Working Paper IDB-WP-301, Inter-American Development Bank. 2012;
136. Maluccio J, Flores R. Impact Evaluation of a Conditional Cash Transfer Program: The Nicaraguan Red de Protección Social. Intl Food Policy Res Inst; 2005. 66 p.
137. Paxson C, Schady N. Does money matter? The effects of cash transfers on child development in rural Ecuador. Econ Dev Cult Change. 2010;59(1):187–229.
138. Porter C, Goyal R. Social protection for all ages? Impacts of Ethiopia's Productive Safety Net Program on child nutrition. Soc Sci Med. 2016 Jun;159:92–9.
139. Case A. Does Money Protect Health Status? Evidence from South African Pensions. In: Wise DA, editor. Perspectives on the Economics of Aging. 2004.
140. Hidrobo M, Hoddinott J, Kumar N, Olivier M. Social Protection, Food Security, and Asset Formation. World Dev. 2018 Jan 1;101:88–103.
141. Behrman JR, Sengupta P, Todd P. Progressing through PROGRESA: An Impact Assessment of a School Subsidy Experiment in Rural Mexico. Econ Dev Cult Change. 2005 Oct 1;54(1):237–75.
142. Behrman Parker Sw JR. Long-term impacts of the Oportunidades conditional cash transfer program on rural youth in Mexico. Ibero America Institute for Economic Research; 2005. Report No. 122.
143. Manley J, Gitter S, Slavchevska V. How effective are cash transfer programmes at improving nutritional status? A rapid evidence assessment of programmes' effects on anthropometric outcomes. Social Science Research Unit, Institute of Education, University of London [Internet]. 2012; Available from: https://www.calpnetwork.org/wp-content/uploads/2020/01/q33-cash-transfers-2012manley-rae.pdf
144. de Groot R, Palermo T, Handa S, Ragno LP, Peterman A. Cash Transfers and Child Nutrition: Pathways and Impacts. Dev Policy Rev. 2017 Apr 18;35(5):621–43.
145. Parappurathu S, Kumar A, Bantilan MCS, Joshi PK. Food consumption patterns and dietary diversity in eastern India: evidence from village level studies (VLS). Food Security. 2015 Oct 1;7(5):1031–42.
146. Kaushal N, Muchomba FM. How Consumer Price Subsidies affect Nutrition. World Dev. 2015 Oct 1;74:25–42.
147. Devereux S, Nzabamwita J. Social Protection, Food Security and Nutrition in Six African Countries [Internet]. Irish Aid, Institute of Development Studies, and Centre for Social Protection; 2018. Available from: https://opendocs.ids.ac.uk/opendocs/handle/20.500.12413/14091
148. OECD. Food Supply Chains and COVID-19: Impacts and Policy Lessons. OECD; 2020.

Chapter 9
Policies Affecting Food Environments and Consumer Behavior

Introduction

Food environment policies affect the places where consumers engage with the food system. Different food environment policies can influence food availability, affordability, and marketing, all of which shape food choice and dietary quality. Food choice and demand are also influenced by a number of other factors: some of these are immediate to an individual, such as price and taste, while others are more distal, such as social customs and norms [1].

The chapter describes how optimal food environments can support healthy diets and nutrition. Select policy areas that influence diets and nutrition are discussed, including food marketing and advertising, market-based subsidies and taxes, labeling, food-based dietary guidelines and mass media campaigns, consumer awareness and nutrition education, and nudge and choice architecture. The application of policy action within physical spaces and places is also described.

How Food Environments Affect the Food Supply and Consumer Demand

Food environments represent the intersection of the food supply and consumer demand. Through these environments, the "demand" side of food systems can shape and influence the food supply. Increases in income and share of disposable income affect food demand, as people have more money to spend on non-food products. Since the proportion of income spent on food decreases as incomes rise, growth in global food demand will be greater if incomes grow faster in developing countries than in high-income countries [2]. Urbanization raises the demand for nutrient-dense foods such as fruits and vegetables, oils, and animal source foods (ASF) [3].

Figure 9.1 shows how an individual's preferences and influences intersect with the food environment to shape decision-making. A person's income, family and friends, religion, and culture all drive decision-making within a food environment. Individual, household, community, and social influences also affect what people choose to consume and how they make those choices [4].

Ideal Food Environments

Ideal food environments promote healthy diets, improve nutrition outcomes, and provide foods that are diverse and of high quality. This diverse set of foods must be convenient and catered to differing tastes without foregoing healthfulness. Food products must also be readily available and safe. If the food environment includes highly-processed, packaged foods, these products should be lower in sodium, sugar, and unhealthy fats.

In ideal food environments, food and nutrition information is accessible and readily available to consumers. Labeling information should be provided on food packages, display cases, or menus. Warning labels must be easy to read. These labels should inform consumers about nutrition information and ingredients.

Food should be affordable and accessible to all. Healthy, high-quality food should not be overly expensive and thus inaccessible for most of the world, especially those with limited incomes. Prices should be stable, and, during times of crisis, there should not be price gouging that impacts the poor.

The physical locations of food environments affect people's ability to access food. The quality of food vendors should be equalized across neighborhoods and income strata, so that the geography of food environments does not discriminate. Road infrastructure and transportation should make food markets easy to access, especially in remote areas where markets are far from residential areas or people have other difficulties in accessing markets. This remoteness is common in rural, agriculture-based societies in low-income countries where the nearest town or market can require a day of travel. For urban places, some parts of cities are disconnected from markets, with very minimal public transport access to get to those markets.

The physical environments of food products are important as well. Unhealthy foods should not comprise the majority of sale or discount products, nor should they be displayed in the front of stores or near cash registers. Junk food should not be advertised, especially not to children who are easily attracted by toys, familiar characters, and colorful displays [6, 7].

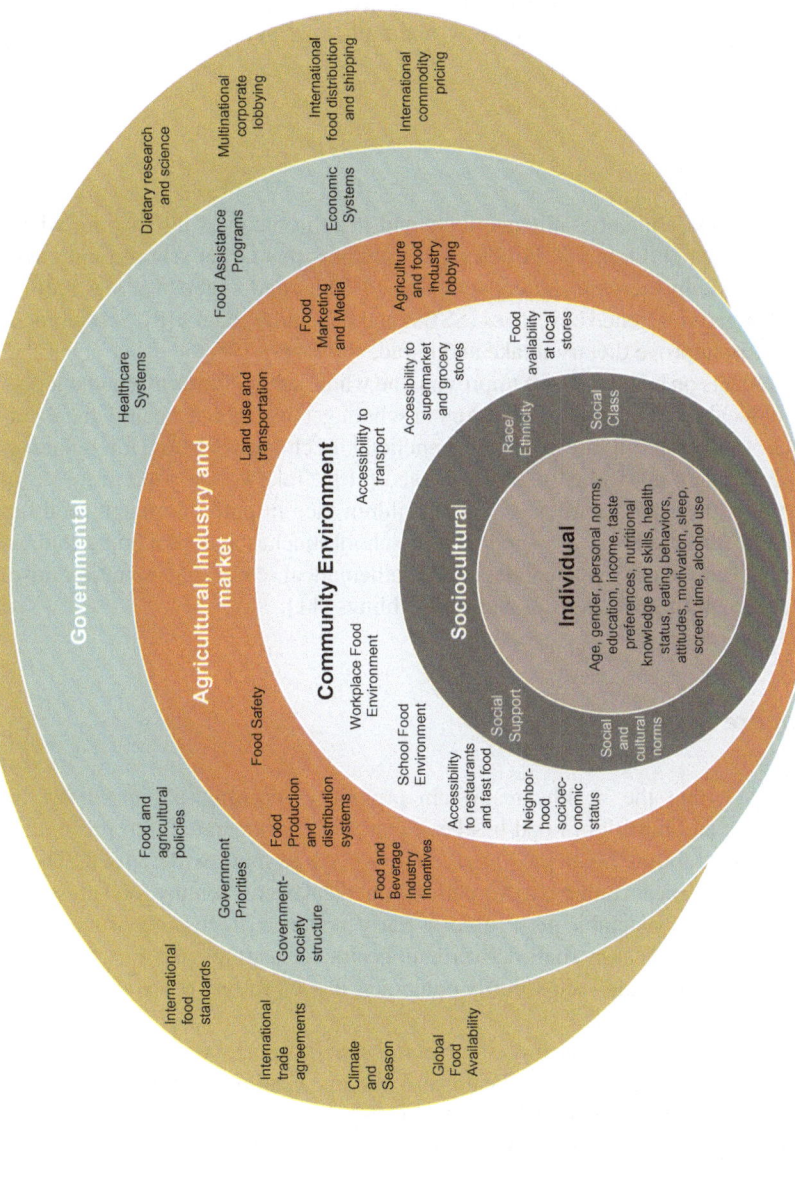

Fig. 9.1 The social determinants of healthy eating [5]

Why Physical Spaces and Places Matter

Food environments include far more than markets, grocery stores, or restaurants. Food can be found everywhere. The provision of food in schools, hospitals, workplaces, and government buildings is commonplace. Food is even sold in bookstores, hardware stores, movie theaters, airports, and train, bus, and gas stations.

Schools

School food environments influence diets and health outcomes by shaping what, where, and when children eat. Policies and programs that target school food environments can help increase the consumption of fruits and vegetables and reduce intakes of sugar-sweetened beverages (SSBs) and unhealthy snacks [8]. School food programs can improve dietary intake and reduce the risk of chronic disease, but the greatest impacts on health require improving the whole school food environment [9].

School meals help ensure that children in school get at least one healthy meal per day. These food programs are especially beneficial for children who are low-income, food-insecure, and nutritionally disadvantaged [10]. "Take home" food rations can alleviate pressures that families of schoolchildren face in putting enough food on the table. In Burkina Faso, a comparison of school lunches and take home rations showed that both improved attendance and mathematical scores, but the rations also improved the nutritional status of students' siblings [11].

Healthcare System

Innovations within the healthcare system provide a meaningful opportunity to improve diets and nutrition. Food has been increasingly integrated into preventive healthcare, as "food as medicine" interventions become more widely used. These programs include meals tailored to the patient's medical needs, healthy food prescriptions, and fruit and vegetable prescriptions. Early evidence suggests that food interventions promoting healthy diets delivered in healthcare settings may be associated with improved health and food security outcomes, though further research is needed [12–14].

In addition to food and nutrition interventions, nutritious food needs to be better incorporated into all levels of the healthcare system. Vending machines and small kiosks at hospitals often sell junk food. Stocking shelves with healthier options is not cost-prohibitive and can promote wellness. Physicians can provide better counsel to promote healthy diets to their patients with low incomes. They can facilitate and help their patients with shopping and preparing nutritious foods that fit into their lifestyles and wellness plans [15–17].

Workplaces

Workplaces serve as a daily food environment for many people. Many office buildings and other workplaces have cafeterias that feed hundreds, or even thousands, of employees every day [18]. Although evidence is limited, increasing the proportion and affordability of healthy food options may help encourage the consumption of healthy foods at worksites [19, 20].

Workplace dietary interventions can benefit both health outcomes and labor engagement, as Ireland's "Food Choice at Work" study showed through a complex intervention of nutrition education and dietary modification [21, 22]. These interventions can also address multiple forms of malnutrition. The "Table for Two" program provides healthy meals to workplace cafeterias and other food providers for a small surcharge, which is used to provide healthy school meals to low-income areas in Africa, Asia, and the United States. Through this exchange, the program works to combat overweight and obesity as well as undernutrition [23].

Policies That Focus on Food Environments and Consumer Demand to Better Shape Diets and Nutrition

Food policies can affect food environments and consumer demand through several different mechanisms, as Fig. 9.2 shows. Policy action can help develop an enabling environment that promotes healthy diets and reduces barriers to the access of healthy foods. These policy mechanisms can also be harnessed to address the structure of food

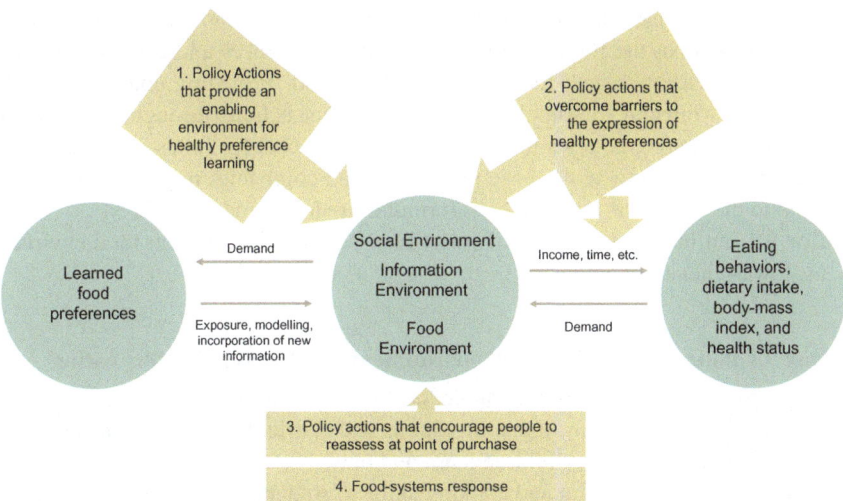

Fig. 9.2 Areas where policies can shape food environments [24]

environments in order to promote healthy eating and provide consumer information. Policies can be implemented through multiple mechanisms to generate cumulative effects throughout the food system [24].

Food environments can help enable people to make dietary choices that support their health and well-being. Policy action that targets food environments can be used to influence people's food preferences. Although some preferences are innate, most are learned from family, friends, role models, and culture. Food availability, information, marketing, and advertising also affect preference [25]. Policy can exert influence on these external factors. For example, policies can limit the advertising and marketing of junk food to youth, which can help prevent children from developing preferences for unhealthy foods.

Structural changes to food environments can also encourage healthy eating. Changes to the way that foods are priced and presented can "nudge" people into making healthier choices [24, 26]. For example, the layout of food products in grocery stores can be redesigned so that healthy foods are presented more prominently, and customers can easily find them without having to search the store. Healthy foods can be made more affordable through promotional "buy one, get one free" sales [27, 28]. Taxes on unhealthy food and beverage products can also discourage purchases and help shift preferences [29].

Policies that shift people's preferences are insufficient to create an enabling food environment. Action is also needed to ensure that healthy, nutritious diets are accessible to all. Many people face extensive barriers to accessing, preparing, and eating healthy foods. These obstacles are especially significant for people with low socioeconomic status [30]. Infrastructure barriers exist in rural and urban areas, where food quality varies across neighborhoods [24, 31, 32]. For example, policy changes to zoning laws can address food deserts and help mitigate issues of limited physical access to healthy foods.

Policy actions that support enabling food environments can lead to cumulative changes throughout the food system. By shifting preferences and ensuring access, these policies can influence food choice and demand. Providing consumers with information is integral to stimulating interdependent actions throughout the food system. For example, policies that require warning labels for foods with trans fats can cause consumers to avoid those products. Food companies might subsequently respond to the decline in demand by reformulating these products [33, 34].

Box 9.1 outlines several areas of smart food policies that reorient food environments toward healthier eating [24].

Box 9.1 Policy actions for food environments that enable healthy eating
- Provide nutrition counseling and education to families and caregivers
- Make healthy foods available in schools and restrict the sales of unhealthy foods in places where children learn and play
- Teach food preparation and cooking skills to students
- Regulate the advertising of unhealthy foods to children

- Reformulate food products to minimize unhealthy ingredients
- Subsidize the cost of nutritious, healthy foods and the transport of foods to more isolated and/or rural areas
- Tax unhealthy foods, such as SSBs
- Implement zoning policies to ensure populations have access to healthy foods
- Offer incentives for retailers to provide healthy food options in underserved, low-income areas
- Deliver healthy foods and meals to elderly and housebound populations
- Inform consumers through food and nutrition labeling [24, 35].

Marketing and Advertising of Certain Foods

Marketing and advertising can influence consumer preferences and increase demands for specific food products. Food can be marketed and advertised to many different audiences through various media channels and messages. These approaches include television and online advertising, packaging, product placement, in-school marketing, branded products, and youth-targeted promotions [36]. Food promotions are a specific type of advertisement that reduce prices for certain foods through special deals, such as "two for one" or "buy one, get one free", coupons, contests, sweepstakes, and events [37, 38].

Some types of marketing can be highly problematic, such as the marketing of junk food or unhealthy products to children. Children require special protection, because they are especially susceptible to the influence of package design, color, and character branding in food marketing. These cues are often advertised as "fun" or "trendy" [37, 38]. Many of the products targeted at children are unhealthy, though there is limited evidence that some child-centric ads can improve children's diets by increasing fruit and vegetable consumption [39].

Over the past decade, steps have been taken to reduce the marketing of junk food to children. The World Health Organization recommended limiting the marketing of foods and non-alcoholic beverages to children, a move which was endorsed by the World Health Assembly in 2010 [40]. Many countries regulate the marketing of food to children, though their methods vary [41]. These regulatory efforts include banning the use of cartoons or toys in unhealthy food promotions and restricting the marketing of fast food and other products high in calories, unhealthy fats, sugar, and sodium. Some countries also require educational labels on advertisements for foods containing added fats, sugars, or sodium [42].

Despite promising action, initiatives to regulate the marketing of unhealthy foods to children have been insufficient. Too few countries have taken substantive action and few regulatory efforts consider the effects of these promotions on public health [41, 43]. To effect meaningful change, policymakers need to prevent the marketing of unhealthy foods to children by regulating child-centric promotional material on product packaging, limiting commercials and messages on television and online, requiring that store checkout areas be free of unhealthy products, and setting nutrition standards for restaurant meals that are sold with toys, among other actions [42, 44].

Market-Based Subsidies and Taxes

Consumer behavior and food consumption can be influenced by making nutritious foods less expensive. For many people, nutritious foods are unaffordable [45, 46]. Price promotions are an effective tool to encourage consumers to purchase more nutritious foods. Reductions in prices are associated with increases in purchases and consumption of fruits, vegetables, and other nutrient-dense foods [29, 47, 48]. Subsidies can also promote healthy eating: subsidies on fruits and vegetables have been shown to increase consumption by 10 to 30% [49].

Making unhealthy foods more expensive is another way to shape diets and nutrition. Taxes and subsidies can be used to affect prices and change dietary intake, as Fig. 9.3 shows [49, 50]. For example, taxes on SSBs can lead to a 20 to 50% reduction in consumption [49]. Price increases of other foods high in sugar, salt, and fat have also been shown to reduce purchasing and consumption [48, 51]. Box 9.2 presents the cases of Denmark and Mexico, where taxes on unhealthy foods led to markedly different outcomes.

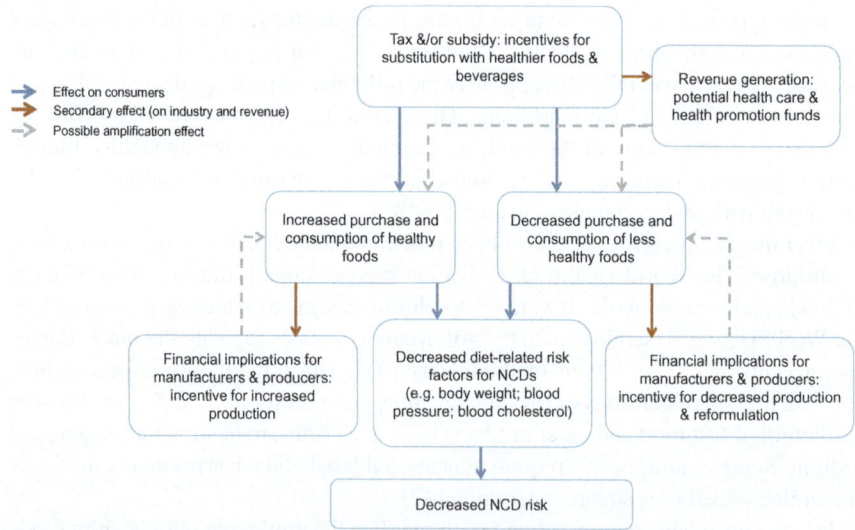

Fig. 9.3 Overall effects of fiscal instruments on consumer behavior and industry [49]

> **Box 9.2 Taxation of unhealthy foods in Denmark and Mexico**
>
> In 2011, Denmark became the first country in the world to implement a tax on saturated fat in food products. The tax resulted in a 4% decline in saturated fat consumption. During the period that the tax was active, vegetable and salt consumption also increased [52]. Consumer demand for some oils and fats shifted from higher-priced supermarkets to lower-priced discount retailers [53]. However, most policy and industry actors opposed the tax on economic grounds. The tax was repealed in 2012, shortly before the publication of research on its dietary effects [54].
>
> In 2014, Mexico imposed taxes on SSBs and nonessential energy-dense foods of approximately 10 and 8%, respectively. As a result of these taxes, purchases of SSBs declined between 8 and 17%, with the highest declines among lower socioeconomic households [55–57]. Purchases of nonessential energy-dense foods declined by approximately 5%. Low socioeconomic households reduced their purchases of taxed foods by more than 10%, while high socioeconomic households did not change their purchasing habits [56, 57].

Food subsidies and taxes can contribute positively to nutrition and health outcomes, although further research is needed on their effects. These policy actions can influence consumption in high-income countries, which may help reduce rates of overweight, obesity, and NCDs [49]. Modeling indicates that these policies could significantly avert disability-adjusted life years (DALYs) and healthcare costs in some contexts [58]. However, food taxes may impose a larger burden on the poor than on wealthier consumers. To prevent this effect, taxes should be combined with subsidies so that consumers can choose healthier products without spending more [59]. Most existing research has focused on the effects of taxes in high-income countries; further study is needed to understand how these policies would drive consumption in developing countries. A summary of the evidence on taxes and subsidies is presented in Fig. 9.4.

Front- and Back-of-Package Labeling

Nutrition labeling provides consumers with information about a food product's nutrient content. These labels are usually found on the back of food packages, though the use of front-of-package labeling is increasing. Back-of-package (BOP) labels include dietary intake or daily value guides that present numerical information. Front-of-package (FOP) labels use visual imagery, such as traffic lights or stars, to evaluate the health of food products.

Although the information provided by BOP labels is highly reliable, these labels are not the most effective way to inform and educate consumers. The Codex Alimentarius Commission, which was established by the FAO and WHO, has helped set the

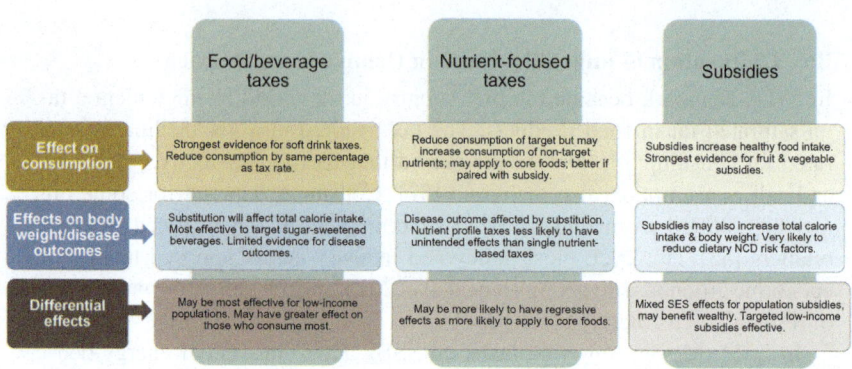

Fig. 9.4 Impact of different fiscal instruments on diets and disease outcomes [49]

standards for the nutrition guidelines found on BOP labels in many countries [60]. Although BOP labels are used in many countries around the world, there is limited evidence that consumers understand these labels or use them in purchasing decisions. These labels, which present information on serving size, calories, and nutritional content through words and numbers, require some level of nutrition literacy and can be difficult for consumers to understand [61].

FOP labels are not well regulated and are an "ungoverned space" where food companies can make claims about the food without scrutiny or penalty. FOP labels are increasingly being considered by many governments. FOP labels often use visual images to convey information on whether a food is beneficial or detrimental for health, which can be easier for consumers to interpret and may help them make better food choices [62–64]. In several European countries, efforts are underway to implement the Nutri-Score, a label that combines colorful imagery with evidence-based nutrient profiling to classify foods [65, 66].

The effect of food labeling on purchasing and consumption remains unclear. The evidence on purchasing behavior and consumption associated with labels is both limited and mixed [62, 67, 68, 69]. Studies using simulated shopping experiences suggest that, of all FOP and BOP label designs, the most effective means of changing consumer behavior are warning labels, multiple traffic light designs, and the Nutri-Score [33, 70]. Figure 9.5 shows the range of labels that are being implemented around the world.

In addition to giving consumers more information, labels also help incentivize industry actors to reformulate products. In Ecuador and Chile, FOP traffic light labels and warning stop signs led to product reformulation by food companies and decreases in purchases of food that had the warning label on their package. More than 20% of companies reformulated at least one product that received a red traffic light label for sugar, fat, or salt [72, 73]. Chile's innovative FOP labeling system is described in Box 9.3.

Fig. 9.5 Policy actions to support enhanced consumer behavior for high-quality diets [71]

Box 9.3 Regulation of marketing, labeling, and the school environment in Chile: A comprehensive policy to tackle obesity and improve the food system

Chile's obesity rate is one of the highest in all of Latin America. As of 2016, approximately two-thirds of adults were overweight and nearly one-third was obese. Chile has the second highest per-capita sales of highly-processed products in Latin America, with a rise of nearly 50% in per-capita sales of these products between 2000 and 2013 [74].

In 2016, Chile implemented the Law of Food Labeling and Advertising to address the country's obesity epidemic and build a healthier food system. The law required the use of FOP labels to warn consumers about products high in energy, sugar, fat, and/or salt. It also prohibited the marketing of unhealthy foods to young children and the sale of such foods in school or daycare settings. This law was the first national regulation to comprehensively standardize the promotion and sale of unhealthy foods [75–77].

The introduction of this law has significantly influenced consumer awareness and purchasing. Since the law's implementation, the warning labels have become well-known among Chileans of diverse socioeconomic backgrounds. Consumer surveys indicate that the warnings have influenced purchasing decisions, with the majority of respondents stating that they choose products with fewer or no warnings [77]. These findings are supported by impact studies that show purchases of unhealthy foods and beverages declined by 7 and 23%, respectively [76, 78].

Food-Based Dietary Guidelines

National food-based dietary guidelines (FBDGs) are science-based, government recommendations for healthy eating. These guidelines are an important consumer resource that provide guidance based on the latest available evidence about the food and nutrient composition of healthy diets. Governments adapt FBDGs to the national context by considering cultural and social norms, among other factors.

Around the world, 83 countries have developed FBDGs that can be used by health and nutrition professionals to provide contextually relevant dietary advice. Worldwide, FBDGs mostly align with WHO guidance on diets [79]. Some countries provide general guidance on what to eat and how much, while others offer more detailed recommendations that include "how-to" tips and strategies [80–82].

The development of FBDGs is both a scientific and political process that incorporates a range of evidence and stakeholder perspectives. These guidelines are informed by dietary data, such as assessments of food and nutrient intakes and national public health priorities to reduce diet-related diseases. Cultural preferences and other national considerations also influence guideline development [79, 83].

FBDGs affect food systems and diets through their integration into national food, agriculture, education, and/health policies and programs. FBDGs influence food environments by setting standards for foods offered in schools, workplaces, hospitals, and restaurants. For instance, in the United States, national guidelines form the basis of federal food and nutrition assistance programs, such as school meal programs. These guidelines inform and influence food system actors, such as policymakers and private companies. In response to FBDGs, the food industry may improve the nutritional quality of food products to better comply with the guidelines or change how products are marketed [84, 85].

However, the guidelines do not necessarily reflect the reality of the food system or support health goals. The FBDGs do not align with the capacity of what the food supply can produce, and they do not necessarily affect consumer behavior or nutrition literacy. There is little evidence that consumers consider FBDGs when making decisions about what foods to purchase and eat [86–88]. Most FBDGs are incompatible with at least one global health target, and approximately one-third do not align with the global agenda for NCDs. To better achieve health goals, FBDGs would need to increase the recommended intake levels for whole grains, fruits and vegetables, nuts and seeds, and legumes, and reduce the recommended intake for red and processed meat [89].

Further, most national guidelines fail to align health and sustainability goals. The majority of the world's FBDGs are incompatible with environmental and sustainability goals, and only four countries have created FBDGs that align both health and sustainability goals [89, 90]. The sustainability of diets is not addressed in most current FBDGs, although it is an important issue that is likely to gain traction. Globally, dietary recommendations will need to address the question of how to provide a sufficient nutritious diet to a population of 9 billion people without depleting natural resources [79].

Additionally, the evidence base used to develop dietary guidelines has been questioned. FBDGs should be informed by the best available evidence, which should be reviewed by accepted methods, rated for quality, and graded. These best practices are not always followed, and many variations and deficiencies exist in the development of FBDGs [89, 91]. A review of guidelines published after 2010 showed that most guidelines were updates of previous FBDGs or were based on other countries' FBDGs. While most guidelines relied on scientific reports, few used systematic reviews or reported review methods [91].

Mass Media and Behavior Change Communication

Mass media campaigns can help promote nutrition education, healthy diets, and behavior change. Different forms of mass media include newspapers, radio, television, billboards, and digital media. Social and behavior change communication (SBCC) uses communication, marketing, and behavior theory to positively change behaviors. Mass media can be used as a tool of SBCC to influence knowledge, attitudes, and social norms. SBCC may involve multicomponent, community-based mass media campaigns that incorporate nutrition strategies. Successful interventions using SBCC help ensure community engagement and positive impacts on dietary behaviors [92–94].

Interventions that use mass media to change behavior can positively affect diets and nutrition. SBCC programs in low-and middle-income countries (LMICs) have improved knowledge of infant and young child feeding practices, rates of exclusive breastfeeding, child health outcomes, and support for nutrition [95–98]. These programs can provide extended benefits when participants share their nutrition knowledge with others. The review of a program in Bangladesh found that, after the intervention, the neighbors of SBCC participants were more likely to feed their children healthy, diverse diets that met the WHO guidelines for minimum dietary diversity and acceptability [99]. In limited contexts, SBCC programs have also been shown to increase consumer awareness of the effects of unhealthy foods, with direct effects on product sales [100]. However, it is difficult to disaggregate the specific contributions of SBCC and media within multicomponent interventions [94]. Although modeling suggests that SBCC programs can improve diets and prevent diet-related deaths, more research is needed to identify effective, context-specific delivery mechanisms [101, 102].

Consumer Awareness and Nutrition Education

Consumer knowledge, awareness, and behavior can be influenced through "agentic" interventions that directly target individual choice and behavior rather than the contexts in which behaviors occur. Agentic interventions focus on an individual's personal agency, or "free will," and are favored by governments around the world [103]. These interventions provide information to individuals, who are expected to use the information to increase their skills, build knowledge, and make healthier choices. Examples include nutrition education, social marketing, and obesity prevention campaigns [103–105].

Agentic nutrition interventions have mixed effects on diets, health, and equity. These interventions may require a great deal of agency, or personal resources, from the intended recipient [103]. In some contexts, agentic approaches may have a limited effect on health outcomes and can even worsen socioeconomic inequality [103, 104]. In LMICs, however, agentic interventions targeted to disadvantaged groups can promote healthy eating and reduce social inequalities in diets [105]. Agentic interventions are more effective when combined with other interventions, such as those that improve access to markets, provide cash transfers, or offer nutrient and food supplements [106–111].

Cooking skills are an aspect of consumer knowledge and behavior that significantly influences diets and health. Learning how to prepare and cook food can have long-term benefits for nutrition and diets. Culinary interventions result in the consumption of healthier diets, increased family socialization, higher confidence, and more positive attitudes [112–118]. However, many people lack the cooking skills and competence needed to ensure optimal nutrition, food handling and storage, and planning and budgeting [116]. This lack of knowledge is a major barrier to healthy eating that can lead people to choose cheaper, more convenient, and less healthy foods.

Traditional food culture has increasingly been recognized as a critical component of nutrition education and knowledge. Adapting nutrition programs to integrate different cultural perspectives can improve acceptance among recipients [119]. These programs help ensure that nutrition educators provide knowledge and skills that are culturally appropriate and acceptable [120, 121]. In some areas, traditional food culture is used to promote nutrition knowledge. For example, in response to rising rates of obesity, South Korea implemented a campaign to promote the traditional Korean diet. The program helped to increase fruit and vegetable consumption and reduce obesity rates [122].

Choice Architecture and Nudges

Along with personal preferences and cultural factors, food environments significantly influence consumer behavior. Consumer knowledge, awareness, and behavior can be altered through interventions that incorporate "choice architecture" [123] and nudges [124]. Instead of trying to convince people to change their behavior, these interventions adjust the surrounding environment so that people are directed toward healthier options [125]. Choice architecture and nudges do not restrict buying options, regulate food choice through bans or taxes, or campaign for behavior change [126].

Choice architecture and nudges help promote preferred behaviors. Choice architecture refers to the physical, social, and psychological aspects of the contexts that influence people's choices. Interventions using choice architecture attempt to influence consumer behavior on sub-conscious levels: this may involve placing healthy products at eye-level in a store, grouping products based on their healthfulness, or changing perceptions through product placement [47, 127].

Nudges are aspects of choice architecture that change behavior in predictable ways. Certain habit-based behaviors can be "nudged" toward better options through interventions that promote ease, do not restrict economic incentives, and require little personal agency from the recipient [103, 125]. Placing healthy foods near a store's cash register is one example of a nudge [125]. Research indicates that most nudge interventions contribute to positive outcomes and increases in the selection and consumption of fruits, vegetables, and other healthy foods [124, 128, 129].

Key Messages and Conclusions

As the places where people engage with the food system, food environments serve to integrate consumer demand and food supply. Policy actions that focus on food environments are an important mechanism to alter diets and nutrition outcomes. These interventions can also contribute to more "upstream" effects on the agriculture, processing, packaging, and retailing stages of the food system.

Ideally, food environments should promote healthy diets and improve nutrition outcomes. Policy actions can help develop and support ideal food environments through many different mechanisms. Food environment policies may increase the accessibility and affordability of healthy foods through structural approaches, such as market-based subsidies and taxes, package labeling, and dietary guidelines. Other policy interventions attempt to influence food choices by improving consumer knowledge and changing behavior. Mass media campaigns, nutrition education, and nudges are examples of these agentic interventions. The physical places where people make food choices provide critical opportunities to intervene in consumer behavior.

Food environment policies can contribute positively to nutrition, diet, and health outcomes, but further research is needed. Evidence shows that certain interventions can influence dietary behaviors and nutritional status. However, people's food choices and behaviors are driven by many complex factors, so it can be difficult to ascertain the influence of one specific policy action on behavior, especially with multicomponent interventions. More study is needed to understand the effectiveness and long-term impacts of food environment policies in different contexts. Additional research can also help policymakers understand how certain policies lead to unintended consequences, such as worsened levels of inequality.

References

1. Shepherd R. Social determinants of food choice. Proc Nutr Soc. 1999 Nov;58(4):807–12.
2. Fukase E, Martin W. Economic Growth, Convergence, and World Food Demand and Supply [Internet]. Policy Research Working Papers. 2017. Available from: https://dx.doi.org/10.1596/1813-9450-8257
3. Warr P. Structural Shifters in the Global Demand for Food: Urbanization and Ageing. In: Hunger and Malnutrition as Major Challenges of the 21st Century. World Scientific; 2018. p. 77–98. (World Scientific Series in Grand Public Policy Challenges of the 21st Century; vol. 3).
4. High Level Panel of Experts. Nutrition and Food Systems. 2017 p. 152.
5. Afshin A, Micha R, Khatibzadeh S, Schmidt LA, Mozaffarian D. Dietary Policies to Reduce Non-Communicable Diseases. In: G. W. Brown GYASW, editor. The Handbook of Global Health Policy. 2014. p. 175–93.
6. Story M, Kaphingst KM, Robinson-O'Brien R, Glanz K. Creating healthy food and eating environments: policy and environmental approaches. Annu Rev Public Health. 2008;29:253–72.
7. Centers for Disease Control and Prevention. Healthier Food Retail: An Action Guide for Public Health Practitioners. U.S. Department of Health and Human Services; 2014.
8. Micha R, Coates J, Leclercq C, Charrondiere UR, Mozaffarian D. Global Dietary Surveillance: Data Gaps and Challenges. Food Nutr Bull. 2018 Jun;39(2):175–205.
9. Welker E, Lott M, Story M. The School Food Environment and Obesity Prevention: Progress Over the Last Decade. Curr Obes Rep. 2016 Jun;5(2):145–55.
10. Smith TA. Do school food programs improve child dietary quality? Am J Agric Econ. 2017;99(2):339–56.
11. Kazianga H, De Walque D, Alderman H, Others. School feeding Programs and the nutrition of siblings: evidence from a randomized trial in rural Burkina Faso. Economics Working Paper Series [Internet]. 2009;908. Available from: https://business.okstate.edu/site-files/docs/ecls-working-papers/0908_Kazianga_SchoolFeeding.pdf
12. Downer S, Berkowitz SA, Harlan TS, Olstad DL, Mozaffarian D. Food is medicine: actions to integrate food and nutrition into healthcare. BMJ. 2020 Jun 29;369:m2482.
13. Downer S, Greenwald R, Broad Leib E, Wittkop K, Hayashi K, Leonce M, and Menchaca M. Food is Prevention: The Case for Integrating Food and Nutrition Interventions into Healthcare. Center for Health Law and Policy Innovation of Harvard Law School (CHLPI); 2015.
14. De Marchis EH, Torres JM, Benesch T, Fichtenberg C, Allen IE, Whitaker EM, et al. Interventions Addressing Food Insecurity in Health Care Settings: A Systematic Review. Ann Fam Med. 2019 Sep;17(5):436–47.
15. Skipper A. How Should Physicians Counsel Patients Who Live in Food Deserts? AMA J Ethics. 2018 Oct 1;20(10):E918–23.
16. Devries S, Dalen JE, Eisenberg DM, Maizes V, Ornish D, Prasad A, et al. A deficiency of nutrition education in medical training. Am J Med. 2014;127(9):804–6.
17. Devries S, Willett W, Bonow RO. Nutrition Education in Medical School, Residency Training, and Practice. JAMA. 2019 Apr 9;321(14):1351–2.
18. Smith SA, Visram S, O'Malley C, Summerbell C, Araujo-Soares V, Hillier-Brown F, et al. Designing equitable workplace dietary interventions: perceptions of intervention deliverers. BMC Public Health. 2017 Oct 16;17(1):808.
19. Pechey R, Cartwright E, Pilling M, Hollands GJ, Vasiljevic M, Jebb SA, et al. Impact of increasing the proportion of healthier foods available on energy purchased in worksite cafeterias: A stepped wedge randomized controlled pilot trial. Appetite. 2019 Feb 1;133:286–96.
20. Tamrakar D, Shrestha A, Rai A, Karmacharya BM, Malik V, Mattei J, et al. Drivers of healthy eating in a workplace in Nepal: a qualitative study. BMJ Open. 2020 Feb 25;10(2):e031404.

21. Geaney F, Scotto Di Marrazzo J, Kelly C, Fitzgerald AP, Harrington JM, Kirby A, et al. The food choice at work study: effectiveness of complex workplace dietary interventions on dietary behaviours and diet-related disease risk - study protocol for a clustered controlled trial. Trials. 2013 Nov 6;14:370.
22. Fitzgerald S, Murphy A, Kriby A, Geaney F, Perry IJ. P49 An economic evaluation of a complex workplace dietary intervention: a cluster controlled trial. J Epidemiol Community Health. 2017 Sep 1;71(Suppl 1):A73–A73.
23. Table for Two [Internet]. Table for Two. 2020. Available from: https://www.tablefor2.org/
24. Hawkes C, Smith TG, Jewell J, Wardle J, Hammond RA, Friel S, et al. Smart food policies for obesity prevention. Lancet. 2015 Jun 13;385(9985):2410–21.
25. Smith R, Kelly B, Yeatman H, Boyland E. Food Marketing Influences Children's Attitudes, Preferences and Consumption: A Systematic Critical Review. Nutrients [Internet]. 2019 Apr 18;11(4). Available from: https://dx.doi.org/10.3390/nu11040875
26. Devine C, Wilkins J. Ecological Approaches to Creating Healthy Local Food Environments in the United States: Push and Pull Forces [Internet]. Local Food Environments. 2015. p. 297–316. Available from: https://dx.doi.org/10.1201/b17351-14
27. Kraak VI, Englund T, Misyak S, Serrano EL. A novel marketing mix and choice architecture framework to nudge restaurant customers toward healthy food environments to reduce obesity in the United States. Obes Rev. 2017 Aug;18(8):852–68.
28. Lake AA. Neighbourhood food environments: food choice, foodscapes and planning for health [Internet]. Vol. 77, Proceedings of the Nutrition Society. 2018. p. 239–46. Available from: https://dx.doi.org/10.1017/s0029665118000022
29. Gittelsohn J, Trude ACB, Kim H. Pricing Strategies to Encourage Availability, Purchase, and Consumption of Healthy Foods and Beverages: A Systematic Review. Prev Chronic Dis. 2017 Nov 2;14:E107.
30. Neff RA, Palmer AM, McKenzie SE, Lawrence RS. Food Systems and Public Health Disparities. J Hunger Environ Nutr. 2009 Jul;4(3–4):282–314.
31. Sedibe HM, Kahn K, Edin K, Gitau T, Ivarsson A, Norris SA. Qualitative study exploring healthy eating practices and physical activity among adolescent girls in rural South Africa. BMC Pediatr. 2014 Aug 26;14:211.
32. Walker RE, Keane CR, Burke JG. Disparities and access to healthy food in the United States: A review of food deserts literature [Internet]. Vol. 16, Health & Place. 2010. p. 876–84. Available from: https://dx.doi.org/10.1016/j.healthplace.2010.04.013
33. Khandpur N, Mais LA, de Morais Sato P, Martins APB, Spinillo CG, Rojas CFU, et al. Choosing a front-of-package warning label for Brazil: A randomized, controlled comparison of three different label designs. Food Res Int. 2019 Jul;121:854–61.
34. Fan S, Pandya-Lorch R. Reshaping agriculture for nutrition and health. Intl Food Policy Res Inst; 2012. 213 p.
35. University of Alberta School of Public Health. Alberta's 2018 Nutrition Report Card on Food Environments for Children & Youth. University of Alberta ; 2018.
36. Story M, French S. Food Advertising and Marketing Directed at Children and Adolescents in the US. Int J Behav Nutr Phys Act. 2004 Feb 10;1(1):3.
37. Vukmirovic M. The effects of food advertising on food-related behaviours and perceptions in adults: A review. Food Res Int. 2015 Sep;75:13–9.
38. Boyland EJ, Whalen R. Food advertising to children and its effects on diet: review of recent prevalence and impact data [Internet]. Vol. 16, Pediatric Diabetes. 2015. p. 331–7. Available from: https://dx.doi.org/10.1111/pedi.12278
39. Kraak VI, Story M. Influence of food companies' brand mascots and entertainment companies' cartoon media characters on children's diet and health: a systematic review and research needs. Obes Rev. 2015;16(2):107–26.
40. WHO. Set of recommendations on the marketing of foods and non-alcoholic beverages to children. WHO; 2010.
41. Hawkes C. Marketing food to children: the global regulatory environment. WHO; 2004.

42. Limits on Marketing to Kids [Internet]. Healthy Food America. Available from: https://www.healthyfoodamerica.org/limits_on_marketing_to_kids
43. Kraak VI, Vandevijvere S, Sacks G, Brinsden H, Hawkes C, Barquera S, et al. Progress achieved in restricting the marketing of high-fat, sugary and salty food and beverage products to children. Bull World Health Organ. 2016 Jul 1;94(7):540–8.
44. Harris J, Graff S. Protecting Children from Harmful Food Marketing: Options for Local Government to Make a Difference [Internet]. The Childhood Obesity Epidemic. 2015. p. 145–56. Available from: https://dx.doi.org/10.1201/b18225-13
45. Hirvonen K, Bai Y, Headey D, Masters WA. Affordability of the EAT-Lancet reference diet: a global analysis. Lancet Glob Health. 2020 Jan;8(1):e59–66.
46. Headey DD, Alderman HH. The Relative Caloric Prices of Healthy and Unhealthy Foods Differ Systematically across Income Levels and Continents. J Nutr [Internet]. 2019 Jul 23 [cited 2019 Jul 23]; Available from: https://academic.oup.com/jn/advance-article-pdf/doi/10.1093/jn/nxz158/28951648/nxz158.pdf
47. Chandon P, Wansink B. Does food marketing need to make us fat? a review and solutions. Nutr Rev. 2012 Oct 1;70(10):571–93.
48. Afshin A, Peñalvo JL, Del Gobbo L, Silva J, Michaelson M, O'Flaherty M, et al. The prospective impact of food pricing on improving dietary consumption: A systematic review and meta-analysis. PLoS One. 2017 Mar 1;12(3):e0172277.
49. Thow AM, Downs S, Jan S. A systematic review of the effectiveness of food taxes and subsidies to improve diets: understanding the recent evidence. Nutr Rev. 2014 Sep;72(9):551–65.
50. Eyles H, Ni Mhurchu C, Nghiem N, Blakely T. Food pricing strategies, population diets, and non-communicable disease: a systematic review of simulation studies. PLoS Med. 2012 Dec 11;9(12):e1001353.
51. Caro JC, Ng SW, Taillie LS, Popkin BM. Designing a tax to discourage unhealthy food and beverage purchases: The case of Chile. Food Policy. 2017 Aug 1;71:86–100.
52. Smed S, Scarborough P, Rayner M, Jensen JD. The effects of the Danish saturated fat tax on food and nutrient intake and modelled health outcomes: an econometric and comparative risk assessment evaluation. Eur J Clin Nutr. 2016 Jun;70(6):681–6.
53. Jensen JD, Smed S. The Danish tax on saturated fat – Short run effects on consumption, substitution patterns and consumer prices of fats. Food Policy. 2013 Oct 1;42:18–31.
54. Vallgårda S, Holm L, Jensen JD. The Danish tax on saturated fat: why it did not survive. Eur J Clin Nutr. 2015 Feb;69(2):223–6.
55. Colchero MA, Rivera-Dommarco J, Popkin BM, Ng SW. In Mexico, Evidence Of Sustained Consumer Response Two Years After Implementing A Sugar-Sweetened Beverage Tax. Health Aff . 2017 Mar 1;36(3):564–71.
56. Colchero MA, Guerrero-López CM, Molina M, Rivera JA. Beverages Sales in Mexico before and after Implementation of a Sugar Sweetened Beverage Tax. PLoS One. 2016 Sep 26;11(9):e0163463.
57. Batis C, Rivera JA, Popkin BM, Taillie LS. First-Year Evaluation of Mexico's Tax on Nonessential Energy-Dense Foods: An Observational Study. PLoS Med. 2016 Jul;13(7):e1002057.
58. Cobiac LJ, Tam K, Veerman L, Blakely T. Taxes and Subsidies for Improving Diet and Population Health in Australia: A Cost-Effectiveness Modelling Study. PLoS Med. 2017 Feb;14(2):e1002232.
59. Thow AM, Jan S, Leeder S, Swinburn B. The effect of fiscal policy on diet, obesity and chronic disease: a systematic review. Bull World Health Organ. 2010 Aug 1;88(8):609–14.
60. Codex Alimentarius Commission. Guidelines on nutrition labelling. FAO; 2012.
61. Mandle J, Tugendhaft A, Michalow J, Hofman K. Nutrition labelling: a review of research on consumer and industry response in the global South. Glob Health Action. 2015 Jan 22;8:25912.
62. Hersey JC, Wohlgenant KC, Arsenault JE, Kosa KM, Muth MK. Effects of front-of-package and shelf nutrition labeling systems on consumers. Nutr Rev. 2013 Jan;71(1):1–14.
63. Vargas-Meza J, Jáuregui A, Pacheco-Miranda S, Contreras-Manzano A, Barquera S. Front-of-pack nutritional labels: Understanding by low- and middle-income Mexican consumers. PLoS One. 2019 Nov 18;14(11):e0225268.

64. Talati Z, Pettigrew S, Neal B, Dixon H, Hughes C, Kelly B, et al. Consumers' responses to health claims in the context of other on-pack nutrition information: a systematic review. Nutr Rev. 2017 Apr 1;75(4):260–73.
65. de Edelenyi FS, Egnell M, Galan P, Druesne-Pecollo N, Hercberg S, Julia C. Ability of the Nutri-Score front-of-pack nutrition label to discriminate the nutritional quality of foods in the German food market and consistency with nutritional recommendations. Arch Public Health. 2019;77(1):28.
66. Chantal J, Hercberg S, Organization WH, Others. Development of a new front-of-pack nutrition label in France: the five-colour Nutri-Score. Public Health Panorama. 2017;3(04):712–25.
67. Leek S, Szmigin I, Baker E. Consumer confusion and front of pack (FoP) nutritional labels. Journal of Customer Behaviour. 2015;14(1):49–61.
68. Mejean C, Macouillard P, Péneau S, Hercberg S, Castetbon K. Consumer acceptability and understanding of front-of-pack nutrition labels. J Hum Nutr Diet. 2013;26(5):494–503.
69. Hamlin R, McNeill L. The Impact of the Australasian "Health Star Rating", Front-of-Pack Nutritional Label, on Consumer Choice: A Longitudinal Study. Nutrients [Internet]. 2018 Jul 16;10(7). Available from: https://dx.doi.org/10.3390/nu10070906
70. Temple NJ. A comparison of strategies to improve population diets: Government policy versus education and advice. J Nutr Metab. 2020 Jun 4;2020:5932516.
71. Global Panel. Policy actions to support enhanced consumer behavior for high-quality diets. Global Panel on Agriculture and Food Systems for Nutrition; Report No.: Policy Brief No. 8.
72. Sandoval LA, Carpio CE, Sanchez-Plata M. The effect of "Traffic-Light"nutritional labelling in carbonated soft drink purchases in Ecuador. PLoS One [Internet]. 2019;14(10). Available from: https://journals.plos.org/plosone/article/file?type=printable&id=10.1371/journal.pone.0222866
73. Kanter R, Reyes M, Swinburn B, Vandevijvere S, Corvalán C. The Food Supply Prior to the Implementation of the Chilean Law of Food Labeling and Advertising. Nutrients [Internet]. 2018 Dec 28;11(1). Available from: https://dx.doi.org/10.3390/nu11010052
74. PAHO. Ultra-processed food and drink products in Latin America: Trends, impact on obesity, policy implications. PAHO; 2015.
75. Reyes M, Garmendia ML, Olivares S, Aqueveque C, Zacarías I, Corvalán C. Development of the Chilean front-of-package food warning label. BMC Public Health. 2019 Jul 8;19(1):906.
76. Taillie LS, Reyes M, Colchero MA, Popkin B, Corvalán C. An evaluation of Chile's Law of Food Labeling and Advertising on sugar-sweetened beverage purchases from 2015 to 2017: A before-and-after study. PLoS Med. 2020 Feb;17(2):e1003015.
77. Correa T, Fierro C, Reyes M, Dillman Carpentier FR, Taillie LS, Corvalan C. "Responses to the Chilean law of food labeling and advertising: exploring knowledge, perceptions and behaviors of mothers of young children." Int J Behav Nutr Phys Act. 2019 Feb 13;16(1):21.
78. Reyes M, Smith Taillie L, Popkin B, Kanter R, Vandevijvere S, Corvalán C. Changes in the amount of nutrient of packaged foods and beverages after the initial implementation of the Chilean Law of Food Labelling and Advertising: A nonexperimental prospective study. PLoS Med. 2020;17(7):e1003220.
79. Herforth A, Arimond M, Álvarez-Sánchez C, Coates J, Christianson K, Muehlhoff E. A Global Review of Food-Based Dietary Guidelines. Adv Nutr [Internet]. 2019 Apr 30; Available from: https://dx.doi.org/10.1093/advances/nmy130
80. Montagnese C, Santarpia L, Iavarone F, Strangio F, Caldara AR, Silvestri E, et al. North and South American countries food-based dietary guidelines: A comparison. Nutrition. 2017 Oct;42:51–63.
81. da Silva Oliveira MS, Silva-Amparo L. Food-Based Dietary Guidelines: a comparative analysis between the Dietary Guidelines for the Brazilian Population 2006 and 2014 - CORRIGENDUM. Public Health Nutr. 2018 Jan;21(1):255.
82. United Nations Children's Fund (UNICEF). Review of national Food Based Dietary Guidelines and associated guidance for infants, children, adolescents, and pregnant and lactating women. UNICEF; 2020.

83. Nestle M. Food Politics: How the Food Industry Influences Nutrition and Health. University of California Press; 2013. 534 p.
84. Mozaffarian D, Ludwig DS. Dietary Guidelines in the 21st Century—a Time for Food. JAMA. 2010 Aug 11;304(6):681–2.
85. Fischer CG, Garnett T. Plates, pyramids, and planets: developments in national healthy and sustainable dietary guidelines: a state of play assessment. Food and Agriculture Organization of the United Nations; 2016.
86. Ahmed S, Downs S, Fanzo J. Advancing an Integrative Framework to Evaluate Sustainability in National Dietary Guidelines [Internet]. 2019. Available from: https://www.frontiersin.org/article/10.3389/fsufs.2019.00076/full
87. Ares G, Aschemann-Witzel J, Vidal L, Machín L, Moratorio X, Bandeira E, et al. Consumer accounts of favourable dietary behaviour change and comparison with official dietary guidelines. Public Health Nutr. 2018 Jul;21(10):1952–60.
88. Webb D, Byrd-Bredbenner C. Overcoming consumer inertia to dietary guidance. Adv Nutr. 2015 Jul;6(4):391–6.
89. Springmann M, Spajic L, Clark MA, Poore J, Herforth A, Webb P, et al. The healthiness and sustainability of national and global food based dietary guidelines: modelling study. BMJ. 2020 Jul 15;370:m2322.
90. Gonzalez Fischer C, Garnett T. Plates, Pyramids, Planet—Developments in National Healthy and Sustainable Dietary Guidelines. FAO; 2016.
91. Blake P, Durão S, Naude CE, Bero L. An analysis of methods used to synthesize evidence and grade recommendations in food-based dietary guidelines. Nutr Rev. 2018 Apr 1;76(4):290–300.
92. Bhutta ZA, Das JK, Rizvi A, Gaffey MF, Walker N, Horton S, et al. Evidence-based interventions for improvement of maternal and child nutrition: what can be done and at what cost? Lancet. 2013 Aug 3;382(9890):452–77.
93. Pelto GH, Martin SL, van Liere MJ, Fabrizio CS. Perspectives and reflections on the practice of behaviour change communication for infant and young child feeding. Matern Child Nutr. 2016 Apr;12(2):245–61.
94. Kennedy E, Stickland J, Kershaw M, Biadgilign S. Impact of social and behavior change communication in nutrition specific interventions on selected indicators of nutritional status. J Hum Nutr. 2018;2(1):34–46.
95. Olney DK, Pedehombga A, Ruel MT, Dillon A. A 2-year integrated agriculture and nutrition and health behavior change communication program targeted to women in Burkina Faso reduces anemia, wasting, and diarrhea in children 3--12.9 months of age at baseline: a cluster-randomized controlled trial. J Nutr. 2015;145(6):1317–24.
96. Martin SL, Omotayo MO, Chapleau GM, Stoltzfus RJ, Birhanu Z, Ortolano SE, et al. Adherence partners are an acceptable behaviour change strategy to support calcium and iron-folic acid supplementation among pregnant women in Ethiopia and Kenya. Matern Child Nutr. 2017;13(3):e12331.
97. Bolles K, Speraw C, Berggren G, Lafontant JG. Ti Foyer (Hearth) community-based nutrition activities informed by the positive deviance approach in Leogane, Haiti: a programmatic description. Food Nutr Bull. 2002 Dec;23(4 Suppl):11–7.
98. Sanghvi T, Haque R, Roy S, Afsana K, Seidel R, Islam S, et al. Achieving behaviour change at scale: Alive & Thrive's infant and young child feeding programme in Bangladesh. Matern Child Nutr. 2016 May;12 Suppl 1:141–54.
99. Hoddinott J, Ahmed I, Ahmed A, Roy S. Behavior change communication activities improve infant and young child nutrition knowledge and practice of neighboring non-participants in a cluster-randomized trial in rural Bangladesh. PLoS One. 2017;12(6):e0179866.
100. Farley TA, Halper HS, Carlin AM, Emmerson KM, Foster KN, Fertig AR. Mass Media Campaign to Reduce Consumption of Sugar-Sweetened Beverages in a Rural Area of the United States. Am J Public Health. 2017 Jun;107(6):989–95.
101. Menon P, Ruel MT, Nguyen PH, Kim SS, Lapping K, Frongillo EA, et al. Lessons from using cluster-randomized evaluations to build evidence on large-scale nutrition behavior change interventions. World Dev. 2020 Mar 1;127:104816.

102. Pearson-Stuttard J, Bandosz P, Rehm CD, Afshin A, Peñalvo JL, Whitsel L, et al. Comparing effectiveness of mass media campaigns with price reductions targeting fruit and vegetable intake on US cardiovascular disease mortality and race disparities. Am J Clin Nutr. 2017;106(1):199–206.
103. Adams J, Mytton O, White M, Monsivais P. Why Are Some Population Interventions for Diet and Obesity More Equitable and Effective Than Others? The Role of Individual Agency. PLoS Med. 2016 Apr;13(4):e1001990.
104. Backholer K, Beauchamp A, Ball K, Turrell G, Martin J, Woods J, et al. A framework for evaluating the impact of obesity prevention strategies on socioeconomic inequalities in weight. Am J Public Health. 2014 Oct;104(10):e43–50.
105. Mayén A-L, de Mestral C, Zamora G, Paccaud F, Marques-Vidal P, Bovet P, et al. Interventions promoting healthy eating as a tool for reducing social inequalities in diet in low- and middle-income countries: a systematic review. Int J Equity Health. 2016 Dec 22;15(1):205.
106. Ruel MT, Alderman H, Maternal and Child Nutrition Study Group. Nutrition-sensitive interventions and programmes: how can they help to accelerate progress in improving maternal and child nutrition? Lancet. 2013 Aug 10;382(9891):536–51.
107. Hirvonen K, Hoddinott J, Minten B, Stifel D. Children's diets, nutrition knowledge, and access to markets. World Dev. 2017;95:303–15.
108. Girard AW, Olude O. Nutrition education and counselling provided during pregnancy: effects on maternal, neonatal and child health outcomes. Paediatr Perinat Epidemiol. 2012 Jul;26 Suppl 1:191–204.
109. Bhandari N, Bahl R, Nayyar B, Khokhar P, Rohde JE, Bhan MK. Food Supplementation with Encouragement to Feed It to Infants from 4 to 12 Months of Age Has a Small Impact on Weight Gain. J Nutr. 2001 Jul 1;131(7):1946–51.
110. Roy SK, Fuchs GJ, Mahmud Z, Ara G, Islam S, Shafique S, et al. Intensive nutrition education with or without supplementary feeding improves the nutritional status of moderately-malnourished children in Bangladesh. J Health Popul Nutr. 2005 Dec;23(4):320–30.
111. Christian P, Mullany LC, Hurley KM, Katz J, Black RE. Nutrition and maternal, neonatal, and child health. Semin Perinatol. 2015 Aug;39(5):361–72.
112. Lautenschlager L, Smith C. Beliefs, knowledge, and values held by inner-city youth about gardening, nutrition, and cooking. Agric Human Values. 2007;24(2):245.
113. Woodruff SJ, Kirby AR. The associations among family meal frequency, food preparation frequency, self-efficacy for cooking, and food preparation techniques in children and adolescents. J Nutr Educ Behav. 2013 Jul;45(4):296–303.
114. Komatsu H, Malapit HJL, Theis S. Does women's time in domestic work and agriculture affect women's and children's dietary diversity? Evidence from Bangladesh, Nepal, Cambodia, Ghana, and Mozambique. Food Policy. 2018 Aug 1;79:256–70.
115. Engler-Stringer R. Food, cooking skills, and health: a literature review. Can J Diet Pract Res. 2010 Autumn;71(3):141–5.
116. Garcia AL, Reardon R, McDonald M, Vargas-Garcia EJ. Community Interventions to Improve Cooking Skills and Their Effects on Confidence and Eating Behaviour. Curr Nutr Rep. 2016 Oct 17;5(4):315–22.
117. Hasan B, Thompson WG, Almasri J, Wang Z, Lakis S, Prokop LJ, et al. The effect of culinary interventions (cooking classes) on dietary intake and behavioral change: a systematic review and evidence map. BMC Nutr. 2019 May 10;5:29.
118. Utter J, Larson N, Laska MN, Winkler M, Neumark-Sztainer D. Self-Perceived Cooking Skills in Emerging Adulthood Predict Better Dietary Behaviors and Intake 10 Years Later: A Longitudinal Study. J Nutr Educ Behav. 2018 May;50(5):494–500.
119. Broyles SL, Brennan JJ, Burke KH, Kozo J, Taras HL. Cultural adaptation of a nutrition education curriculum for Latino families to promote acceptance. J Nutr Educ Behav. 2011 Jul;43(4 Suppl 2):S158–61.
120. Hassel C. Nutrition Education: Toward a Framework of Cultural Awareness? Proceedings Whole Grains Summit [Internet]. 2012; Available from: https://online.cerealsgrains.org/publications/plexus/cfwplexus/library/books/Documents/WholeGrainsSummit2012/CPLEX-2013-1001-27B.pdf

121. Cultural Diversity as Part of Nutrition Education and Counseling [Internet]. National Resource Center on Nutrition, Physical Activity, and Aging. 2001. Available from: https://nutrition.fiu.edu/creative_solutions/nutrition_ed.asp
122. Lee M-J, Popkin BM, Kim S. The unique aspects of the nutrition transition in South Korea: the retention of healthful elements in their traditional diet. Public Health Nutr. 2002 Feb;5(1A):197–203.
123. Hollands GJ, Shemilt I, Marteau TM, Jebb SA, Kelly MP, Nakamura R, et al. Altering microenvironments to change population health behaviour: towards an evidence base for choice architecture interventions. BMC Public Health. 2013 Dec 21;13:1218.
124. Vecchio R, Cavallo C. Increasing healthy food choices through nudges: A systematic review. Food Qual Prefer. 2019 Dec 1;78:103714.
125. Kroese FM, Marchiori DR, de Ridder DTD. Nudging healthy food choices: a field experiment at the train station. J Public Health . 2016 Jun;38(2):e133–7.
126. Thaler RH, Sunstein CR. Nudge: Improving Decisions about Health, Wealth, and Happiness. Penguin; 2009. 312 p.
127. Arno A, Thomas S. The efficacy of nudge theory strategies in influencing adult dietary behaviour: a systematic review and meta-analysis. BMC Public Health. 2016 Jul 30;16:676.
128. Marcano-Olivier MI, Horne PJ, Viktor S, Erjavec M. Using Nudges to Promote Healthy Food Choices in the School Dining Room: A Systematic Review of Previous Investigations. J Sch Health. 2020 Feb 18;90(2):143–57.
129. Broers VJV, De Breucker C, Van den Broucke S, Luminet O. A systematic review and meta-analysis of the effectiveness of nudging to increase fruit and vegetable choice. Eur J Public Health. 2017 Oct 1;27(5):912–20.

Part IV
New Challenges to Achieving Healthy Diets for Nutrition

Chapter 10
Sustainable Diets: Aligning Food Systems and the Environment

Introduction

The need to ensure sufficient nutritious diets for all the world's people without putting undue further pressure on the environment presents a monumental challenge for the global community. The need to achieve this dual goal is heightened by the commitments made in the 2030 Sustainable Development Goals and the twenty-first Conference of the Parties on Climate Change that took place in Paris in 2015 (COP21). Food systems depend on natural resources and the environment, yet agriculture is a major driver of environmental degradation and climate change. Given the impending challenges posed by population growth, migration, and climate change, securing a sustainable future will require dietary patterns to shift significantly in coming decades.

The concept of "sustainable diets" attempts to achieve these goals by bridging the divide between agriculture and the environment. This chapter discusses the health and environmental outcomes of sustainable diets, as well as research and policy implications. Over time, the concept of sustainable diets has evolved to encompass nutrition, health, environmental, and economic dimensions. Yet there is still little guidance on how to define and implement these diets. Research on the health and environmental impacts of diets indicates that more plant-based diets support human and planetary health. However, these findings are nuanced and highly context-specific. Researchers and policymakers must also contend with various practical and ethical conundrums, such as recommendations to limit the consumption of some animal source foods (ASF) within some populations. Implementing these dietary shifts will require further research to better assess dietary outcomes and trade-offs, as well as to understand what policies and interventions work best.

The Agriculture–Environment Connection

The relationship between agriculture and the environment is highly complex and bidirectional. Natural resources are integral to agricultural production and food systems, but food system activities can impair environmental health. Agriculture acts as a major driver of adverse global environmental change: production contributes up to 25% of the planet's greenhouse gas emissions (GHGe), requires 40% of the earth's land surface, and accounts for 70% of freshwater withdrawals [1, 2]. Figure 10.1 provides more detail about how the agricultural sector uses landmass and contributes to GHGe.

As part of the two-way relationship between food systems and the environment, the ramifications of environmental damage also directly affect agricultural production. Blighted natural resources, such as polluted soil, depleted freshwater reserves, or biodiversity loss, can lower agricultural productivity and carry ramifications that extend to landscapes far beyond the original point of impact [2, 4–6]. Climate change also impairs agriculture, a situation which will only intensify over time. The effects of climate change reduce the productivity and, in some cases, nutritional quality of crops, livestock, and aquatic foods [7–10]. These repercussions threaten the overall production of sufficient high-quality, nutritious food for the world's growing population, which will likely lead to more deaths from poor diets and nutrition [2, 11]. Box 10.1 describes how agricultural production has contributed to deforestation and wildfires in the Amazon rainforest, a situation that will likely further exacerbate the effects of climate change and lead to cumulative harms.

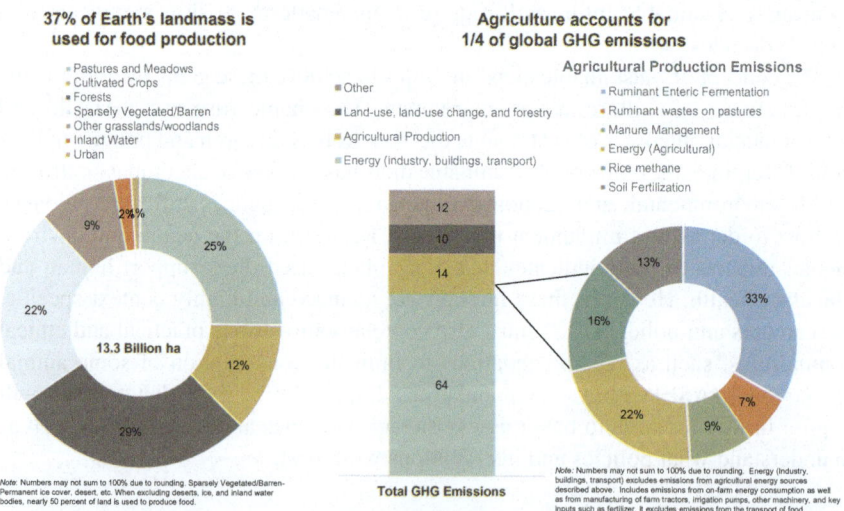

Fig. 10.1 Food systems contribute to climate change [3]

Box 10.1 The burning of the Amazon: Threats to human diets and health
Over the last 10 years, the Amazon rainforest has been burning. In 2018–2019, the fires gained international attention, as did wildfires surging across the planet in places like California and the Pacific Northwest in the United States and New South Wales in Australia [12, 13].

What sparked these destructive fires? Some of these wildfires were spurred on by nature—be it extremely dry conditions, droughts, heatwaves, or lightning storms. In a vicious cycle, climate change can reinforce and exacerbate the risk of wildfires, while, in turn, wildfires contribute to greenhouse gas emissions and hamper the planet's ability to absorb carbon dioxide [14, 15]. Many wildfires, including those in the Amazon, are also directly triggered by humans, largely due to farmers and ranchers clearing forests and shrublands to grow more food, log, or mine.

In the Amazon, the production of beef and soybeans are major drivers of mass deforestation. Soybeans are grown to feed cattle, which is a massive industry in Brazil—the country is the world's top exporter of beef [16]. The global demand for meat has directly led to deforestation as pasture lands are expanded to feed cattle in Brazil and other parts of the Amazon [17–19]. Between 2015 and 2017, cattle ranching was a major driver of the annual loss of 5,800 square kilometers in the Amazon [20]. Since 2010, JBS, the world's largest meat processing company, has been linked to one-third of all deforestation in the Amazon [16].

Between 2010 and 2019, the number of fires in the Amazon increased by 35% [21]. In places like the Amazon, these fires destroy wild habitats and biodiversity that are critical for food security and diets, as well as ecosystem resilience [22]. As the "lungs of the earth," the Amazon plays a major role in carbon sequestration and the production of oxygen [15]. By damaging the planet's "lungs," these fires hinder climate mitigation efforts and potentially worsen the effects of climate change.

The History of Sustainable Diets

The concept of sustainable diets aims to address both human well-being and environmental sustainability. Sustainable diets contribute to food security and nutrition for current and future generations while simultaneously lowering the environmental impacts of diets and food system activities [23]. This definition has evolved over time and expanded to include the economic, ethical, and cultural aspects of diets [1, 23–25].

The origins of the sustainable diet concept lie in the early environmental and "econutrition" movements of the 1960s and 1970s. The dialogue began during the counterculture movement of the 1960s, as Rachel Carson's *Silent Spring* and Francis Moore Lappe's *Diet for a Small Planet*, among other seminal titles, began to influence societal understanding of environmental well-being and degradation. Joan Dye Gussow's work on ecological nutrition in the 1970s and her book *Chicken Little, Tomato Sauce, and Agriculture: Who Will Produce Tomorrow's Food?* sparked further discussions about the connection between environmental resources and agricultural production. Later publications by Gussow and colleagues helped to formalize and clarify the term "sustainable diets" [26–28].

Over time, the meaning and policy implications of sustainable diets have undergone much debate and development by diverse scientific disciplines. Beginning in the 2000s, the concept became more prominently used to describe diets that met recommended dietary requirements and contributed to environmental health. The concept has since evolved to promote both economic and environmental stability through low-impact and affordable foods that simultaneously improve public health and nutrition. The importance of sustainable diets has also been increasingly recognized by the international community. Sustainable diets and food systems are featured in international commitments, such as the UN's 2030 Agenda for Sustainable Development, and national dietary guidelines as a means of addressing hunger, food insecurity, malnutrition, global health, sustainable development, and climate change [24, 29–32].

Despite the growing recognition of the importance of sustainable diets, there is little agreement on how to define or apply the term. The FAO and WHO have proposed an official definition for sustainable diets that acknowledges the concept's breadth and complexity, but the United Nations has not yet reached consensus on it. Generally, sustainable diets are understood to be healthy, plant-based diets that are less environmentally impactful. However, it remains unclear what, exactly, this type of diet would look like "on the plate." Given the ongoing discussion of the term's meaning, different stakeholders within the food systems may choose to interpret the term's meaning—and its policy implications—in varying ways that reflect their own priorities [33].

The EAT-*Lancet* Report

In an effort to increase public awareness of the challenges facing food systems, the *Lancet* journals created the Eat-*Lancet* Commission on Food, Planet, and Health. The Commission was a diverse, interdisciplinary group of experts from the fields of human health, agriculture, political science, and environmental sustainability. In partnership with EAT, a global non-profit focused on food system transformation, the Commission published the *2019 Eat-Lancet Report on Healthy Diets for Sustainable Food Systems*. The report explored whether diets could maintain and improve human health while remaining within the boundaries of planetary sustainability.

As the first scientific review examining how to achieve a healthy diet produced from a sustainable food system, the Commission's groundbreaking report described a universal healthy reference diet, established measurable targets for sustainable food systems, and called for a "Great Food Transformation." The report's reference diet, or "Planetary Health Diet," aimed to meet the nutritional needs of the planet's future population with a healthy, plant-based diet while restraining global warming to 1.5 °C, as specified in the Paris Agreement. The diet includes large amounts of vegetables, fruits, whole grains, legumes, nuts, and unsaturated fats; some seafood and poultry; and little to no red meat, processed meat, added sugar, or refined grains. The report also proposed scientific targets for the safe operation of food systems within the six key earth processes of climate change, land-system change, freshwater use, nitrogen cycling, phosphorus cycling, and biodiversity. The report's authors acknowledged that implementing the Planetary Health Diet and achieving transformation to sustainable food production by 2050 would require significant shifts in dietary patterns and natural resource use [2].

The Planetary Health Diet is based on evidence from the published literature made up of randomized controlled feeding studies with cardiovascular disease risk factor outcomes, observational cohort studies with long follow-up and disease outcomes, and randomized controlled trials of dietary patterns with cardiovascular disease risk factors and disease outcomes. Pulling together the evidence of this literature, the Commission also employed three different risk models to assess the health benefits of the Planetary Health Diet. The three models showed that roughly the same estimated number of adult deaths could be averted by the Diet—11 million per year.

Although the Eat-*Lancet* Commission's report filled a critical gap in global nutrition and sustainable diet strategy, it also sparked significant debate and criticism from scientific and political circles. One review of the Commission's Planetary Health Diet found that nearly 1.6 million people do not have the financial means to follow the diet, which is especially concerning given that malnutrition is concentrated among economically poorer populations [34, 35]. Other critics noted that meeting people's nutritional needs through the Diet would lead to unexpected environmental trade-offs and require doubling yields of fruits, vegetables, and nuts globally by 2050, yet the effects of climate change on agriculture will make it challenging to achieve this goal [2, 36–40]. The report's potential impacts on the livestock sector were especially contentious, with many criticizing the diet as being protein deficient and insufficiently science-based [41, 42]. Though some critics acknowledged that significant reductions in meat consumption could benefit populations in high- and middle-income countries, they noted that ASF can be a valuable source of nutrients for people experiencing undernutrition [43].

Despite its limitations, the report helped forge consensus and inspire discussion among many in the international community. The report's findings were widely welcomed by those in the public health, nutrition, and environmental fields [44]. The report's dietary recommendations aligned with existing research showing that plant-based diets promote health and environmental outcomes in middle- and high-income countries [1] as well as with the United States Dietary Guidelines, with some divergences in key food groups, such as red meat and whole grains [45]. These findings also spurred governments and stakeholders to more closely examine food systems in the context of climate change. The report encouraged these actors to consider potential guidance on sustainable diets and policies, as well as secondary effects for agriculture and food production. By challenging the current status of diets and food systems, the report asked policymakers to consider what changes would be needed to shift diets and create sustainable food systems, who would benefit from such changes, and the acceptability of potential trade-offs.

Health and Environmental Implications of Sustainable Diets

The concept of sustainable diets is based on research into the health and environmental implications of diets and foods. Existing studies suggest that plant-dominant diets are better for both human and environmental health. These diets include more fruits and vegetables, whole grains, legumes, and fish, and fewer ASF, sugars, and vegetable oils [2, 46, 47]. Replacing ASF with more plant-based foods can benefit both health and the environment, as can replacing ruminant meat products, such as beef, with animal foods with lower environmental footprints like poultry or seafood [1, 2, 48–51]. However, nutritional needs and environmental outcomes are highly context-specific depending on how and where food is grown, and health and environmental priorities do not always converge [1].

Sustainable diets can support human health, but the relationship between health and environmental gains is nuanced. Plant-dominant diets can help lower the incidence of mortality, obesity, and DR-NCDs. Dietary patterns such as the Mediterranean (a plant-based diet with minimal amounts of red meat inspired by traditional eating habits in Spain, Italy, and Greece), pescatarian, and vegetarian diets have been shown to help reduce rates of diabetes, cancer, and mortality from coronary heart disease [1, 2, 50]. However, environmentally sustainable diets do not necessarily support health outcomes. Diets high in sugar, salt, and refined starches and grains have lower environmental footprints but do not provide sufficient micronutrients and some are detrimental to health [33, 48, 52–54]. Further, some have argued that the health benefits of sustainable diets are not statistically significant [48]. Recommendations for sustainable diets can be especially problematic for populations in low- and middle-income countries (LMICs) that experience nutrient deficiencies.

From an environmental perspective, plant-based diets confer more environmental benefits than other diet types. The most commonly studied dietary patterns include vegan, vegetarian, pescatarian, Mediterranean, and omnivorous diets. Of these diets, plant-based dietary patterns have the lowest adverse effects on the environment [48, 49, 51, 52, 55–57]. Vegan and vegetarian diets are associated with the most significant reductions in greenhouse gas emissions (GHGe) and land use. Vegetarian diets are also associated with the most significant reductions in water use, with median reductions of approximately 20–30% [52, 58]. Omnivorous diets that replace ruminant meat with fish, poultry, and pork can lead to lower environmental impacts, but these reductions are less significant than those of plant-based diets [49, 51].

Research examining the environmental footprints of specific foods or food groups is less conclusive, but existing studies indicate that the impacts of specific food groups

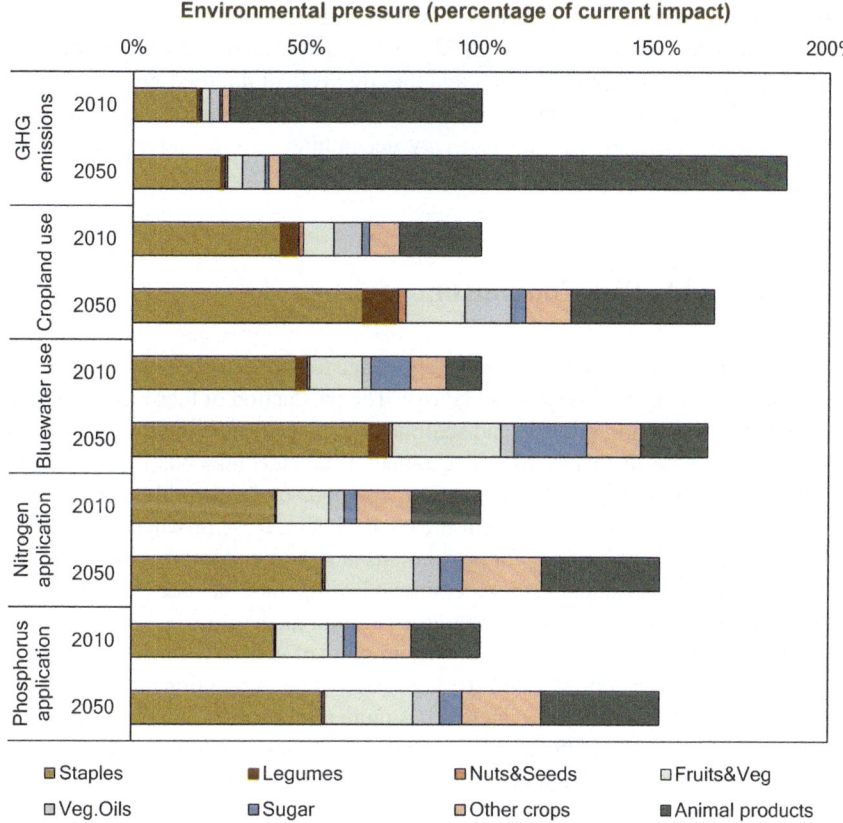

Fig. 10.2 Impact of food groups on five environmental pressures [64]

vary widely. As Fig. 10.2 shows, the production of ASF generates the majority of food-related GHGe (72–78% of total agricultural emissions). These foods can also negatively affect crop diversity, forests, water use, land use and land-use change, and pollution. While staple crops generally have lower environmental footprints than animal products, they account for 30–50% of cropland use, blue water use, and nitrogen and phosphorus application, and more than 50% of grains are used as feed for animals [59]. Fish and seafood production and harvesting can negatively contribute to GHGe, land and water quality, and biodiversity. In some cases, fruit, vegetable, and nut production requires more water and generates more GHGe than certain meat products [50, 52, 60–62]. Overall, foods with lower impacts in one environmental area tend to have lower impacts on other areas as well [63].

As with research on the health impacts of sustainable diets, the findings on environmental impacts of diets are nuanced. Research comparing the impacts of specific foods is limited due to the inconsistent methods and metrics used to assess environmental, dietary, and health outcomes [31, 48, 49, 51, 65]. Relatively few studies examine dimensions of sustainability other than GHGe, such as land use, land-use changes, water use, and biodiversity [2, 52, 66, 67]. These metrics can have differing impacts based on geographical region and the life cycle of the food product, which consists of all the inputs and energy needed to produce the food [68]. The environmental impacts of different foods also vary depending on how and where food is grown [33, 52, 69–71].

The Sustainable Diet Conundrum

The consumption of ASF presents a major challenge for sustainable diets. Around the world, the consumption of ASF is on the rise. The production of these foods, which include dairy, beef, pork, poultry, and seafood, can be environmentally detrimental and highly resource-intensive. Many sustainable diet recommendations advocate for plant-based diets with little to no meat, seafood, or dairy. Although limiting consumption of these foods can benefit the environment, these products can also be nutritionally valuable, especially for populations at risk of undernutrition. To ensure healthy diets for all, sustainable diet recommendations must balance environmental and nutritional needs for diverse communities around the world.

In recent decades, the production and consumption of ASF has grown significantly around the world. Between 1961 and 2014, global poultry production increased more than 12-fold, while beef cattle production has more than doubled. ASF consumption is concentrated in many middle- and high-income countries. Americans, who account for only 4.5% of the world's population, consume approximately 15% of the meat produced globally. Demand for meat has also risen in countries like China, where consumption has grown 15-fold since 1961 and its meat imports are expected to grow from USD $2.9 billion in 2007 to USD $149 billion in 2050 [72–75]. In wealthy contexts, meat consumption often far exceeds daily nutrient requirements [72].

Given the adverse health and environmental implications of diets high in ASF, dietary shifts are needed now more than ever before. Yet sustainable diet recommendations that reduce or eliminate ASF can also be highly problematic, especially for nutritionally vulnerable groups. ASF provides micronutrients that are difficult to obtain in sufficient amounts from plant-based foods, especially vitamin A, vitamin B-12, riboflavin, calcium, and iron. Inadequate intake of these nutrients can cause anemia, poor growth, rickets, impaired cognitive performance, blindness, neuromuscular deficits, and eventually, death. The nutrients in ASF are critical for healthy childhood development, growth, and maintenance, yet many people in lower- and middle-income countries cannot afford these foods [76]. Countries that have the highest burdens of undernutrition also consume the least meat. Instead of plant-based diets, higher ASF intake can improve health outcomes for populations in regions like sub-Saharan Africa and Southeast Asia, where undernutrition still contributes more to the burden of disease than DR-NCDs [57, 64, 67, 77].

Recommendations to shift diets away from ASF present other ethical complexities as well. The livestock, aquaculture, and fishing sectors provide a source of livelihood for millions of people around the world [78–81]. In many regions, ASF are an important component of culture and religion [52, 78]. These foods are also meaningful to individual identity and taste preference; for some, eating meat is associated with strength, health, masculinity, and indulgence [82].

Research Limitations and Policy Opportunities

Achieving the goal of sustainable food systems and diets requires a better understanding of what constitutes a sustainable diet for different populations and contexts. Additional research is needed to characterize and define the key environmental, biological, cultural, and health determinants of sustainable diets, as well as to provide guidance on what sustainable diets look like "on the plate" [31, 33, 49]. This work requires better indicators to measure the health, environmental, and economic outcomes of these diets, which in turn can help inform decision-making around trade-offs [24, 49]. Monitoring and evaluation tools can inform research and policy-making, but political will and consensus is also critical to achieving the dietary and environmental goals underlying sustainable diets [83].

To meet key dietary and environmental goals in coming decades, further research and intervention will be needed to understand and reduce the adverse environmental effects of food systems. The agricultural sector has long been focused on increasing agricultural yields and supplies of food without sufficient consideration to the environmental ramifications of production. However valid, this focus on food security has contributed to biodiversity loss, increased GHGe, and water pollution. Moving forward, agricultural efficiency must be balanced with environmental health in order to reduce GHGe from agriculture and land use, minimize biodiversity loss, phase out unsustainable water withdrawals, and curtail air and water pollution. Many different coordinated actions will be required to produce a sufficient amount of nutritious food for all the world's people while respecting planetary boundaries. "Climate-smart" agriculture that addresses food security needs along with climate mitigation and adaptation will be critical. Additional measures and indicators include dietary shifts, improvements in technology and management, and reductions in food loss and waste. Further study is also needed to ascertain how environmental outcomes differ based on geographic context and production method [64, 84].

Policies can shift populations toward more sustainable diets, but more research is required to understand what interventions work best and how to implement them. Policymakers must also better integrate sustainability issues into dietary and nutrition policies in order to create "policy coherence." Few national food-based dietary guidelines (FBDGs) incorporate elements of environmental sustainability [85, 86]. Instead, most recommendations are incompatible with the Paris Climate Agreement and other environmental targets [87]. To overcome these limitations, the FAO and WHO jointly released their "Guiding Principles on Sustainable Healthy Diets," which outlines 16 key principles related to health, environmental, and sociocultural aspects of sustainable diets. These principles are meant to inform governments and other actors in policy-making and communications from low- to high-income countries. The guidance represents foundational elements of healthy and sustainable diets by considering nutrient recommendations alongside environmental, social-cultural, and economic sustainability [88].

Ultimately, achieving goals in one domain will present challenges for other domains, a problem which is often exacerbated by interactions between different aspects of the food system. The process of setting goals and prioritizing thresholds to meet competing objectives presents ethical concerns. It is essential that thresholds and constraints in one area, such as the environment, be balanced to account for limits in other domains, such as health. The global community must realistically optimize risks in different domains to find ways for humanity to responsibly inhabit the planet. Thresholds should be determined by assessing the value of these risks and negotiating concerns among stakeholders. Is it acceptable to take risks that might exacerbate adverse health outcomes now in order to protect environmental outcomes now and in the future? What thresholds can reasonably be achieved by the current population?

Key Messages and Conclusions

Over the last 50 years, the concept of sustainable diets has evolved from a singular focus on environmental outcomes to an approach that more broadly considers the nutrition, health, environmental, and economic implications of diets and food systems. Ongoing discussions of sustainable diets center around nuanced, rigorous research that evaluates the many different dimensions of dietary outcomes. Now, amidst the rising pressures of climate change and population growth, the shift to more sustainable diets is arguably more important than ever before.

Although sustainable diets can lead to mutual benefits for human and environmental health, achieving dietary change will be a daunting feat. Harnessing these dietary benefits requires an integrated approach to health and sustainability that considers the complex linkages between food systems, diets, human health, and the environment. No single concept of sustainable diets can be applied to all settings, as sustainability is highly context-specific and nuanced. Approaches to sustainability must be tailored to differing needs across diverse countries, communities, and homes. The ethical complexities posed by dietary recommendations will require careful consideration to ensure fairness and equity for all. Further research will be needed to provide more definitive guidance on sustainable diets and recommendations for policy interventions.

References

1. Springmann M, Wiebe K, Mason-D'Croz D, Sulser TB, Rayner M, Scarborough P. Health and nutritional aspects of sustainable diet strategies and their association with environmental impacts: a global modelling analysis with country-level detail. The Lancet Planetary Health. 2018 Oct;2(10):e451–61.
2. Willett W, Rockström J, Loken B, Springmann M. Food in the Anthropocene: the EAT–Lancet Commission on healthy diets from sustainable food systems. Lancet [Internet]. 2019; Available from: https://www.thelancet.com/journals/lancet/article/PIIS0140-6736(18)31788-4/fulltext?fbclid=IwAR2ftk_lpUKlVbQ-B93qUXmWnm6bA4dfFA5paVFCG0vExt5c516oikYOCsk
3. World Resources Institute. Creating a Sustainable Food Future. 2018; Available from: https://wriorg.s3.amazonaws.com/s3fs-public/creating-sustainable-food-future_2.pdf
4. DeClerck FAJ, Fanzo J, Palm C, Remans R. Ecological approaches to human nutrition. Food Nutr Bull. 2011 Mar;32(1 Suppl):S41–50.
5. Calicioglu O, Flammini A, Bracco S, Bellù L, Sims R. The Future Challenges of Food and Agriculture: An Integrated Analysis of Trends and Solutions. Sustain Sci Pract Policy. 2019 Jan 4;11(1):222.
6. Vogel E, Donat MG, Alexander LV. The effects of climate extremes on global agricultural yields. Environmentalist [Internet]. 2019; Available from: https://iopscience.iop.org/article/10.1088/1748-9326/ab154b/meta
7. Toreti A, Deryng D, Tubiello FN, Müller C, Kimball BA, Moser G, et al. Narrowing uncertainties in the effects of elevated CO_2 on crops. Nature Food. 2020 Dec 1;1(12):775–82.
8. Smith MR, Myers SS. Impact of anthropogenic CO_2 emissions on global human nutrition. Nature Climate Change. 2018;8(9):834–9.
9. Beach RH, Sulser TB, Crimmins A, Cenacchi N, Cole J, Fukagawa NK, et al. Combining the effects of increased atmospheric carbon dioxide on protein, iron, and zinc availability and projected climate change on global diets: a modelling study. The Lancet Planetary Health. 2019 Jul 1;3(7):e307–17.
10. Myers SS, Zanobetti A, Kloog I, Huybers P, Leakey ADB, Bloom AJ, et al. Increasing CO_2 threatens human nutrition. Nature. 2014 Jun 5;510(7503):139–42.
11. Fanzo J, Davis C, McLaren R, Choufani J. The effect of climate change across food systems: Implications for nutrition outcomes. Global food security [Internet]. 2018; Available from: https://www.sciencedirect.com/science/article/pii/S2211912418300063
12. Liverpool L. Burning of Amazon may get a lot worse. New Sci. 2020 Jan;245(3265):16.
13. Take action to stop Amazon burning. Nature. 2019 Sep;573(7773):163.
14. Hopke JE. Connecting Extreme Heat Events to Climate Change: Media Coverage of Heat Waves and Wildfires. Environmental Communication. 2020 May 18;14(4):492–508.
15. Xu R, Yu P, Abramson MJ, Johnston FH, Samet JM, Bell ML, et al. Wildfires, Global Climate Change, and Human Health. N Engl J Med. 2020 Nov 26;383(22):2173–81.
16. Ermgassen EKHJ z., Godar J, Lathuillière MJ, Löfgren P, Vasconcelos A, Gardner T, et al. The origin, supply chain, and deforestation footprint of Brazil's beef exports [Internet]. 2020. Available from: http://dx.doi.org/10.31220/osf.io/efg6v
17. DeFries R, Herold M, Verchot L, Macedo MN, Shimabukuro Y. Export-oriented deforestation in Mato Grosso: harbinger or exception for other tropical forests? Philos Trans R Soc Lond B Biol Sci. 2013 Jun 5;368(1619):20120173.
18. Richards PD, VanWey L. Farm-scale distribution of deforestation and remaining forest cover in Mato Grosso [Internet]. Vol. 6, Nature Climate Change. 2016. p. 418–25. Available from: http://dx.doi.org/10.1038/nclimate2854
19. VanWey LK, Spera S, de Sa R, Mahr D, Mustard JF. Socioeconomic development and agricultural intensification in Mato Grosso. Philos Trans R Soc Lond B Biol Sci. 2013 Jun 5;368(1619):20120168.
20. Andrew Wasley, Alexandra Heal, Dom Phillips, Daniel Camargos, Mie Lainio, André Campos, Diego Junqueira. Revealed: How the global beef trade is destroying the Amazon. The Bureau of Investigative Journalism. 2019.

21. Symonds A. Amazon rainforest fires: here's what's really happening. New York Times. 2019;
22. Hattersley L, Cogill B, Hunter D, Kennedy G. Evidence for the Role of Biodiversity in Supporting Healthy, Diverse Diets and Nutrition. In: Hunter D, Borelli T, Gee E, editors. Biodiversity, Food and Nutrition. Routledge; 2020.
23. Bioversity and FAO. Sustainable Diets and Biodiversity: Directions and Solutions for Policy, Research and Action. Burlingame B DS, editor. 2012.
24. Meybeck A, Gitz V. Sustainable diets within sustainable food systems. Proc Nutr Soc. 2017 Feb;76(1):1–11.
25. Green H, Broun P, Cook D, Cooper K, Drewnowski A, Pollard D, et al. Healthy and sustainable diets for future generations. J Sci Food Agric. 2018 Jul;98(9):3219–24.
26. Gussow JD. Chicken little, tomato sauce, and agriculture: who will produce tomorrow's food? Bootstrap Press; 1991.
27. Herrin M, Gussow JD. Designing a sustainable regional diet. J Nutr Educ. 1989;21(6):270–5.
28. Lang T. Sustainable Diets: another hurdle or a better food future? Development. 2015;57(2).
29. Johnston JL, Fanzo JC, Cogill B. Understanding sustainable diets: a descriptive analysis of the determinants and processes that influence diets and their impact on health, food security, and environmental sustainability. Adv Nutr. 2014 Jul;5(4):418–29.
30. Mason P, Lang T. Sustainable Diets: How Ecological Nutrition Can Transform Consumption and the Food System. Taylor & Francis; 2017. 354 p.
31. Jones AD, Hoey L, Blesh J, Miller L, Green A, Shapiro LF. A Systematic Review of the Measurement of Sustainable Diets. Adv Nutr. 2016 Jul 11;7(4):641–64.
32. UNICEF. Transforming our World: The 2030 Agenda for Sustainable Development. UNICEF; 2015.
33. Garnett T. What is a sustainable healthy diet? Food Climate Research Network (FCRN); 2014.
34. Hirvonen K, Bai Y, Headey D, Masters WA. Affordability of the EAT-Lancet reference diet: a global analysis. Lancet Glob Health. 2020 Jan;8(1):e59–66.
35. Drewnowski A. Analysing the affordability of the EAT-Lancet diet. Lancet Glob Health. 2020 Jan;8(1):e6–7.
36. Tuomisto HL. The complexity of sustainable diets. Nat Ecol Evol. 2019 May;3(5):720–1.
37. Vanham D, Mekonnen MM, Hoekstra AY. Treenuts and groundnuts in the EAT-Lancet reference diet: Concerns regarding sustainable water use. Glob Food Sec. 2020 Mar;24:100357.
38. Semba RD, de Pee S, Kim B, McKenzie S, Nachman K, Bloem MW. Adoption of the "planetary health diet" has different impacts on countries' greenhouse gas emissions. Nature Food. 2020 Aug 1;1(8):481–4.
39. Lawrence MA, McNaughton SA. Vegetarian diets and health. BMJ. 2019 Sep 4;366:l5272.
40. Sanchez PA. Viewpoint: Time to Increase Production of Nutrient-rich Foods. Food Policy [Internet]. 2020 [cited 2021 Jan 13];91(C). Available from: https://ideas.repec.org/a/eee/jfpoli/v91y2020ics0306919220300270.html
41. Zagmutt FJ, Pouzou JG, Costard S. The EAT-Lancet Commission's Dietary Composition May Not Prevent Noncommunicable Disease Mortality. J Nutr. 2020 May 1;150(5):985–8.
42. Verkerk R. EAT-Lancet—Is there such a thing as "one- size-fits-all" sustainability? Journal of holistic healthcare [Internet]. 2019;16(3). Available from: https://bhma.org/wp-content/uploads/2019/10/EAT-Lancet-response-.pdf
43. Adesogan AT, Havelaar AH, McKune SL, Eilittä M, Dahl GE. Animal source foods: Sustainability problem or malnutrition and sustainability solution? Perspective matters. Global Food Security. 2020 Jun 1;25:100325.
44. Lawrence MA, Baker PI, Pulker CE, Pollard CM. Sustainable, resilient food systems for healthy diets: the transformation agenda. Public Health Nutr. 2019 Nov;22(16):2916–20.
45. Blackstone NT, Conrad Z. Comparing the Recommended Eating Patterns of the EAT-Lancet Commission and Dietary Guidelines for Americans: Implications for Sustainable Nutrition. Curr Dev Nutr. 2020 Mar;4(3):nzaa015.
46. Mozaffarian D. Dietary and Policy Priorities for Cardiovascular Disease, Diabetes, and Obesity: A Comprehensive Review. Circulation. 2016;133(2):187–225.
47. Garnett T. Plating up solutions. Science. 2016 Sep 16;353(6305):1202–4.

48. Payne CL, Scarborough P, Cobiac L. Do low-carbon-emission diets lead to higher nutritional quality and positive health outcomes? A systematic review of the literature. Public Health Nutr. 2016 Oct;19(14):2654–61.
49. Auestad N, Fulgoni VL 3rd. What current literature tells us about sustainable diets: emerging research linking dietary patterns, environmental sustainability, and economics. Adv Nutr. 2015 Jan;6(1):19–36.
50. Tilman D, Clark M. Global diets link environmental sustainability and human health. Nature. 2014 Nov 27;515(7528):518–22.
51. Hallström E, Carlsson-Kanyama A, Börjesson P. Environmental impact of dietary change: a systematic review. J Clean Prod. 2015;91:1–11.
52. Aleksandrowicz L, Green R, Joy EJM, Smith P, Haines A. The Impacts of Dietary Change on Greenhouse Gas Emissions, Land Use, Water Use, and Health: A Systematic Review. PLoS One. 2016 Nov 3;11(11):e0165797.
53. Drewnowski A, Rehm CD, Martin A, Verger EO, Voinnesson M, Imbert P. Energy and nutrient density of foods in relation to their carbon footprint [Internet]. Vol. 101, The American Journal of Clinical Nutrition. 2015. p. 184–91. Available from: http://dx.doi.org/10.3945/ajcn.114.092486
54. Baker P, Machado P, Santos T, Sievert K, Backholer K, Hadjikakou M, et al. Ultra-processed foods and the nutrition transition: Global, regional and national trends, food systems transformations and political economy drivers. Obes Rev. 2020;21(12):e13126.
55. Joyce A, Hallett J, Hannelly T, Carey G. The impact of nutritional choices on global warming and policy implications: examining the link between dietary choices and greenhouse gas emissions. Energy Emission Contr Technol. 2014 Dec;33.
56. Nelson ME, Hamm MW, Hu FB, Abrams SA, Griffin TS. Alignment of Healthy Dietary Patterns and Environmental Sustainability: A Systematic Review. Adv Nutr. 2016 Nov;7(6):1005–25.
57. Perignon M, Vieux F, Soler L-G, Masset G, Darmon N. Improving diet sustainability through evolution of food choices: review of epidemiological studies on the environmental impact of diets. Nutr Rev. 2017 Jan;75(1):2–17.
58. Le LT, Sabaté J. Beyond meatless, the health effects of vegan diets: findings from the Adventist cohorts. Nutrients. 2014 May 27;6(6):2131–47.
59. Kim SW, Less JF, Wang L, Yan T, Kiron V, Kaushik SJ, et al. Meeting Global Feed Protein Demand: Challenge, Opportunity, and Strategy. Annu Rev Anim Biosci. 2019 Feb 15;7:221–43.
60. Farmery AK, Gardner C, Jennings S, Green BS, Watson RA. Assessing the inclusion of seafood in the sustainable diet literature. Fish Fish . 2017 May;18(3):607–18.
61. Downs SM, Fanzo J. Is a Cardio-Protective Diet Sustainable? A Review of the Synergies and Tensions Between Foods That Promote the Health of the Heart and the Planet. Curr Nutr Rep. 2015 Oct 2;4(4):313–22.
62. Garnett T, Godde C, Muller A, Röös E, Smith P. Grazed and confused?: ruminating on cattle, grazing systems, methane, nitrous oxide, the soil carbon sequestration question-and what it all means for greenhouse …. 2017; Available from: https://library.wur.nl/WebQuery/wurpubs/529441
63. Clark MA, Springmann M, Hill J, Tilman D. Multiple health and environmental impacts of foods. Proc Natl Acad Sci U S A. 2019 Nov 12;116(46):23357–62.
64. Springmann M, Clark M, Mason-D'Croz D, Wiebe K, Bodirsky BL, Lassaletta L, et al. Options for keeping the food system within environmental limits. Nature. 2018 Oct;562(7728):519–25.
65. Clune S, Crossin E, Verghese K. Systematic review of greenhouse gas emissions for different fresh food categories. J Clean Prod. 2017 Jan 1;140:766–83.
66. Heller MC, Keoleian GA, Willett WC. Toward a life cycle-based, diet-level framework for food environmental impact and nutritional quality assessment: a critical review. Environ Sci Technol. 2013 Nov 19;47(22):12632–47.
67. Murray CJL, Aravkin AY, Zheng P, Abbafati C, Abbas KM, Abbasi-Kangevari M, et al. Global burden of 87 risk factors in 204 countries and territories, 1990–2019: a systematic analysis for the Global Burden of Disease Study 2019. Lancet. 2020 Oct 17;396(10258):1223–49.

68. Clark M, Tilman D. Comparative analysis of environmental impacts of agricultural production systems, agricultural input efficiency, and food choice. Environ Res Lett. 2017;12(6):64016.
69. Harris F, Moss C, Joy EJM, Quinn R, Scheelbeek PFD, Dangour AD, et al. The Water Footprint of Diets: A Global Systematic Review and Meta-analysis. Adv Nutr [Internet]. 2019 Sep 6 [cited 2019 Sep 10]; Available from: https://academic.oup.com/advances/advance-article-pdf/doi/10.1093/advances/nmz091/29807543/nmz091.pdf
70. Mekonnen MM. The Green, Blue and Grey Water Footprint of Farm Animals and Animal Products: Volume 1: Main Report. UNESCO-IHE; 2010. 43 p.
71. Mekonnen MM, Hoekstra AY. A Global Assessment of the Water Footprint of Farm Animal Products. Ecosystems. 2012 Apr 1;15(3):401–15.
72. Ranganathan J, Vennard D, Waite R, Searchinger T, Dumas P, Lipinski B. Shifting Diets: Toward a Sustainable Food Future. In IFPRI; 2016. (2016 Global Food Policy Report, International Food Policy Research Institute [IFPRI]).
73. Ritchie H, Roser M. Micronutrient deficiency [Internet]. Our World in Data. 2017. Available from: https://ourworldindata.org/micronutrient-deficiency
74. Sans P, Combris P. World meat consumption patterns: An overview of the last fifty years (1961–2011). Meat Sci. 2015 Nov;109:106–11.
75. Gale F, Hansen J, Jewison M. China's Growing Demand for Agricultural Imports. United States Department of Agriculture Economic Research Service; 2015.
76. Headey DD, Alderman HH. The Relative Caloric Prices of Healthy and Unhealthy Foods Differ Systematically across Income Levels and Continents. J Nutr [Internet]. 2019 Jul 23 [cited 2019 Jul 23]; Available from: https://academic.oup.com/jn/advance-article-pdf/doi/10.1093/jn/nxz158/28951648/nxz158.pdf
77. Imamura F, Micha R, Khatibzadeh S, Fahimi S, Shi P, Powles J, et al. Dietary quality among men and women in 187 countries in 1990 and 2010: a systematic assessment. The Lancet Global health. 2015 Mar;3(3):e142.
78. Neo H And Emel J. Geographies of Meat: Politics, Economy and Culture. Taylor & Francis; 2017.
79. Lowder SK, Skoet J, Raney T. The Number, Size, and Distribution of Farms, Smallholder Farms, and Family Farms Worldwide. World Dev. 2016 Nov 1;87:16–29.
80. Graeub BE, Chappell MJ, Wittman H, Ledermann S, Kerr RB, Gemmill-Herren B. The State of Family Farms in the World. World Dev. 2016 Nov 1;87:1–15.
81. Food and Agriculture Organization of the United Nations. The State of World Fisheries and Aquaculture 2020. FAO; 2020.
82. de Bakker E, Dagevos H. Reducing Meat Consumption in Today's Consumer Society: Questioning the Citizen-Consumer Gap. J Agric Environ Ethics. 2012 Dec 1;25(6):877–94.
83. Lawrence M, Burlingame B, Caraher M, Holdsworth M, Neff R, Timotijevic L. Public health nutrition and sustainability. Public Health Nutr. 2015 Sep;18(13):2287–92.
84. Neufeldt H, Jahn M, Campbell BM, Beddington JR, DeClerck F, De Pinto A, et al. Beyond climate-smart agriculture: toward safe operating spaces for global food systems. Agriculture & Food Security. 2013 Aug 30;2(1):12.
85. Herforth A, Arimond M, Álvarez-Sánchez C, Coates J, Christianson K, Muehlhoff E. A Global Review of Food-Based Dietary Guidelines. Adv Nutr [Internet]. 2019 Apr 30; Available from: http://dx.doi.org/10.1093/advances/nmy130
86. Fischer CG, Garnett T. Plates, pyramids, and planets: developments in national healthy and sustainable dietary guidelines: a state of play assessment. Food and Agriculture Organization of the United Nations; 2016.
87. Springmann M, Spajic L, Clark MA, Poore J, Herforth A, Webb P, et al. The healthiness and sustainability of national and global food based dietary guidelines: modelling study. BMJ. 2020 Jul 15;370:m2322.
88. Food and Agriculture Organization of the United Nations, World Health Organization. Sustainable healthy diets: Guiding principles. Food & Agriculture Org.; 2019. 44 p.

Chapter 11
The Future of Food: Shaping Diets and Nutrition

Introduction

The future is now. Technology holds the power to transform the way people produce, transport, prepare, and consume food. As lifestyles and incomes change around the world, people are accessing food in many new ways. The availability of the internet and mobile devices has fundamentally reshaped expectations about convenience and consumerism. Emerging technologies can help address these dynamic shifts at both the producer and consumer levels of the food system. Technological innovations abound at every stage of the food supply chain. These technologies hold the potential to let farmers produce food more efficiently, processors store and transport products more safely, and companies develop unique foods. Whether consumers want more information or simply more convenience, these advances promise to deliver a more transparent, digitally connected eating experience personalized to their needs. This chapter focuses on new technologies that are changing the operation of food supplies, demand for certain types of foods, and culture shared around food.

Agriculture 4.0: Revolutionizing Food Supplies for Better Diets

Over the last 100 years, the growth and pace of technological innovations has changed dramatically. In the early twentieth century, the telephone, electricity, and automobiles were exciting new inventions, though it took a long time for all households to have access to those technologies. In the last 30 years, transformative technologies have taken hold across the world and profoundly changed how people live. The internet, mobile technology, and shared economies have significantly changed the way that people communicate, function, and socialize. Unlike the innovations of the early twentieth century, these modern technologies have been rapidly adopted over the last decade [1].

Many modern innovations are intended to improve food systems, diets, and nutrition. These new technologies will ultimately affect every chain in the food supply [2]. Advances in nanotechnology, 3D printing, and robotics will affect food production and supply chains to deliver healthy foods [3]. High-tech solutions are being developed to make tasty, plant-based proteins and lab-grown meat alternatives that could eventually preclude the need to raise large numbers of livestock. The taste, texture, and smell of these products have improved, which has already led to greater acceptance in high-income contexts [4].

The term "Agriculture 4.0" refers to technologies that hold the potential to transform different aspects of agriculture and the food system. These innovations include developing or already operational technologies, such as precision, digital, and vertical agriculture; robotics; gene editing; blockchain; the "internet of things;" bio-economies; and big data [5]. As Fig. 11.1 shows, some of these innovations have already been implemented, while others will require more time and development to bring to market.

Despite the promising nature of these technologies, vast inequities in access still remain. In many regions of the world, electricity, vehicular transport, and irrigation are unattainable. In remote villages and other settings where subsistence farmers rely on rain-fed agriculture, access to blockchain or nanotechnology to improve

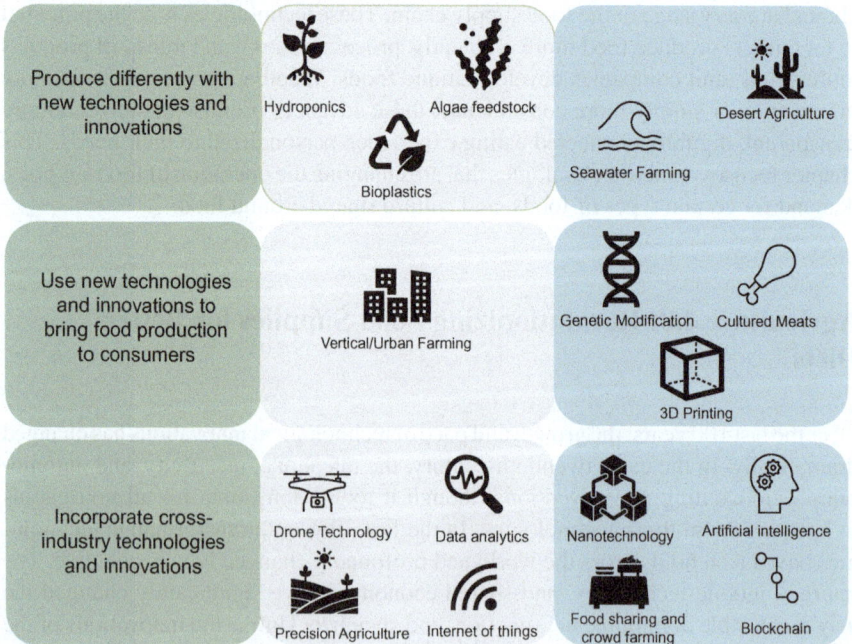

Fig. 11.1 Technologies and their readiness for markets [6]

supply chains is unlikely, to say the least. The "digital divide," which represents the gap between those who stand to benefit from internet technologies and those who do not, threatens to worsen already existing inequities between the world's people [7]. Many food system innovations are trialed, tested, and adapted in high-income contexts with little adoption in low-income countries. Lab-grown meat products remain prohibitively expensive and inaccessible to populations in low-income countries [4]. These issues of access and affordability stand in stark contrast to certain high-income contexts, where large-scale monocropping systems test robotics and drones to deliver the highest quality crops to urban consumers with an abundance of choice and income to spend on specialty foods.

Digital, Precision, and Vertical Farming

Digital and precision technologies can be used to help improve the accuracy and efficiency of agricultural production. Many farms use digital technologies to provide real-time data on weather and market prices. Precision agriculture allows farmers to use high-resolution data to apply site-specific fertilizers or pesticides to crops in specific, efficient amounts. Farms employ driverless tractors and other unmanned equipment to till land and carry out other labor. Some utilize robotics and drones to be more precise in how food is grown. Digital imagery can also be used to determine the optimal time to harvest crops.

Vertical farms function as an energy-efficient, self-contained method of producing food. These farms consist of multi-story buildings with environments conducive to growing crops, such as fruits, vegetables, and non-edible plants [8]. The concept takes advantage of stacked farm levels, where the building captures all the stages from inputs and growing of food to harvest, to effectively create an autonomous supply chain. One of the benefits of vertical farming is its use of renewable energy resources, such as solar panels to generate energy, biomass for fuel, and wind for power [9]. Less energy is required overall, since there is less need for plowing, transporting, and using other fossil-fuel dependent processes. However, questions remain about the cost of vertical production, the foods that can be grown besides horticultural crops and microgreens, and the capacity to feed a significant number of people [10]. Cost is one of the most significant controversies of vertical farms because the inputs necessary to generate vast quantities of food require significant up-front investment, and the types of crops that can be grown at scale are not always profitable [11, 12].

Middle of the Chain Technologies

Many technologies have been developed to improve efficiency along the "middle" of the food supply chain, which includes the storage, transport, processing, and packaging stages. These innovations include efforts to reduce food loss and improve the quality or sustainability of food products. At the storage and transport stages, micro-cold transport and evaporative cooling systems are used to keep perishable products, like fruits and vegetables, for extended periods of time. Micro-warehousing is utilized to store foods in smaller, local distribution centers that are close to the final point of delivery.

At the processing stage, near-farm mobile processing helps to improve the shelf life of foods before shipment. Both new and old technologies use dehydration, snap freezing, and solar drying techniques in order to minimize the loss of perishable foods that easily rot or go rancid. More sustainable packaging options, such as biodegradable material or edible packaging, are in development to reduce the use of plastic and harmful by-products [13].

Producing New and Varied Foods: 3D Printing, GMOs, and Lab-Grown Meat

New technologies are underway to formulate and produce new foods or variations of foods in order to withstand adverse growing conditions or improve nutrition. By helping to produce foods outside of traditional climate zones and under diverse conditions, these innovations can support the dual goals of food security and climate change adaptation. 3D printed food technology uses Computer Aided Design software to make a three-dimensional object from a film fabrication technique [14]. This technology improves on traditional cooking processes by mixing and processing food ingredients into different shapes and designs with new textures and flavors. 3D printed foods face considerable uncertainty with consumers, as many are either unfamiliar with the concept or express concerns about the "realness" of the food product, its sensory qualities, and over-processing [15, 16].

Genetic modification (GM) is a technology that involves editing the DNA of cells to change, remove, or add genes. This technology is intended to resolve agricultural or nutrition challenges through genetically modified organisms (GMOs). The first generation of GM crops aimed to produce higher yields from certain food crops and improve resilience to environmental conditions. Across 25 countries, 17 million farmers have adopted GM crops [17], and in the United States alone, 90% of all corn, soy, and cotton is GM [18]. The second generation of GM crops is intended to address nutrition issues that still prevail in some areas of the world [19]. To address micronutrient deficiencies, biofortification through GM technology or conventional breeding could be used to increase the nutritional content of staple crops [20]. In the case of Golden Rice, beta carotene was built into the rice grain to produce a food rich in vitamin A [21]. As with other GM food products, the debut of Golden Rice was met with skepticism and resistance from consumers for cultural and ethical reasons.

As its name implies, lab-grown, or "cultured," meat is produced in a laboratory. This technology involves replicating muscle stem cells from livestock animals in a petri dish and then differentiating them into muscle tissue [22]. The nutritional composition of these foods can be modified, enriched, and fortified in the lab to match the nutritional content of conventionally produced foods [4]. Lab-grown meat is considered a major disruptor to traditional livestock agriculture [4], but cost and consumer acceptance remain as significant challenges. Although costs have declined significantly in recent years due to technological advances, Memphis Meats indicates that a quarter-pound of lab-grown beef costs $600 USD [23]. It is unclear whether consumers will accept lab-grown meat, since they have historically been suspicious of "unnatural" foods [24, 25]. Taste and food safety will also be critical to ensuring market approval and acceptance [26].

The Disappearing Grocery Store, Restaurant, and Kitchen

Over time, supermarkets have displaced smaller chains and "mom and pop" shops in both rural and urban areas in many countries. In cities, these same businesses are now threatened by digital platforms that provide consumers with new experiences and enhanced convenience. These platforms can engage consumers with a "tap" on a mobile screen or a "click" on a browser. These digital platforms, which are termed "direct-to-consumer (D2C) models," disrupt conventional food supply chains by displacing the middle of the chain, along with the traditional "brick-and-mortar" grocery store. These models are designed for consumers who know what they want and when—and usually, they want it immediately [1]. In the modern age, having groceries or a prepared meal delivered to the doorstep only requires a mobile phone and the willingness to subscribe to a service. Privacy concerns are a major obstacle for these services, which collect vast amounts of data from consumers. In using these services, consumers provide extensive information about their personal preferences, tastes, and aspirations, which can be used by companies for future targeted marketing and advertising.

Physical food environments are also being reimagined with the goal of improved convenience. Amazon, the online retail giant, has introduced a new type of physical store that eliminates the checkout process. With Amazon's "Just Walk Out" technology, shoppers only need a mobile device—no cash, no credit card, and no checkout lines. The technology uses weight sensors to detect what products shoppers take from or return to the shelves and tracks them in a virtual cart. The technology is powered by computer vision and deep learning to detect motion and object movement and activity, much like driverless car technology. Emerging concerns with this technology include job elimination and excessive, unnecessary plastic waste [27, 28].

Food Delivery and Meal Services: Concierge Convenience

More and more, consumers want "concierge convenience" when it comes time to prepare their foods. This concierge style involves having food delivered directly to the consumers' homes whenever they want and bypassing the in-person grocery shopping. In the first six months of 2017, meal delivery services earned $781 million USD globally [1]. Many of these online food shopping experiences allow for "one-stop shopping," where food and other household items can be purchased at once, delivered quickly, and all transactions occur on a mobile device. Box 11.1 describes how the COVID-19 pandemic heightened consumers' reliance on contactless online grocery shopping and food delivery.

> **Box 11.1 Effects of the COVID-19 pandemic on online food shopping and delivery**
>
> As the COVID-19 pandemic gripped the world in 2020, quarantine orders, lockdowns, and concerns about personal health and safety led many consumers to abandon in-person shopping and dining out. Instead, many people turned to online ordering to purchase food and have it delivered. Consumer surveys show that 43% of shoppers bought groceries online during 2020, a two-fold increase from 2018 [29]. While food service sales in the United States declined by nearly 8% during the early months of the pandemic, grocery store sales rose by 16% as compared to the same period in 2019 [30]. In addition to the rise in online shopping, the pandemic also changed in-person shopping behavior. Consumers who continued to shop in grocery stores reported making fewer, larger trips that maximized efficiency and limited browsing [31].
>
> The pandemic transformed the retail landscape as stores and restaurants were forced to abandon traditional sales models. Retailers hurried to set up online ordering platforms, establish contactless points of turnover, and comply with changing health and safety regulations. To meet the growing demand for online ordering, some retailers increased ordering capacity and pickup services by more than 60% [30]. The expansion of "ghost kitchens," a delivery-only food service model, allowed restaurateurs to avoid the expenses associated with traditional in-person dining, such as rent, utilities, and employee wages. Amidst high unemployment, many turned to the "gig economy" to work as grocery shoppers or delivery drivers for food shopping and delivery apps.
>
> The pandemic resulted in global upheaval both sudden and massive in scale, but it remains to be seen whether the impacts on food retail will last. Many consumers, especially younger generations, are expected to continue using e-commerce and contactless shopping due to their convenience, and market research suggests that online grocery sales will represent more than one-fifth of the grocery sector's sales by 2025 [30, 32, 33]. However, e-commerce accounted for only 7% of grocery shopping in 2020, and 78% of surveyed consumers indicated a preference for traditional brick-and-mortar shopping.

Online shopping presents a significant challenge for those without computer skills or access to the internet, such as the elderly, poor, and others affected by the digital divide. There are also concerns that online shopping may encourage the purchase of less healthy foods, especially among low-income consumers, as nutrition information is not universally available online and digital purchasing makes it easier for retailers to track consumer preferences and deliver targeted marketing [31].

While the major food delivery service apps doubled their revenue due to the rise in online orders, these companies face many challenges to their profitability, including growing concerns about the high commissions charged to restaurants and the employment status of their workers. In several municipalities, newly introduced legislation has limited the commissions they can collect from restaurants. Proposed legislation has attempted to address the issue of whether low-paid delivery service workers are independent contractors or employees entitled to benefits and higher pay. As the economic decline spurred by the pandemic leads to the widespread closure of small businesses, there are concerns that the most profitable retailers and restaurants will be large corporate outfits and chains that can develop their own ordering apps, outsource food preparation to third-party operators in ghost kitchens, and employ low-paid gig workers as kitchen staff to maximize profits [34].

The Lure of Street Food and Fast Casual

From food trucks to market stalls, street food is an important feature of the urban landscape everywhere in the world. This type of food includes ready-to eat foods and beverages that are prepared and/or sold by vendors in the streets or other similar places [35]. On average, about 2.5 billion people eat street food every day [36]. Street and informal food vendors meet the growing demand for inexpensive, convenient, and fast-food options in urban settings, as their offerings are cheap and readily available around the clock.

Although street food helps to address food security for populations in large cities, concerns remain about the safety and healthfulness of these foods. The quality and hygiene of street foods are normally unregulated, as most street food vendors operate as part of an informal economy. Concerns over poor sanitation and unsafe, poor food quality have led some governments to eradicate informal street vending [37, 38]. There are also concerns that the fried, oily foods typically offered by street vendors contribute to obesity and do not align with a healthy diet [39]. While some governments have blamed street vendors for outbreaks of foodborne illness and subsequently banned them, others have tried to integrate informal vending in the regulated food environment and encourage the provision of healthy foods, as with Singapore's Healthy Hawkers Program [40].

Fast-casual restaurants were launched in the 1990s to offer higher-quality, healthy food as compared to typical fast-food restaurants, such as McDonalds or KFC. In 2009, there were 17,300 fast-casual restaurants in the United States with sales of $19 billion. By 2018, the sector had more than doubled to reach 34,800 restaurants with sales of $47.5 billion [41]. These outlets allow customers to design their own meals, such as burritos, rice bowls, or pizzas, which often use organic, seasonal ingredients and locally produced foods. Many fast-casual restaurants have shifted toward more sustainable packaging and serving containers in lieu of plastic. In recent years, many have transitioned to using smartphone apps to allow customers to order food ahead of time and avoid waiting in line, which served them well throughout the COVID-19 pandemic.

Changing Palates, Changing Demands

More than ever before, consumers care about where their food comes from, who prepares it, and what it contains. For many, food serves as a means of self-expression and an important source of connection between communities. Food can convey values and priorities, such as concerns about animal welfare, fair trade and labor practices, and the environment. Younger generations are especially engaged and embrace technological innovations to help them personalize their health and nutrition goals.

Food has become ubiquitous within society. Blogs, podcasts, documentaries, travel shows, and other television programs about food and cooking have become more popular than ever before [42]. Professional chefs have become television stars and household names, as have journalists and authors writing about historical and present-day food culture and politics. Millions of books describing the ills of the food system have been sold: for many consumers, Michael Pollan's advice in *The Omnivore's Dilemma* to "Eat food, mostly plants, not too much" has become a personal mantra [43]. These cultural vanguards have effectively sparked a new dialogue about how people can make conscious decisions to eat healthier, more nutritious foods within a healthier food system [44].

Consumer Engagement and the Foodie Generation

Consumers are increasingly demanding more from their foods—more alignment with their priorities and values, more creativity, and more options. The novelty and entertainment value of food has grown as people have become less concerned with eating healthy and spending quality time on preparing food. In the United States, Americans spend 27 minutes preparing food and 58% still prepare dinner regularly, although that figure has been declining since the 1980s [42]. More time is spent working and watching cooking on television than actually doing cooking.

Many of these engaged consumers are self-professed "foodies" who seek out new culinary experiences rather than simply eating out of convenience or hunger. Foodies express an avid interest in food and often prefer locally grown, organic, and high-quality options. The "Foodie Generation" of young adults aged 18 to 35 pursue information about their food choices through social media and the internet. This new type of consumerism has forced food suppliers to rethink everything from ingredients to promotional marketing.

Overall, new models of consumerism will have long-term consequences for how society addresses health and nutrition, as well as how the food system operates. Younger generations are more informed about nutrition and food, especially what their food contains and how it is produced. They want more transparency from the food industry and are willing to pay more for higher-quality food [45–47]. Although food preferences and consumption behaviors are shifting, these trends do not necessarily represent all consumers. Young people are not a unified cohort with a singular identity and set of priorities. These consumer trends are more prevalent in high-income settings than in low-income contexts, where concerns and priorities are rightfully different.

Personalized Nutrition

Personalized, or precision, nutrition aims to address nutrition problems through detailed health data. These data, which include multidimensional genomic and metabolic information, can be used to better understand differences in how human metabolism responds to diet [48]. Precision nutrition relies on a wide range of tools, including high-throughput analytical chemistry techniques, longitudinal tracking, data science, and behavioral interventions, to provide highly personalized and targeted dietary guidance [49]. Recent research has evaluated how personalized health data and dietary guidance can affect various outcomes, such as blood glucose and cardiovascular risk [50, 51]. The growth of personalized nutrition reflects the rising interest in using technology to track personal health. To help manage their diets and health in a more personalized way, many people have turned to technological innovations that include wearable devices, smartphone apps that track food consumption, online diaries, water bottles that monitor fluid intake, and even video games [52–54].

However promising, there are many caveats to personalized nutrition and related technologies. Personalized nutrition is in the early stages of development and may not be feasible in all settings, especially resource-poor settings [50]. The collection and analysis of personal health information presents concerns about genetic profiling and privacy [55]. In addition, the individual-centric approach of these technologies does not address the underlying determinants of poor nutrition outcomes, such as socioeconomic inequities or unhealthy food environments. Unlike public health efforts that emphasize policies and programs, these technologies are unlikely to affect overall population health [56].

The Implementation of Technologies

Across the food system, technological innovations are being developed and implemented at a rapid rate. As Fig. 11.2 shows, these technologies span the production, processing, packaging, distribution, consumption, and waste sectors. These innovations include many of those discussed in this chapter, as well as artificially made products, nano-drones, holobiomes and many others. Some technologies, such as digital agriculture, are fully developed or near-ready interventions, while others, such as nanotechnologies, remain in the research stage [57].

These technologies present an opportunity to address food system challenges by engendering significant systematic changes. However, any potential change depends on the acceptance of these technologies by various food system actors. While some innovations could be implemented in low- and middle-income settings, the cost and infrastructure needed for others would prohibit widespread use. Incentives to encourage adoption and regulations to ensure technologies are appropriately used are required to help guarantee equitable distribution.

Key Messages and Conclusions

Technology holds the potential to transform the food system. With emerging innovations, the grand challenge of feeding the world a sufficient, healthy diet while staying within planetary boundaries may be attainable. Technological advances encompass the entire food supply chain, from the agricultural level to the processing and retail stages in the middle and finally on to the consumer side. While technologies can shape food environments and consumer preferences, demand for certain foods also influences how new ideas take hold and thrive within society.

Despite the promise of new technologies, the future of food systems remains uncertain. Many emerging innovations only exist in the early stages of development and implementation. Some advances are scalable, while others will likely be too costly to be widely applied. Without consumer acceptance for novel technologies, these advances will never come to fruition. Some innovations pose ethical issues and threaten to worsen existing inequities. While the world's changing food culture has inspired some consumers to learn more about their food, others prioritize convenient, inexpensive options, often at the expense of health and nutrition. Achieving the goal of a sustainable food system will require that cultural and technological advances prioritize the fair distribution of healthy, nutritious, responsibly produced food in tandem with knowledge and resources.

Key Messages and Conclusions 179

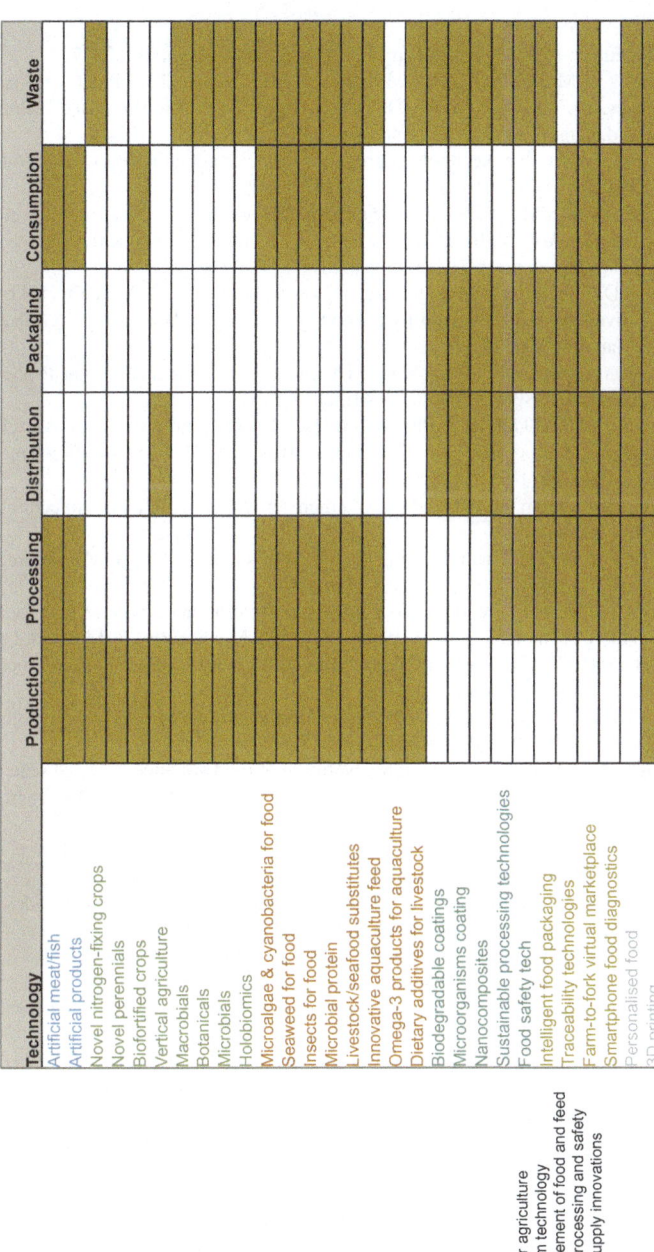

Fig. 11.2 Technological innovations across the food system [57]

References

1. Accenture. The Future of Food: New realities for the industry. Accenture; 2017.
2. Fanzo JC, Downs S, Marshall QE, de Pee S, Bloem MW. Value Chain Focus on Food and Nutrition Security. In: de Pee S, Taren D, Bloem MW, editors. Nutrition and Health in a Developing World. Cham: Springer International Publishing; 2017. p. 753–70.
3. Gruère GP. Implications of nanotechnology growth in food and agriculture in OECD countries. Food Policy. 2012 Apr 1;37(2):191–8.
4. Sergelidis D. Lab Grown Meat: The Future Sustainable Alternative to Meat or a Novel Functional Food? [Internet]. Vol. 17, Biomedical Journal of Scientific & Technical Research. 2019. Available from: http://dx.doi.org/10.26717/bjstr.2019.17.002930
5. Klerkx L, Rose D. Dealing with the game-changing technologies of Agriculture 4.0: How do we manage diversity and responsibility in food system transition pathways? Global Food Security. 2020 Mar 1;24:100347.
6. De Clercq M, Vats A, Biel A. Agriculture 4.0: The future of farming technology. Proceedings of the World Government Summit, Dubai, UAE. 2018;11–3.
7. Peláez AL. From the Digital Divide to the Robotics Divide? Reflections on Technology, Power, and Social Change [Internet]. The Robotics Divide. 2014. p. 5–24. Available from: http://dx.doi.org/10.1007/978-1-4471-5358-0_2
8. Despommier D. Farming up the city: the rise of urban vertical farms. Trends Biotechnol. 2013 Jul;31(7):388–9.
9. Despommier D. The Vertical Farm: Feeding the World in the 21st Century. Macmillan; 2010. 320 p.
10. Gruner RL, Orazi D, Power D. Global versus local: an exploration on how vertical farms can lead the way to more sustainable supply chains. IEEE Eng Manage Rev. 2013;41(2):23–9.
11. Kvaløy O, Tveterås R. Cost Structure and Vertical Integration between Farming and Processing. J Agricultural Economics. 2008 Jun;59(2):296–311.
12. Banerjee C, Adenaeuer L. Up, up and away! The economics of vertical farming. Journal of Agricultural Studies. 2014;2(1):40–60.
13. Farley S, Vuillaume R, Keenan C. Innovating the future of food systems: A global scan for the innovations needed to transform food systems in emerging markets by 2035. Washington DC. 2017.
14. Yang F, Zhang M, Bhandari B. Recent development in 3D food printing. Crit Rev Food Sci Nutr. 2017 Sep 22;57(14):3145–53.
15. Lupton D, Turner B. "I can't get past the fact that it is printed": consumer attitudes to 3D printed food. Food, Culture & Society. 2018 May 27;21(3):402–18.
16. Brunner TA, Delley M, Denkel C. Consumers' attitudes and change of attitude toward 3D-printed food. Food Qual Prefer. 2018 Sep;68:389–96.
17. Hefferon KL. Nutritionally enhanced food crops; progress and perspectives. Int J Mol Sci. 2015 Feb 11;16(2):3895–914.
18. United States Department of Agriculture. Recent Trends in GE Adoption [Internet]. 2018 [cited 2019 Apr 25]. Available from: https://www.ers.usda.gov/data-products/adoption-of-genetically-engineered-crops-in-the-us/recent-trends-in-ge-adoption.aspx
19. Glass S, Fanzo J. Genetic modification technology for nutrition and improving diets: an ethical perspective. Curr Opin Biotechnol [Internet]. 2017; Available from: https://www.sciencedirect.com/science/article/pii/S0958166916302488
20. Bouis HE, Saltzman A. Improving nutrition through biofortification: A review of evidence from HarvestPlus, 2003 through 2016. Glob Food Sec. 2017 Mar;12:49–58.
21. Stokstad E. After 20 years, golden rice nears approval. Science. 2019 Nov 22;366(6468):934.
22. Penn J. Cultured Meat: Lab-Grown Beef and Regulating the Future Meat Market. UCLA J Envtl L & Pol'y. 2018;36:104.
23. Schaefer O. Lab-grown meat. Sci Am. 2018;14.
24. Chriki S, Hocquette J-F. The Myth of Cultured Meat: A Review. Frontiers in Nutrition. 2020;7:7.

25. Bryant CJ, Barnett JC. What's in a name? Consumer perceptions of in vitro meat under different names. Appetite. 2019 Jun 1;137:104–13.
26. Servick K. As lab-grown meat advances, U.S. lawmakers call for regulation [Internet]. Science. 2018. Available from: http://dx.doi.org/10.1126/science.aau1426
27. Polacco A, Backes K. The amazon go concept: Implications, applications, and sustainability. Journal of Business and Management. 2018;24(1):79–92.
28. Ives B, Cossick K, Adams D. Amazon Go: Disrupting retail? Journal of Information Technology Teaching Cases. 2019 May 1;9(1):2–12.
29. Fowler GA. In 2020, we reached peak Internet. Here's what worked—and what flopped. The Washington Post. 2020 Dec 28;
30. OECD. E-commerce in the time of COVID-19. OECD; 2020.
31. Reiley L. Bigger hauls, fewer choices: How the pandemic has changed our grocery shopping habits forever. The Washington Post. 2020 Sep 1.
32. The great consumer shift: Ten charts that show how US shopping behavior is changing [Internet]. McKinsey and Co. 2020. Available from: https://www.mckinsey.com/business-functions/marketing-and-sales/our-insights/the-great-consumer-shift-ten-charts-that-show-how-us-shopping-behavior-is-changing
33. The Evolution of the Grocery Customer [Internet]. Mercatus. 2020. Available from: https://info.mercatus.com/egrocery-shopper-behavior-report?utm_source=ketner&utm_medium=media&utm_campaign=fy21-q3-shopper-survey-report-ketner-press-release
34. Reiley L. A pandemic surge in food delivery has made ghost kitchens and virtual eateries one of the only growth areas in the restaurant industry. The Washington Post. 2020 Sep 17.
35. FAO. Food for the Cities: Street Foods. FAO; 2017.
36. The Economist. South-East Asian cities are waging war on street food. The Economist. 2017 Mar 16.
37. Resnick D. Why brutalising food vendors hits Africa's growing cities where it hurts. The Conversation. 2017 May.
38. FAO. Street Foods the Way Forward for Better Food Safety and Nutrition. FAO; 2011.
39. FAO. Summary: Influencing food environments for healthy diets. FAO; 2016.
40. Ghani A. A recipe for success: How Singapore hawker centres came to be. Institute of Policy Studies. 2011;3:1–15.
41. Carman T. Why fast-casual restaurants became the decade's most important food trend. The Washington Post. 2019;
42. Pollan M. Cooked: A Natural History of Transformation. Penguin; 2014. 468 p.
43. Pollan M. In Defense of Food: An Eater's Manifesto. Penguin; 2008. 244 p.
44. Zimmerman H. Caring for the middle class soul: Ambivalence, ethical eating and the Michael Pollan phenomenon. Food, culture & society. 2015;18(1):31–50.
45. Bollani L, Bonadonna A, Peira G. The millennials' concept of sustainability in the food sector. Sustain Sci Pract Policy. 2019;11(10):2984.
46. Lerro M, Raimondo M, Stanco M, Nazzaro C, Marotta G. Cause Related Marketing among Millennial Consumers: The Role of Trust and Loyalty in the Food Industry. Sustain Sci Pract Policy. 2019 Jan 20;11(2):535.
47. Barska A. Millennial consumers in the convenience food market. Management. 2018 Jun 1;22(1):251–64.
48. Ferguson LR, De Caterina R, Görman U, Allayee H, Kohlmeier M, Prasad C, et al. Guide and Position of the International Society of Nutrigenetics/Nutrigenomics on Personalised Nutrition: Part 1 - Fields of Precision Nutrition [Internet]. Vol. 9, Lifestyle Genomics. 2016. p. 12–27. Available from: http://dx.doi.org/10.1159/000445350
49. O'Sullivan A, Henrick B, Dixon B, Barile D, Zivkovic A, Smilowitz J, et al. 21st century toolkit for optimizing population health through precision nutrition. Crit Rev Food Sci Nutr. 2018;58(17):3004–15.
50. Toro-Martín J de, de Toro-Martín J, Arsenault B, Després J-P, Vohl M-C. Precision Nutrition: A Review of Personalized Nutritional Approaches for the Prevention and Management of Metabolic Syndrome [Internet]. Vol. 9, Nutrients. 2017. p. 913. Available from: http://dx.doi.org/10.3390/nu9080913

51. Zeevi D, Korem T, Zmora N, Israeli D, Rothschild D, Weinberger A, et al. Personalized Nutrition by Prediction of Glycemic Responses. Cell. 2015 Nov 19;163(5):1079–94.
52. Baranowski T, Blumberg F, Buday R, DeSmet A, Fiellin LE, Green CS, et al. Games for Health for Children—Current Status and Needed Research. Games for Health Journal. 2016 Feb 1;5(1):1–12.
53. Shih PC, Han K, Poole ES, Rosson MB, Carroll JM. Use and adoption challenges of wearable activity trackers. IConference 2015 Proceedings [Internet]. 2015; Available from: http://www.ideals.illinois.edu/handle/2142/73649
54. Deng Y, Liu N-Y, Tsow F, Xian X, Krajmalnik-Brown R, Tao N, et al. Tracking Personal Health-Environment Interaction with Novel Mobile Sensing Devices. Sensors [Internet]. 2018 Aug 14;18(8). Available from: http://dx.doi.org/10.3390/s18082670
55. Gibney, M., Walsh, M., Goosens, J. Chapter 5.1 Personalized Nutrition: Paving the way to better population health. In: Eggersdorfer M, Kraemer K, Cordaro JB, Fanzo J, Gibney M, Kennedy E, et al., editors. Good Nutrition: Perspectives for the 21st Century. 2016. p. 235–48.
56. Chatelan A, Bochud M, Frohlich KL. Precision nutrition: hype or hope for public health interventions to reduce obesity? [Internet]. Vol. 48, International Journal of Epidemiology. 2019. p. 332–42. Available from: http://dx.doi.org/10.1093/ije/dyy274
57. Herrero M, Thornton PK, Mason-D'Croz D, Palmer J, Benton TG, Bodirsky BL, et al. Innovation can accelerate the transition towards a sustainable food system. Nature Food. 2020 May 1;1(5):266–72.

Chapter 12
Conclusion and Ways Forward

Importance of Food Policy for Diets and Nutrition

In recent years, many have called for a transformation to our food systems for the benefit of present and future generations [1–6]. This book has illustrated how important food is to society, human health, the planet, and economic prosperity. Food is central to every aspect of society. However, the systems that make, mold, move, and monetize our food need to be nurtured, governed, and maintained if they are to generate positive outcomes for society. Various actors and interventions are needed to shape food systems in ways that benefit everyone and the planet. In this book, we have highlighted the plethora of actors engaged in this work, some of whom hold more power while others have less.

Malnutrition burdens remain universal—every country is affected, and for many of the forms of malnutrition, in many parts of the world, little progress has been achieved in tackling the burden or, in some cases, preventing further decline [7]. If no action is taken on climate change or inequities, these burdens could further regress. Diets and the foods consumed by people contribute to the multiple forms of malnutrition. Thus, food systems and the policies that shape diets are critical to making a considerable positive impact on malnutrition.

Policies can influence the functioning of food supply chains, the architecture of food environments, and the behaviors of consumers, as well as the drivers that shape food systems in various ways. As this book has demonstrated, some policies, such as agricultural subsidies or trade interventions, can benefit one aspect of food systems without necessarily benefiting diets and nutrition. Conversely, some policies can create powerful benefits for human health and break down inequities that affect health disparities.

Challenges Remain

Many significant and sometimes intractable challenges and controversies remain amidst decision-making about how food systems should function and which actors should be responsible for change. Policies that improve one set of outcomes may harm another, as there will always be trade-offs and constraints. Policymakers must determine how to ensure the most benefit, while at the same time mitigating against the most harmful aspects of each and every decision. These decisions involve significant trade-offs between protecting economic growth, the natural resource base of the planet, and human nutrition and health. Successful policy-making requires a careful evaluation of what trade-offs the world is willing to live with in order to avoid detrimental damage to human populations and the planet [6, 8, 9].

The COVID-19 global pandemic, which is ongoing at the time of this writing, has now become a social, economic, health, and food system crisis with a significant death toll. Research suggests that SARS-CoV-2, the virus that causes the disease COVID-19, infected people through a zoonotic spillover event, in which the disease jumped from animals, most likely bats, to humans [10, 11]. Data shows that of emerging infectious diseases, 60% are zoonotic, and of that 60%, 72% originate in wildlife [12]. Case tracing indicates that that the virus originated in Wuhan, China and specifically implicates a seafood wet market, although this origin remains unresolved [13, 14].

Food and agriculture play a significant role in the rise of zoonotic disease. Just two centuries ago, humans only used about 5% of arable land for agriculture. Now, we use 40% of the earth's land for agriculture [1, 15]. This expansion of agriculture is spurred by the need to feed a growing human population, much of which lives in an urbanized world with growing demands for animal-sourced foods [16, 17]. Though our global agricultural system is a very efficient system that produces plenty of food, it carries costs for humans, the environment, and social equity [18, 19]. As a result of expanded agriculture, the natural habitats where much of the world's wildlife live have declined and been outright destroyed, leading humans, domesticated animals, and wildlife to live in closer proximity with each other [20].

Modeling suggests that if the global community does not take action on mitigating the effects of food systems on climate change, we will not achieve the 1.5°C Paris COP agreement target made in 2015 or, by the end of the century, the 2°C target [21]. Necessary action involves shifting diets toward more plant-based foods, avoiding the overconsumption of calories, reducing food loss and waste, and producing food with fewer greenhouse gases per unit of food produced and on less land. To address the grand challenges facing food systems, these goals must be achieved in unison using all available resources and tools, including technology and social change. These "socio-technical innovation bundles" require strong political and institutional enabling environments [4].

To resolve the complex issues inherent to food systems, many obstacles must be overcome. Agricultural production systems are homogenous and dominated by too few food crops and animals, including maize, rice, wheat, soy, chickens, and cattle

[22]. This profound loss of diversity puts the planet at a multiplicity of risks that include climate, nutrition, and zoonotic threats. The foods that predominate across the agricultural landscape are often misaligned with human health and environmental sustainability goals [1]. Over the last decade, violent conflicts have risen significantly, with hotspots in some parts of Africa and Asia [23]. Along with climate change, conflict is a major push factor for migration and urbanization. As those trends evolve, dietary patterns and consumer demand are changing in different ways. Not all of these changes are negative, however, as the movement of people results in a blending of cultures and traditions, diversity, and opportunity.

Growing societal inequities also pose a serious challenge for food systems [24]. The marginalization and discrimination of some populations around the world can amplify poor nutrition and health outcomes, with significant disparities becoming increasingly noticeable amidst the COVID-19 pandemic. Many of the world's poor cannot access a healthy diet and have been systemically marginalized within food systems and, more broadly, in society [25]. Approximately 65% of Africans and South Asians can only purchase enough food to meet their very basic caloric needs [25]—anything above and beyond that is unattainable.

We live in a world where technology, innovation, communication, and big data are rapidly changing the ways we engage and cooperate. Technologies like GMOs or lab-grown meat could be potential game-changers that transform food systems for better diets, ensuring systems are sustainable and saving us from significant climate-related natural disasters. When the impacts of these technologies on the Sustainable Development Goals are considered, however, there are significant trade-offs [6]. The outstanding challenge remains to identify available technological options that are ethically permissible and acceptable, and which can be considered and distributed in fair and justifiable ways [4].

The directive to improve diets and nutrition lacks fixed leadership. At the end of the day, who is responsible for ensuring adequate food security and nutrition? Achieving optimal nutrition for the world's people requires the engagement of multiple sectors, disciplines, and institutions. This book has highlighted the many necessary actors and interventions, but, historically, there has been an absence of accountability within the nutrition sector, as illustrated by the common refrain that "nutrition is everybody's business, nobody's responsibility" [26]. Why is this so? Is the problem that other competing priorities are more readily visible than nutrition challenges, or that the multiple solutions required to resolve nutrition issues seem too complex and daunting? Whatever the case may be, food is relevant to every sector, every discipline, and every person, and resolving issues with our food system is an "all hands-on deck" challenge that is ripe for opportunity.

With Challenges Come Opportunities

In and of itself, the cost of inaction justifies the scaling up of policies to improve food systems for diets and nutrition. Given that the burden of malnutrition and diets is now a major risk factor for death globally, the social and economic costs of inadequate food systems alone should elicit action. Addressing food insecurity and malnutrition does not have to be difficult or expensive. Through better legislation, coherent policies, political will, commitment, and accountability, change can happen.

As this book has illustrated, solutions exist. Policy success is a matter of investing in and scaling these solutions to ensure that no one is left behind. Food supplies and environments can be reshaped to improve diets and nutrition. The behaviors and actions of actors are malleable and subject to change. Incentives can help to nudge stakeholders and actors toward interventions with more beneficial outcomes. If we are to ensure that food systems work for human and planetary health, governments and other actors must take on the following actions:

1. Governments and private sector food actors must recognize the importance of public health and nutrition in the food system policies that they enact. In doing so, these actors need to create a sustained enabling environment and generate political will and action with public health goals in mind.
2. Power asymmetries must be addressed to bring about stewardship. The private sector has an important role in providing the foods that we consume every day, but it should be held to account to benefit public health and environmental sustainability while earning a profit. If companies do not prioritize these mutual goals and act responsibly, they must be penalized. Governments should shepherd food system actors in directions that align with overarching policies.
3. Governments and investors must invest in food systems, which goes hand-in-hand with rebalancing power. Governments and funders invest very little in public health nutrition or food systems, which is astounding when the burden of disease hinges on changing the types of foods available and accessible in food systems.
4. Civil society groups should act as advocates for communities, particularly those being left behind. These groups can create new movements and coalitions that build substantive social networks to call out the challenges and inequities faced by marginalized communities. This work can ensure that communities have agency and power to shape food systems in ways that work for them.
5. Researchers who work to gather, share, and communicate evidence must not be undermined or discouraged when data are disregarded. Research can chart a positive path for food systems and bring about meaningful changes in political thought and action [27].

References

1. Willett W, Rockström J, Loken B, Springmann M, Lang T, Vermeulen S, et al. Food in the Anthropocene: the EAT-Lancet Commission on healthy diets from sustainable food systems. Lancet. 2019 Feb 2;393(10170):447–92.
2. Watson RT, Noble IR, Bolin B, Ravindranath NH, Verardo DJ, Dokken DJ. IPCC special report on land use, land-use change, and forestry [Internet]. Intergovernmental Panel on Climate Change; 2000. Available from: http://edepot.wur.nl/78643

References

3. Fanzo J, Bellows AL, Spiker ML, Thorne-Lyman AL, Bloem MW. The importance of food systems and the environment for nutrition. Am J Clin Nutr [Internet]. 2020 Nov 24; Available from: http://dx.doi.org/10.1093/ajcn/nqaa313
4. Barrett CB, Benton TG, Cooper KA, Fanzo J, Gandhi R, Herrero M, et al. Bundling innovations to transform agri-food systems. Nat Sustain. 2020 Dec 1;3(12):974–6.
5. Béné C, Fanzo J, Haddad L, Hawkes C, Caron P, Vermeulen S, et al. Five priorities to operationalize the EAT–Lancet Commission report. Nat Food. 2020 Aug 1;1(8):457–9.
6. Herrero M, Thornton PK, Mason-D'Croz D, Palmer J, Bodirsky BL, Pradhan P, et al. Articulating the effect of food systems innovation on the Sustainable Development Goals. Lancet Planet Health. 2021 Jan;5(1):e50–62.
7. Luo H, Zyba SJ, Webb P. Measuring malnutrition in all its forms: An update of the net state of nutrition index to track the global burden of malnutrition at country level. Global Food Security. 2020 Sep 1;26:100453.
8. Mausch K, Hall A, Hambloch C. Colliding paradigms and trade-offs: Agri-food systems and value chain interventions. Glob Food Sec. 2020 Sep 1;26:100439.
9. Herrero M, Thornton PK, Mason-D'Croz D, Palmer J, Benton TG, Bodirsky BL, et al. Innovation can accelerate the transition towards a sustainable food system. Nat Food. 2020 May 1;1(5):266–72.
10. Alluwaimi AM, Alshubaith IH, Al-Ali AM, Abohelaika S. The Coronaviruses of Animals and Birds: Their Zoonosis, Vaccines, and Models for SARS-CoV and SARS-CoV2. Front Vet Sci. 2020 Sep 24;7:582287.
11. Mackenzie JS, Smith DW. COVID-19—A Novel Zoonotic Disease: A Review of the Disease, the Virus, and Public Health Measures. Asia Pac J Public Health. 2020 May 1;32(4):145–53.
12. Cutler SJ, Fooks AR, van der Poel WHM. Public health threat of new, reemerging, and neglected zoonoses in the industrialized world. Emerg Infect Dis. 2010 Jan;16(1):1–7.
13. Cohen J. Wuhan seafood market may not be source of novel virus spreading globally. Science [Internet]. 2020 Jan 26; Available from: https://www.sciencemag.org/news/2020/01/wuhan-seafood-market-may-not-be-source-novel-virus-spreading-globally
14. Li J, Wu C, Zhang X, Chen L, Wang X, Guan X, et al. Post-pandemic testing of SARS-CoV-2 in Huanan Seafood Market area in Wuhan, China. Clin Infect Dis [Internet]. 2020 Jul 25; Available from: http://dx.doi.org/10.1093/cid/ciaa1043
15. Nelson GC, Rosegrant MW, Palazzo A, Gray I, Ingersoll C, Robertson R, et al. Food Security, Farming, and Climate Change to 2050: Scenarios, Results, Policy Options. Intl Food Policy Res Inst; 2010. 131 p.
16. Searchinger T, Waite R, Hanson C, Ranganathan J, Dumas P, Matthews E. Creating a sustainable food future: a menu of solutions to feed nearly 10 billion people by 2050. World Resources Institute [Internet]. 2019; Available from: https://www.voced.edu.au/content/ngv:83748
17. Hanson M, Barker M, Dodd JM, Kumanyika S, Norris S, Steegers E, et al. Interventions to prevent maternal obesity before conception, during pregnancy, and post partum. Lancet Diabetes Endocrinol. 2017 Jan;5(1):65–76.
18. Turvey ST, Crees JJ. Extinction in the Anthropocene. Curr Biol. 2019 Oct 7;29(19):R982–6.
19. Ceballos G, Ehrlich PR, Raven PH. Vertebrates on the brink as indicators of biological annihilation and the sixth mass extinction. Proc Natl Acad Sci U S A. 2020 Jun 16;117(24):13596–602.
20. Hassell JM, Begon M, Ward MJ, Fèvre EM. Urbanization and Disease Emergence: Dynamics at the Wildlife–Livestock–Human Interface. Trends Ecol Evol. 2017 Jan 1;32(1):55–67.
21. Clark MA, Domingo NGG, Colgan K, Thakrar SK, Tilman D, Lynch J, et al. Global food system emissions could preclude achieving the 1.5° and 2°C climate change targets [Internet]. Vol. 370, Science. 2020. p. 705–8. Available from: http://dx.doi.org/10.1126/science.aba7357
22. Khoury CK, Bjorkman AD, Dempewolf H, Ramirez-Villegas J, Guarino L, Jarvis A, et al. Increasing homogeneity in global food supplies and the implications for food security. Proc Natl Acad Sci U S A. 2014 Mar 18;111(11):4001–6.
23. Mwesigye F, Matsumoto T. The Effect of Population Pressure and Internal Migration on Land Conflicts: Implications for Agricultural Productivity in Uganda. World Dev. 2016 Mar 1;79:25–39.

24. Christian P, Smith ER, Zaidi A. Addressing inequities in the global burden of maternal undernutrition: the role of targeting. BMJ Glob Health. 2020 Mar 18;5(3):e002186.
25. FAO, IFAD, UNICEF, WFP. The State of Food Security and Nutrition in the World 2020 [Internet]. 2020. Available from: http://www.fao.org/3/ca9692en/CA9692EN.pdf
26. Nisbett N, Gillespie S, Haddad L, Harris J. Why Worry About the Politics of Childhood Undernutrition? World Dev. 2014 Dec 1;64:420–33.
27. Fanzo J, Covic N, Dobermann A, Henson S, Herrero M, Pingali P, et al. A research vision for food systems in the 2020s: Defying the status quo. Glob Food Sec. 2020 Sep;26:100397.

Index

A

acceptability, food
   and culture, 10, 88, 172
   and food promotions, 21
   of GM foods, 14, 172
   of technological innovations, 170, 172, 173, 178
access to quality foods and healthy diets
   access defined, 19
   and built environment, 19, 95
   and costs, 19, 20, 78–79, 185
   and COVID-19, 76
   and food environments, 19–20, 95, 132, 136
   and food security, 53, 54
   and ideal diet, 10, 78–79
   and inequities, 2
   role in food systems, 11
   and technological innovations, 170–71, 175, 178
   and urbanization, 95
adequacy in assessing diet, 42
adolescents
   catch-up growth by, 62, 64
   and COVID-19 pandemic, 76
   diet needs, 43
   underweight rates, 55
advertising. *See* marketing and advertising

Africa
   birth rates, 94
   cash assistance programs in, 122
   and costs of ideal diet, 79, 185
   food insecurity rates, 55
   hunger rates, 53
   income spent on food away from home, 72
   influence of multinational food companies in, 78
   and multiple burden of malnutrition, 58
   packaged and processed foods in, 72, 73, 121
   smallholder farms in, 16, 121
   stunting rates, 55–56
   suboptimal diets in, 45, 47
   traditional diets in, 47
   undernutrition in, 55, 162
   urbanization in, 95
agentic interventions, 143–44
agricultural inputs
   and environment, 86, 94, 162, 171
   and organic farming, 17
   role in food supply chains, 15, 16
   role in food systems, 10, 11
   and value chain, 111
agriculture
   agriculture 4.0, 169–73

climate-smart, 163
and conflicts and crises, 92
digital, 170, 171, 178
diversified farming, 17, 110
and diversity of crops, 76–77, 86–87, 110, 114, 184–85
effects of environment and climate change on, 87–88, 97, 156–57
effects on environment, 86–87, 156–57, 161
employment in, 12, 13, 89
farming systems, described, 15–17
feminization of, 89
land use from, 12, 86, 156, 184
and migration, 89, 96–97
monoculture, 16, 77, 113
and nutrition transition, 72, 74
policy, 77, 110–15, 120–21, 184–85
precision, 170, 171
role in food supply chains, 15–17
role in food systems, 10, 11
smallholder, 12, 16–17, 74, 120–21
subsidies, 13, 89, 113–15
and sustainable diets, 155–64
technological innovations in, 97–98, 169–73, 178
and urbanization, 95–96
vertical, 170, 171, 179
agrobiodiversity, 86
agroecosystems, 15–17
Amazon [company], 173
Amazon rainforest, 156, 157
anemia, 61, 119
animal source foods (ASF)
consumption by children, 43, 44
costs of and access, 79
and employment, 16
and environment, 16, 87, 161
increase in consumption and demand, 94, 131, 162, 184
nutrition from, 16, 162
and nutrition transition, 75
and subsidies, 113
and sustainable diets, 155, 159, 160, 162–63
See also livestock; meat
aquaculture, 13, 16, 17, 162–63, 179
aquatic ecosystems, 16
ASF. *See* animal source foods (ASF)
Asia
birth rates, 94
and costs of ideal diet, 79, 185
feminization of agriculture in, 89
hunger rates, 53
income spent on food away from home, 72
influence of multinational food companies in, 78
micronutrient deficiencies in, 43
and multiple burden of malnutrition, 58
packaged foods consumption in, 72, 73
red meat consumption in, 71
smallholder farms in, 16
suboptimal diets in, 45, 46, 47
undernutrition in, 53, 55, 162
urbanization in, 95
wasting rates, 55
availability, food
and consumer behavior, 13, 21, 136
defined, 19
and food environments, 19–20, 78
and food security, 53
and policy, 89, 91–92, 110, 131, 136
and trade, 77, 115–16

B

back-of-package label policies, 139. *See also* labels
balance as measure in assessing diet, 42
Bangladesh
feminization of agriculture, 89
SBCC programs in, 143
biodiversity, 12, 85, 86–87, 96, 156, 161, 163, 184
bio-economies, 170
biofortification, 110, 172, 179
biophysical drivers of food systems, 85–88
bioplastics, 170, 172
birth defects, 61, 120
birth rates, 94
blindness, 14, 61
blockchain, 170
"blue zone" diets, 46–47
Brazil
deforestation in, 156, 157
demand for animal source foods in, 79
influence of multinational food companies in, 78
breastfeeding, 43, 44, 62, 94, 143
built environment, 19, 62, 95, 98–99
Burkina Faso, take home rations in, 134

C

cafeterias, 135

Index

CAFOs (concentrated animal feeding operations), 113
calories, general increase in, 72
Canada
    traditional diets in, 46
    trans fats policy, 33
cancer, 2, 12, 33, 46, 52, 61, 160
cardiovascular disease, 33, 46, 47, 52, 61, 63, 159
Caribbean
    and costs of ideal diet, 79
    food insecurity rates, 55
    hunger rates, 53
    income spent on food away from home, 72
    suboptimal diets in, 45
Carson, Rachel, 158
cash assistance, 122, 123
catch-up growth, 62, 64
child mortality, 61
child obesity, 2, 52, 56, 57, 58, 59
children
    and animal source foods, 43, 44, 162
    cognitive development of, 52, 61, 63
    diet needs, 43, 44
    feeding practices, 59–60, 143
    and food diversity, 3
    and intergenerational cycle of malnutrition, 63–64
    marketing and advertising to, 132, 136, 137–38, 141
    and micronutrient deficiencies, 56, 61
    obesity and overweight in, 2, 52, 56, 57, 58, 59
    and school food environments, 134, 135, 136
    undernutrition of, 3, 55–56, 59, 60, 61, 62
    wasting rates, 52, 57
    See also stunting
Chile
    consumption of processed foods in, 141
    labels in, 31, 140–41
    obesity rates, 141
choice architecture, 144–45
choices, food. *See* consumer behavior
civil society, 13–14, 30, 33, 90, 186
climate change
    defined, 87
    as driver of food systems, 85, 87–88, 97
    effect of agriculture on, 86–87, 156–57
    effect on agriculture, 87–88, 97, 156–57
    and migration, 88, 97

    as policy challenge, 183, 184–85
    and sustainable diets, 155–64
climate-smart agriculture, 163
Codex Alimentarius Commission, 139–40
cognitive development, 52, 61, 63
Common Agricultural Policy (EU), 113
Common Food Policy (EU), 35, 37
concentrated animal feeding operations (CAFOs), 113
Conference of the Parties on Climate Change (COP21), 155
conflicts, 92–94, 96, 97, 185
consumer behavior
    and agentic interventions, 143–44
    and choice architecture, 144–45
    as component of food systems, 9, 12, 15, 21
    consumers as food system actors, 13, 21, 33
    and convenience, 19, 20, 21, 42
    and culture, 9–10, 19, 88, 132, 133, 136
    and dietary guidelines, 21
    and food environments, 18–20, 131–32, 133, 144–45
    and food supply chains, 15
    and interest in food, 176–77
    and labels, 21, 136, 137, 140, 141
    and life stages, 21, 41–42
    and marketing and advertising, 21, 136, 137–38
    and media, 143
    and nudges, 136, 145
    and nutrition education and information, 132, 136, 137, 142, 143–44
    and policies, 112, 131, 135–45
    and prices, 79, 136, 138
    social and behavior change communication (SBCC), 143
    and taxes, 136, 137, 138–39, 140
    and technology and innovation, 169, 172, 176–78
consumerism, 176–78
convenience
    and consumer behavior, 19, 20, 21, 42
    and food environments, 20
    and recent changes in food systems, 75, 78
    and technological innovation, 98, 169, 173, 174, 175
    and urbanization, 95
cooking
    skills, 136, 144
    time spent preparing food, 176–77

COP21 (Conference of the Parties on Climate Change), 155
Costa Rica, trans fats policy in, 33
costs
    and access to healthy diets, 19, 20, 78–79, 185
    and food environments, 20, 132
    of sustainable diets, 79, 159
    and technological innovations, 171, 173, 178
    and trade policy, 115
    See also prices
COVID-19 pandemic, 1, 65, 75–76, 174–75, 176, 184, 185
crises. *See* humanitarian crises
culture
    and animal source foods, 163
    and dietary guidelines, 142
    as driver of food systems, 88–89
    and interest in food, 176–77
    role in food choices, 9–10, 19, 88, 132, 133, 136
    role in nutrition education, 144
    role of food in, 9–10
    and technological acceptability, 172

D

dairy products, 43, 44, 117, 162
deaths
    from cardiovascular disease, 33, 47, 61
    child mortality, 61
    deaths and disability-adjusted life years (DALYs) lost, 2, 47, 139
    from food-borne illness, 20
    infant mortality, 56, 63
    maternal mortality, 61, 62
    and nutrition transition, 74
    and obesity, 61
    and suboptimal diets, 2, 47
    and sustainable diets, 159
    and vitamin A deficiency, 14, 63
    and zinc deficiency, 63
deforestation, 86, 117, 156–57
dementia, 46
demographic drivers of food systems, 94–97
Denmark
    labels in, 141
    taxes on unhealthy foods, 138–39
    trans fats policy, 33
diabetes
    gestational, 62
    and malnutrition, 12, 59, 64
    and obesity, 61
    and suboptimal diets, 2, 33, 47, 52, 91
diet
    and agentic interventions, 144
    assessing quality of, 42
    changes in recent decades, 71–75
    components of, 10
    defined, 41
    effect of climate change on, 87
    effect of dietary guidelines on, 142
    increase in calories, 72
    influence of globalization and trade on, 90–92
    and market policies, 121
    Mediterranean diet, 46, 160
    and microbiome, 60
    needs and life stages, 42, 43, 44
    and nutrition transition, 71, 72–75, 90
    overview of, 41–48
    price support effects on, 139
    and public procurement policies, 122–23
    role in malnutrition, 10
    sustainable diets, 155–64
    and trade policy, 116
    traditional diets, 46–47, 144
    types, 41–47
    and urbanization, 72, 74, 75, 95
    vegan/vegetarian diets, 160
    and zoning laws, 121
    See also access to quality foods and healthy diets; diversity, food
diet, healthy
    and accessibility, 10, 78–79
    assessing, 42
    described, 42–43
    diversity of foods in, 42, 77
    ideal, 10
    Planetary Health Diet, 43, 79, 159
    and social determinants, 133
diet, suboptimal
    effect on health, 2, 10, 47, 52
    global rates of, 43–47
    and influence of globalization and trade, 90–91
    and influence of multinational food companies, 78
    regional variations in, 47
dietary guidelines, 21, 142–43, 163–64
digital agriculture, 170, 171, 178
digital divide, 170–71, 175. *See also* inequities
disease

Index 193

"Fetal Origins of Adult Disease" hypothesis, 63
  malnutrition from, 59, 60
  risks from undernutrition, 61
  zoonotic diseases as policy challenge, 184
  See also noncommunicable diseases (NCDs)
distribution
  and climate change, 87
  in Common Food Policy, 35
  and COVID-19, 75
  and food safety, 20, 42
  in food value chain, 111
  and globalization, 77
  role in food systems, 11
  technological innovations in, 178, 179
  and trade, 116
  and urbanization, 96
diversified farming, 17, 110
diversity, food
  and agricultural diversity, 76–77, 86–87, 110, 114, 184–85
  and food insecurity, 2
  in healthy diets, 42, 77
  and humanitarian crises, 116
  and social and behavior change communication (SBCC), 143
  and subsidies, 114
  and trade, 116
  and undernutrition, 3
double burden of malnutrition, 57–59
drivers of food systems
  biophysical, 85–88
  demographic, 94–97
  economic, 89–94
  environmental, 85–88
  political, 89–94
  sociocultural, 88–89
drones, 170, 171, 178
dumping, 91
Dutch famine cohort, 63, 64

E

eating anxiety, 76
Eat-*Lancet* Commission on Food, Planet, and Health, 42–43, 79, 158–60
Eat-Lancet Report on Healthy Diets for Sustainable Food Systems,, 43, 158–60
economic development and nutrition transition, 72, 74

economic drivers of food systems, 89–94
econutrition movement, 157–58
ecosystems as drivers of food systems, 85–88, 110
ecosystem services, 86
Ecuador
  labels and reformulation in, 140, 141
  and quinoa, 16
education
  and consumer behavior, 142, 143–44
  and cooking skills, 136, 144
  and food environments, 136
  and food waste, 112
  nutrition education, 136, 142, 143–44
  and reformulation, 119
educational attainment, 59, 89
Egg Products Inspection Act, 30
eggs, 44
emotional eating, 76
employment
  in agriculture, 12, 13, 89
  and animal source foods, 16
  fair labor policies, 112, 115
  by food delivery systems, 175
  in food systems, 12, 13
  migration for, 96–97
  and nutrition transition, 74
  and sustainable diets, 162–63
  of women, 89, 97, 98
  See also workplaces
environment
  and diversified farming, 17
  effect of agriculture on, 86–87, 156–57, 161
  effect of animal source foods on, 16, 87, 161
  effect of food systems on, 12, 86–88
  effect on agriculture, 87–88, 97, 156–57
  effect on food systems, 10, 85–88, 97
  environmental drivers of food systems, 85–88
  and monocrops, 77
  as policy challenge, 183, 184–85
  and sustainable diets, 155–64
  and trade policy, 117
  See also built environment; food environments
Ethiopia
  smallholder farms and traditional crops in, 121
  and stunting, 55–56
Europe
  agriculture subsidies in, 113

Common Food Policy, 35, 37
Farm to Fork initiative, 113
Nutri-Score labels, 140
packaged foods in, 72, 73
suboptimal diets in, 45, 46
evaporative cooling systems, 172
external domain of food environments, 19, 20

F
famine
Dutch famine cohort, 63, 64
in Ethiopia, 55
and intergenerational cycle of malnutrition, 64
and nutrition transition, 74
in South Sudan, 93
FAO (Food and Agriculture Organization of the United Nations), 139–40, 158, 163–64
Farm Bill (US), 113
farmers
diversity of, 13
as food system actors, 13, 33
global numbers of, 13
and nutrition transition, 72, 74
See also agriculture; smallholder agriculture
Farm Input Subsidy Policy (Malawi), 114
Farm to Fork initiative (2020), 113
fast-casual restaurants, 176
fast food, 18, 46, 78, 98, 121, 137–38, 175
fat
increase in consumption, 72
tax on saturated fat in Denmark, 139
trade in fatty meats, 90, 91–92
trans fats, 32, 33–34, 45, 46, 71, 117
FDA (Food and Drug Administration), 30
feeding practices, 59–60, 143
fertilizers. *See* agricultural inputs
"Fetal Origins of Adult Disease" hypothesis, 63
Fiji, trade in fatty meats, 91–92
fish and fisheries, 13, 16, 31, 43, 161, 162–63
consumption by children, 43
environmental impact of, 161
in food supply chains, 16
as food systems actors, 13
policy examples, 31
and sustainable diets, 162–63
folate, 31, 116
Food, Drug, and Cosmetic Act of 1938, 30

Food and Agriculture Organization (FAO), 139–40, 158, 163–64
Food and Drug Administration (FDA), 30
"food as medicine" interventions, 134
food assistance programs, 122, 142
food-based dietary guidelines (FBDGs), 21, 142–43, 163–64
foodborne illness, 20, 98
"Food Choice at Work" (Ireland), 135
food crops. *See* agriculture
food delivery systems, 174–75, 176
food deserts, 19–20, 111, 121–22, 136, 137
food eaten away from home
and delivery services, 174–75
increase in, 72, 79
and street food, 175
food environments
and access, 19–20, 95, 132, 136
and availability, 19–20, 78
and choice architecture, 144–45
as component of food systems, 9, 11, 12, 18–20
and consumer behavior, 18–20, 131–32, 133, 144–45
effect on supply, 131–32
entry points, 19
external environment, 19, 20
and globalization, 77–78
ideal, 132
and infrastructure, 98
and market policies, 120–22
obesogenic, 98
overview of, 18–20
personal environment, 19, 20
policies, 112, 120–22, 131, 135–45
and supermarket revolution, 78, 121
technological innovations in, 173–76
types of, 134–35
and urbanization, 77, 78, 95
zoning laws, 121–22, 136
foodies, 176–77
food insecurity
and climate change, 88, 97
and COVID-19, 65, 76
dimensions of food security, 53
and food diversity, 2
food security, defined, 53
and fruit and vegetable consumption, 121
and humanitarian crises, 93–94, 97
and malnutrition, 53, 54, 59–60, 62, 93
and migration, 97
and public procurement policies, 122
rates of, 2, 55

Index   195

and sustainable diets, 157
and undernutrition, 3
and women, 55
food policy
    actors in, 13, 14, 29–30
    and agriculture, 77, 110–15, 120–21, 184–85
    challenges in, 183, 184–86
    and civil society, 14, 30, 186
    and consumer behavior, 112, 131, 135–45
    defined, 29–30
    and dietary guidelines, 142–43
    diversity of, 30
    as driver of food systems, 89–90
    evolution of, 34–35
    examples of, 31
    and food environments, 112, 120–22, 131, 135–45
    on food supply chains, 109–23
    and governance, 32, 90
    holistic, 34–37
    importance of, 1–2, 29, 183–86
    influences on, 32–34
    levers of policy, 112
    on markets and distribution, 120–22
    measuring success of, 30
    need for collaboration on, 14
    need for leadership, 185
    overview of and key concepts, 29–37
    political economy approach to, 31
    price and income support, 115, 137, 138–39
    on processing and packaging, 112, 117–20
    on production, 113–15
    and public procurement, 120, 122–23, 142
    role of government in, 13, 30
    stakeholders in, 31, 32–34
    suggested actions, 186
    and sustainability, 186
    and sustainable diets, 163–64
    systems approach, 34
    trade-offs in, 184, 185
food promotions, 21, 137, 138
food quality
    components quality of diet, 42
    and consumer behavior, 21
    defined, 21
    as measure in assessing diet, 42
    and street food, 175
    technological innovations in, 172

    See also access to quality foods and healthy diets
food safety
    and consumer behavior, 21
    defined, 20
    and distribution and storage, 20, 42
    and foodborne illness, 20, 98
    as measure in assessing diet, 42
    policies and regulations, 13, 112
    and street food, 175
    technological innovations in, 179
food security. *See* food insecurity
food supply chains
    activities in, 15
    actors and stages in, 15–18
    as component of food systems, 9, 12, 15–18
    and direct-to-consumer models, 173
    effects of conflicts/crises on, 92
    food value chains, 18, 110–12
    and globalization, 1, 15, 109
    ideal, 109–12
    and income, 15, 77, 78
    increased complexity of, 75, 109
    as interconnected, 15
    overview of, 15–18
    policies affecting, 109–23
    recent changes in, 75, 76–77, 109–10
    technological innovations in, 97–98, 169–73, 178
    and urbanization, 15, 96
    value chain analysis, 110–12
food swamps, 19–20, 111, 121–22
food systems
    actors in, 9, 10, 12–14
    changes in recent decades, 75–80
    components overview, 9, 12, 15–21
    defined, 9, 10–12
    diagram of general, 11
    effect on environment, 12, 86–88
    environment's effect on, 12, 86–87
    food systems approach, 11
    importance of, 1–3, 12
    interconnectedness of, 10–11, 75
    overview and key concepts, 9–22
    and sustainable diets, 155–64
    See also consumer behavior; drivers of food systems; food environments; food policy; food supply chains; technology and innovation
food value chains, 18, 110–12
food waste, 98, 111, 112, 172, 178
forced displacement, 96–97

fortification, 110, 119–20. *See also* biofortification
front-of-package labels, 118, 139–41. *See also* labels
fruits and vegetables
    and agricultural diversity, 77
    consumption of, 43, 44, 45, 46, 47, 71
    costs of and access to, 79
    and declines in undernutrition, 59
    in dietary guidelines, 142
    environmental impact of farming, 161
    and food insecurity, 121
    lack of subsidies for, 113
    and nutrition transition, 74
    prescriptions for, 134
    price supports for, 138
    and reformulation, 117
    in schools, 134
    and sustainable diets, 159
    and urbanization, 95
    and zoning laws, 121

G

gender
    equality and food systems, 12
    norms, 89
    and obesity rates, 56
    See also men; women
genetically modified (GM) foods, 14, 110, 170, 172
Ghana, influence of multinational food companies in, 78
GHGe. *See* greenhouse gas emissions (GHGe)
ghost kitchens, 174, 175
globalization
    as driver of food systems, 90–92
    and food environments, 77–78
    and food supply chains, 1, 15, 109
    increased access to foods from, 115, 116
    and nutrition transition, 72, 74, 90
    and recent changes in food systems, 71, 75, 77–78
GM (genetically modified) foods, 14, 110, 170, 172
Golden Rice, 14, 172
governance
    defined, 29, 30–32, 90
    influences on, 32–34
    role in food systems, 90
governments
    and dietary guidelines, 142–43
    as food systems actors, 13
    role in policy, 13, 29, 186
grains
    and climate change, 87
    in dietary guidelines, 142
    global consumption of, 43, 44, 45
    percentage grown for animal feed, 161
    and reformulation, 117
    and subsidies, 113
    and trade policies, 116
    and urbanization, 95
Green Deal (EU), 113
greenhouse gas emissions (GHGe)
    and agriculture, 86, 156, 161, 163
    and animal source foods, 16, 161
    and food systems, 5, 12
    and urbanization, 95
    and vegetarian/vegan diets, 160
"Guiding Principles on Sustainable Healthy Diets" (FAO/WHO), 163–64
Gussow, Joan Dye, 158

H

habitat loss, 184
health
    and healthy diets, 42
    and suboptimal diets, 2, 10, 47, 52
    and sustainable diets, 159–60
    and traditional diets, 46
    See also disease; malnutrition; noncommunicable diseases (NCDs); stunting; wasting
health care
    "food as medicine" interventions, 134
    systems and policies, 122, 142
    systems as food environments, 134
Healthy Hawkers Program (Singapore), 176
height. *See* stunting
hidden hunger. *See* micronutrient deficiencies
high-income countries
    and children's diets, 43
    food deserts and food swamps in, 20
    and market policies, 121
    percentage of income spent on food, 20, 79, 115
    and technological innovations, 171
    and trans fats, 34
    and urbanization, 96
    and value chain analysis, 112
high-pressure processing, 112
holobiomes, 178, 179

Index

humanitarian crises, 92–94, 96, 97, 116
hunger
    and conflicts/humanitarian crises, 97
    defined, 53
    and empowerment of women, 89
    increase in, 53, 65
    and price increases, 79
    rates of, 2, 53
    See also famine; malnutrition; micronutrient deficiencies
hunger, hidden. *See* micronutrient deficiencies

I

income
    and food choices, 132, 133
    and food environments, 77, 78
    and food supply chains, 15, 77, 78
    from food systems, 12
    increase in, 79
    and multiple burden of malnutrition, 58, 59
    and obesity, 59
    percentage spent on food, 20, 79
    percentage spent on food eaten away from home, 72
    support policies for, 115
    See also high-income countries; low-and middle-income countries (LMICs)
India
    and multiple burden of malnutrition, 58, 59
    public procurement policy, 122
    wasting in, 55
Indigenous peoples and traditional diets, 46–47
inequities
    and access to healthy diet, 2
    and COVID-19, 185
    as policy challenge, 185
    and sustainable diets, 159, 160, 164
    and taxes on unhealthy foods, 139
    and technological innovations, 170–71, 175, 178, 185
infant mortality, 56, 63
infants
    breastfeeding, 43, 44, 62, 94, 143
    feeding practices, 59–60, 143
    and food prices, 115
    low birth weight, 56, 62, 63, 64
    and suboptimal diets, 44, 54
infrastructure

    and access and availability, 19–20, 136
    as driver of food systems, 97, 98–99
    and food environments, 98
    and food supply chains, 111
    and market policies, 120–21
    role of policy in, 111
    See also built environment
in-kind assistance programs, 122
innovation. *See* technology and innovation
International Panel of Experts on Sustainable Food Systems, 35
International Rice Research Institute, 14
internet of things, 170, 171
iodine deficiency, 2, 56, 61, 119
Ireland, "Food Choice at Work" initiative, 135
iron
    and animal source foods, 162
    and climate change, 87
    fortification, 119
    iron deficiency, 2, 56, 61
Italy and COVID-19 pandemic, 76

J

Japan and Okinawan diet, 46

K

Kentucky Fried Chicken (KFC), 78
kitchens, ghost, 174, 175

L

labels
    back-of-package labels, 139
    and consumer behavior, 21, 136, 137, 140, 141
    front-of-package labels, 118, 139–41
    and ideal food environments, 132
    policy, 112, 118, 139–41
    and reformulation, 118, 119
    warning labels, 21, 31, 118, 132, 136, 140–41
lab-grown meat, 170, 171, 172–73, 179
labor policies, fair, 112, 115
Lancet Commission on Food, Planet, and Health, Eat-, 42–43, 79, 158–60
land use
    and agriculture, 12, 86, 156, 184
    and population growth, 94
    and urbanization, 96
    and vegetarian/vegan diets, 160
Lappe, Francis Moore, 158

Latin America
  cash assistance programs in, 122
  and costs of ideal diet, 79
  food insecurity rates, 55
  hunger rates, 53
  income spent on food away from home, 72
  influence of multinational food companies in, 78
  labels in, 31, 140–41
  nuts and seeds consumption in, 45, 47
  packaged foods increase in, 73
  smallholder farms and traditional crops in, 16–17, 121
  suboptimal diets in, 45, 46
Law of Food Labeling and Advertising (Chile), 141
laws. *See* regulations and laws
LBW. *See* low birth weight (LBW)
leadership, need for, 185
legumes
  and climate change, 87
  and declines in undernutrition, 59
  and dietary guidelines, 142
  environmental impact of, 161
  global consumption of, 44, 45, 46
life expectancy, 61, 62, 74
livestock
  concentrated animal feeding operations (CAFOs), 113
  and deforestation, 157
  in diversified farming, 17
  in food supply chains, 16
  as food systems actors, 13
  and reformulation, 117
  and subsidies, 113
  and sustainable diets, 159, 162–63
  See also animal source foods (ASF)
livestock producers, 13, 16, 113
low-and middle-income countries (LMICs)
  access to foods in, 19, 116
  access to technological innovations in, 171
  and agentic interventions, 144
  children's diets in, 43
  and demographic drivers of food systems, 94
  fast food in, 18
  food-borne illness in, 20
  food eaten away from home in, 72
  food subsidies in, 114
  fortification programs in, 119
  marketplace changes in, 18, 77, 121
  and micronutrient deficiencies, 56, 63, 119
  obesity in, 47, 57
  percentage of income spent on food, 20, 79, 115
  and school meals, 134
  and social and behavior change communication (SBCC), 143
  stunting and underweight in, 57
  and sustainable diets, 160
  and trans fats, 34
  undernutrition in, 47, 52, 63
  and urbanization, 96
  and value chain analysis, 112
  and women's empowerment and hunger, 89
low birth weight (LBW), 56, 62, 63, 64

M

Malawi, subsidies in, 114–15
malnutrition
  causes of, 59–60
  and cognitive development, 52, 63
  and DALYs (deaths and disability-adjusted life years) lost, 47
  defined, 52
  and Dutch famine cohort, 63, 64
  and food insecurity, 53, 54, 59–60, 62, 93
  forms of, 2, 52
  as global problem, 2, 51–65, 183, 185–86
  health impact of, 12, 47, 52, 53, 57–64
  and humanitarian crises, 93–94
  intergenerational cycle of, 63–64
  and life stages, 61
  and microbiome, 60
  multiple or double burden of, 57–59
  and processed foods, 60
  and productivity, 47, 52, 61, 63, 65
  rates of, 64
  and suboptimal diets, 10, 47
  and sustainable diets, 159
  See also micronutrient deficiencies; undernutrition
mandatory reformulation, 118–19
marketing and advertising
  to children, 132, 136, 137–38, 141
  and consumer behavior, 21, 136, 137–38
  and food choices, 21
  and food environments, 20, 132, 136
  and food promotions, 21, 137, 138
  in food value chain, 111
  online food shopping and delivery services, 173, 175

policies, 21, 111, 112, 137–38
markets and retailers
    and COVID-19, 174–75
    in food supply chains, 15, 18
    as food systems actor, 10, 13
    in food value chain, 111
    and food waste, 112
    and online food shopping and delivery, 174–75, 176
    and policies, 120–22, 136, 137
    and price and income supports, 115
    and supermarket revolution, 78, 121
    and technological innovations, 173–76
    and urbanization, 95
    wet markets, 75
    and zoning laws, 121–22
Masai peoples and traditional diet, 47
maternal anemia, 61
maternal mortality, 61, 62
maternal undernutrition, 3, 61, 62, 63–64
meal services, 174–75
meat
    and deforestation, 157
    in dietary guidelines, 142
    global consumption of, 43, 45, 46, 71
    lab-grown meat, 170, 171, 172–73, 179
    laws and regulations, 30
    production *vs.* ideal consumption of, 114
    and sustainable diets, 159, 160, 162
    trade in fatty meats, 90, 91–92
    See also animal source foods (ASF); processed meats; red meat
Meat Inspections Act, 30
media
    and consumer behavior, 143
    interest in food, 176
Mediterranean diet, 46, 160
men
    obesity rates, 56
    underweight rates, 59
Mexico
    cash assistance programs in, 31
    fast-food policies, 121
    influence of multinational food companies in, 78
    taxes on unhealthy foods in, 138–39
microbiome, 60
micro-cold transport, 172
micronutrient deficiencies
    and animal source foods, 162
    defined, 52
    and food insecurity, 54
    as global problem, 2, 56

and GM crops, 172
health effects of, 61, 62, 63
and maternal malnutrition, 63
rates of, 2, 56
and role of micronutrients, 51
types of, 56
micro-warehousing, 172
migration, 72, 88, 89, 96–97, 185
milk, 43, 44, 45, 114
mixed crop-landscape systems. *See* diversified farming
moderation as measure in assessing diet, 42
monoculture, 16, 77, 113
mortality. *See* deaths
multinational food companies
    influence of, 77–78
    and subsidies, 113
multiple burden of malnutrition, 57–59
mutton flaps, 91–92

N

natural resources. *See* environment
near-farm mobile processing, 172
Nestle, 78
nitrogen application, 161
noncommunicable diseases (NCDs)
    and diet, 42, 52
    and malnutrition, 52, 57–59, 61, 64
    and nutrition transition, 74, 75
    and productivity, 63
non-governmental organizations. *See* civil society
Nordic diet, 46
North America
    packaged food sales in, 72, 73, 78
    suboptimal diets in, 45, 46
    sugar-sweetened beverages in, 72, 78
North American Free Trade Agreement, 78
nudges, 136, 145
Nutri-Score, 140
nutrition
    and agentic interventions, 144
    from animal source foods, 16, 162
    and climate change, 87
    and food value chains, 110, 111
    fortification and biofortification, 110, 119–20, 172, 179
    in healthy diets, 42–43
    and life stage, 42, 43, 51
    and market policies, 121
    nutrition transition, 71, 72–75, 90
    and organic farming, 17

personalized/precision nutrition, 177–78, 179
policy, 34, 35
and price supports, 139
and public procurement policies, 122–23
reformulation, 110, 117–20, 137, 140–41
role in food systems, 11
role in health, 51–52
role of micronutrients, 51
and subsidies, 113–15
and sustainable diets, 157, 159–60, 161–62
and take home rations, 134
and trade policy, 90–91, 116
and zoning laws, 121
See also malnutrition; undernutrition
nutritional research, 52
nutrition education, 136, 142, 143–44
nutrition information and consumer behavior, 132, 136, 137, 177
nutrition transition, 71, 72–75, 90
nuts and seeds
in dietary guidelines, 142
environmental impact of farming, 161
global consumption of, 43, 44, 45, 47
and sustainable diets, 159

O

obesity and overweight
child obesity, 2, 52, 56, 57, 58, 59
in Chile, 141
and deaths, 61
defined, 53
and food insecurity, 54
as form of malnutrition, 52, 56–57
and gender, 56
health effects of, 61
increases in, 2, 52, 57, 59, 64
in India, 59
in low- and middle-income countries, 47, 57
and multiple burden of malnutrition, 57–59
and nutrition transition, 74, 75
and pregnancy, 62, 63
and productivity, 63
rates of, 2, 56–57
with stunting, 58, 59
and suboptimal diets, 47
and urbanization, 57
obesogenic environments, 98
Oceania

packaged food consumption in, 72, 73
suboptimal diets in, 45
See also Pacific Island nations
Okinawan diet, 46
organic food and farming, 17

P

Pacific Island nations
and multiple burden of malnutrition, 58
obesity rates, 57
trade in fatty meats, 90, 91–92
packagers and packaging
and children, 137, 138
and fast-casual restaurants, 176
as food systems actor, 13
packaged food sales, 72, 73
policy on, 112, 117–20
role in food supply chains, 15, 17–18
technological innovations in, 97, 170, 172, 178, 179
See also labels; processed foods
Pakistan and COVID-19 pandemic, 76
personal domain of food environments, 19, 20
personalized nutrition, 177–78, 179
pescatarian diet, 160
pesticides. *See* agricultural inputs
phosphorous application, 161
physical activity
and COVID-19 pandemic, 76
and nutrition transition, 74, 75, 90
Planetary Health Diet, 43, 79, 159
policy. *See* food policy; trade policy
political drivers of food systems, 89–94
political economy approach to food governance, 32
Pollan, Michael, 176
population growth, 1, 94–95
portion sizes, 72
Poultry Products Inspection Act, 30
poverty
and conflicts, 93
and malnutrition, 59–60, 62, 63, 65, 93
and migration, 96
and public procurement policy, 122–23
and women's empowerment, 89
power and policy, 90, 186
precision agriculture, 170, 171
precision nutrition, 177–78, 179
pregnancy, 61, 62, 63–64
prices
and climate change, 87

and consumer behavior, 79, 136, 138
and COVID-19 pandemic, 76
and food value chains, 18
and ideal food environments, 132
and increases in hunger, 79
stability of, 132
support policies for consumers, 115, 137, 138–39, 140
and trade policy, 115–16
See also costs
privacy, 173, 177
private sector
  as food systems actor, 13, 33
  influence and power of, 77–78, 186
  role in governance, 90
  role in policy, 30, 186
private standards and certifications, 112
processed foods
  consumption of, 45, 46, 47, 71, 72, 73, 121, 141
  degrees of, 18
  in dietary guidelines, 142
  increase in sales, 78
  and influence of multinational food companies, 78
  and malnutrition, 60
  and nutrition transition, 74, 75, 90
  and obesity, 59
  policies on, 112, 117–20, 121
  reformulation of, 117–20
  trans fats in, 33
  and urbanization, 95
processed meats
  described, 2, 41
  in dietary guidelines, 142
  global consumption of, 45, 46, 47, 71, 73
  and sustainable diets, 159
processors and processing
  and climate change, 87
  and conflicts and crises, 92
  in food supply chains, 15, 17–18
  as food systems actor, 11, 13
  in food value chain, 110, 111
  forms of, 17
  policy on, 112, 117–20
  and price and income supports, 115
  technological innovations in, 97, 112, 169, 171–72, 178, 179
  and urbanization, 95–96
productivity, human, 47, 52, 61, 63, 65, 74
protein
  from animal source foods, 16
  and climate change, 87

  increase in consumption, 72
  and sustainable diets, 159
  technological innovations in, 170, 179
Public Distribution System (India), 122
public procurement policy, 120, 122–23, 142

Q

quality. *See* food quality
quinoa, 16–17

R

red meat
  consumption of, 45, 46, 71
  in dietary guidelines, 142
  in sustainable diets, 159, 160
  trade in fatty meats, 90, 91–92
reformulation, 110, 117–20, 137, 140–41
regulations and laws
  and food policy, 30
  on marketing to children, 137
  as part of food environment, 20
renewable energy and vertical agriculture, 171
REPLACE initiative, 34
research
  limitations of on sustainable diets, 163
  role in governance, 90
  role in policy, 186
restaurants
  and COVID-19, 174–75, 176
  and dietary guidelines, 142
  fast-casual, 176
  fast-food, 18, 46, 78, 98, 121, 137–38, 175
  in food supply chains, 15
  increase in food eaten away from home, 72, 79
  and meal delivery services, 174–75, 176
  and zoning laws, 121
retailers. *See* markets and retailers
robotics, 170, 171

S

safety net. *See* public procurement policy
salt
  iodine fortification, 119
  and reformulation, 117, 118–19
  sodium consumption, 43, 45, 46, 118
Samoa
  obesity in, 57
  trade in fatty meats, 91–92

SBCC (social and behavior change communication), 143
schools, 122, 134, 135, 136, 141, 142
SDGs (Sustainable Development Goals), 5, 155, 158
shocks, climate, 97
shocks, food, 1, 75–76
Singapore, Healthy Hawkers Program, 176
smallholder agriculture
    defined, 16
    employment in, 12
    and market policies, 120–21
    and nutrition transition, 74
    role in food supply chains, 16–17
snacking, 72, 76, 79
social and behavior change communication (SBCC), 143
sociocultural drivers of food systems, 88–89
soda. *See* sugar-sweetened beverages (SSBs)
sodium, 43, 45, 46, 117, 118–19
South Korea, traditional diet in, 144
South Sudan conflict, 93–94
Spain and COVID-19 pandemic, 76
SSBs. *See* sugar-sweetened beverages (SSBs)
stability dimension of food security, 53
standards and certifications, private, 112
storage
    and climate change, 87
    and food safety, 20, 42
    in food value chain, 111, 112
    and market policies, 121
    role in food systems, 11
    technological innovations in, 171–72
street food, 175
stunting
    and conflicts/crises, 93
    decline in, 2, 57, 64
    defined, 52, 53
    and Ethiopia, 55–56
    and food insecurity, 54
    and low birth weight, 63
    and maternal malnutrition, 63
    and nutrition transition, 74
    with obesity, 58, 59
    rates of, 2, 52, 55, 57, 58
subsidies
    agricultural, 13, 79, 89, 113–15
    price supports for consumers, 115, 137, 138–39, 140
sugar-sweetened beverages (SSBs)
    consumption of, 43, 45, 46, 71–72, 78
    and reformulation, 118
    and schools, 134
    taxes on, 118, 137, 138, 139
supermarket revolution, 78, 121
supermarkets
    direct-to-consumer models, 173
    in food supply chain, 15
    rise of in low-and middle-income countries, 18–19, 77, 121
    supermarket revolution, 78, 121
    and technological innovations, 173
    and urbanization, 95
sustainability
    and dietary guidelines, 142, 162–63
    Eat-*Lancet* Commission on Food, Planet, and Health, 42–43, 79, 158–60
    and holistic food policy, 35, 37
    importance of, 155
    policies, 112, 113, 186
    sustainable diets, 155–64
    sustainable diet term, 158
    technological innovations in, 172
    2030 Agenda for Sustainable Development, 158
    2030 Sustainable Development Goals, 5, 155, 158
Syngenta, 14

T
"Table for Two" program, 135
take home rations, 134
taxes
    and consumer behavior, 136, 137, 138–39, 140
    and costs of healthy diets, 79
    as driver of food systems, 89
    policies, 118, 136, 137, 138–39, 140
    and reformulation, 118
technology and innovation
    in agriculture, 97–98, 169–73, 178
    and consumers, 169, 172, 176–78
    as driver of food systems, 97–98
    in food environments, 173–76
    in food supply chains, 97–98, 169–73, 178
    future of, 169–79
    implementation of, 178, 179
    inequities in, 170–71, 175, 178, 185
    in packagers and packaging, 97, 170, 172, 178, 179
    in processors and processing, 97, 112, 169, 171–72, 178, 179
tobacco, 114

Tonga, trade in fatty meats, 91–92
trade
    as driver of food systems, 90–92
    dumping, 91
    and environment, 117
    in food supply chains, 15
    importance of international, 116
    and nutrition transition, 72
    policy, 13, 77, 90–91, 113, 115–17
    role of government in, 13
trade policy, 13, 77, 90–91, 113, 115–17
traditional diets, 46–47, 144
trans fats, 32, 33–34, 45, 46, 71, 117
transportation
    in food supply chains, 15, 18
    and ideal food environments, 132
    and improvements in infrastructure, 98
    and market policies, 120–21
    technological innovations in, 171–72
turkey tails, 92

0–9

3D printing, 170, 172, 179
2019 Eat-Lancet Report on Healthy Diets for Sustainable Food Systems, 43, 158–60
2030 Agenda for Sustainable Development, 158
2030 Sustainable Development Goals, 5, 155, 158

T

tobacco, 114
Tonga, trade in fatty meats, 91–92
trade
    as driver of food systems, 90–92
    dumping, 91
    and environment, 117
    in food supply chains, 15
    importance of international, 116
    and nutrition transition, 72
    policy, 13, 77, 90–91, 113, 115–17
    role of government in, 13
trade policy, 13, 77, 90–91, 113, 115–17
traditional diets, 46–47, 144
trans fats, 32, 33–34, 45, 46, 71, 117
transportation
    in food supply chains, 15, 18
    and ideal food environments, 132
    and improvements in infrastructure, 98
    and market policies, 120–21
    technological innovations in, 171–72

turkey tails, 92

0–9

2019 Eat-Lancet Report on Healthy Diets for Sustainable Food Systems, 43, 158–60
2030 Agenda for Sustainable Development, 158
2030 Sustainable Development Goals, 5, 155, 158

U

Ultraviolet irradiation, 112
undernutrition
    of children, 3, 55–56, 59, 60, 61, 62
    and conflicts/crises, 93–94
    and COVID-19 pandemic, 76
    deaths from, 61
    defined, 52, 53
    and food diversity, 3
    and food insecurity, 3
    health effects of, 55, 57–59, 61–64
    increase in, 65
    maternal undernutrition, 3, 61, 62, 63–64
    and multiple burden of malnutrition, 57–59
    and public procurement policies, 122
    rates of, 52, 53, 59
    and sustainable diets, 159, 160, 162
    UNICEF child undernutrition framework, 59, 60
    of women, 3, 55, 61, 62, 63–64
    See also malnutrition; stunting; wasting
underweight
    defined, 52
    and low birth weight, 63
    and maternal malnutrition, 63
    rates of, 52, 55, 57, 59
    rates of for women, 55, 57, 59
    as sign of undernutrition, 42
UNICEF child undernutrition framework, 59, 60
United Kingdom, sodium reformulation in, 118–19
United Nations
    Food and Agriculture Organization (FAO), 139–40, 158, 163–64
    2030 Agenda for Sustainable Development, 158
    2030 Sustainable Development Goals, 5, 155, 158
United States

agricultural policy, 113, 144
and COVID-19, 76, 174
dietary guidelines in, 142
fast-casual restaurants in, 176
food assistance programs in, 142
food eaten away from home, 72
GM crops in, 172
labeling in, 33
regulations in, 30
small-scale farms in, 16
subsidies in, 113, 114
time spent preparing food in, 176–77
United States Department of Agriculture (USDA), 30
urbanization
and consumer demand, 131
diet changes from, 72, 74, 75, 95
as driver of food systems, 95–96
and food environments, 77, 78, 95
and food supply chains, 15, 96
increase in, 95, 96
and nutrition transition, 72, 74
and obesity, 57
USDA (United States Department of Agriculture), 30
utilization dimension of food security, 53

V

value chain analysis, 110–12
vegan diet, 160
vegetables. *See* fruits and vegetables
vegetarian diet, 160
vertical agriculture, 170, 171, 179
vitamin A deficiency
in adolescent girls, 43
and animal source foods, 162
as common, 2, 56
deaths and blindness from, 14
and fortification, 119
Golden Rice, 14, 172
health effects of, 14, 61
and international trade, 116
vitamin B12, 116, 162
voluntary reformulation, 118

W

war and conflicts. *See* conflicts

warning labels, 21, 31, 118, 132, 136, 140–41
wasting
and conflicts/crises, 93
defined, 52, 53
and food insecurity, 54
and maternal malnutrition, 63
rates of, 52, 55, 57, 58
water use, 12, 86, 156, 160, 161
Western diet. *See* diet, suboptimal
wet markets, 75
whole grains
in dietary guidelines, 142
global consumption of, 43, 44, 45
and reformulation, 117
wildfires, 156, 157
women
and anemia, 61
employment in agriculture, 89
empowerment of, 89, 97, 98, 115
and food insecurity, 55
and intergenerational cycle of malnutrition, 63–64
maternal undernutrition, 3, 61, 62, 63–64
obesity rates, 56
undernutrition of, 3, 55, 61, 62, 63–64
underweight rates, 55, 57, 59
workplaces
and dietary guidelines, 142
food environments in, 135
and public procurement policy, 122
World Health Assembly
and marketing to children, 137
and sodium guidelines, 119
World Health Organization (WHO)
and back-of-package labels, 139–40
Codex Alimentarius Commission, 139–40
on marketing to children, 137
optimal diet guidelines, 42
and sustainable diets, 158, 163–64
trans fats initiative, 34

Z

zinc deficiency, 2, 43, 56, 61, 87
zoning laws, 121–22, 136, 137
zoonotic diseases as policy challenge, 184

The manufacturer's authorised representative in the EU is Springer Nature Customer Service Centre GmbH, Europaplatz 3, 69115 Heidelberg, Germany. If you have any concerns regarding our products, please contact ProductSafety@springernature.com

Printed and bound by CPI Group (UK) Ltd, Croydon, CR0 4YY

25/03/2026

02078196-0014